"I do not know another series quite like Theology in Community. Each volume is grounded in both the Old and New Testaments, and then goes on to wrestle with the way the chosen theme has been developed in history, shaped the lives of men and women, and fits in the scheme of confessionally strong Christian theology. The volumes are characterized by rigor and reverence and, better yet, they remain accessible to all serious readers. If we are to pursue more than unintegrated biblical data, but what Paul calls 'the pattern of sound teaching,' this is an excellent place to begin."

—**D. A. Carson**, Research Professor of New Testament, Trinity Evangelical Divinity School; Cofounder, The Gospel Coalition

"This distinguished series brings together some of the best theological work in the evangelical church on the greatest themes of the Christian faith. Each volume stretches the mind and anchors the soul. A treasury of devout scholarship not to be missed!"

—**Timothy George**, Founding Dean, Beeson Divinity School; General Editor, Reformation Commentary on Scripture

"This series tackles some big and juicy topics on theology, ranging from kingdom to suffering to sin to glory. Some of the best theological thinkers in the world explain what it means to have a 'faith seeking understanding' in our contemporary age. The volumes are full of solid teaching in biblical, historical, systematic, and practical theologies and contain a wealth of immense learning. A valuable resource for any thinking Christian."

—**Michael F. Bird**, Lecturer in Theology, Ridley College, Melbourne, Australia; author, *Evangelical Theology*

THE LOVE OF GOD

Other Crossway Books in the Theology in Community Series

The Deity of Christ (2011)

Fallen: A Theology of Sin (2013)

The Glory of God (2010)

Heaven (2014)

The Kingdom of God (2012)

Suffering and the Goodness of God (2008)

THE LOVE OF GOD

Christopher W. Morgan, editor

WHEATON, ILLINOIS

The Love of God

Copyright © 2016 by Christopher W. Morgan

Published by Crossway
1300 Crescent Street
Wheaton, Illinois 60187

All rights reserved. No part of this publication may be reproduced, stored in a retrieval system, or transmitted in any form by any means, electronic, mechanical, photocopy, recording, or otherwise, without the prior permission of the publisher, except as provided for by USA copyright law. Crossway® is a registered trademark in the United States of America.

Chapter 1 is adapted from "On Distorting the Love of God," chapter 1 in *The Difficult Doctrine of the Love of God* (Crossway), copyright 2000 by D. A. Carson, 9–24.

Cover design: Studio Gearbox

Cover image: The Fall on the Road to Calvary, 1517, Raphael Sanzio of Urbino / Prado, Madrid, Spain / Bridgeman Images

First printing 2016

Printed in the United States of America

Unless otherwise indicated, Scripture quotations are from the ESV® Bible (The Holy Bible, English Standard Version®), copyright © 2001 by Crossway, a publishing ministry of Good News Publishers. Used by permission. All rights reserved.

Scripture references marked JB are from *The Jerusalem Bible*. Copyright © 1966, 1967, 1968 by Darton, Longman & Todd Ltd. and Doubleday & Co., Inc.

Scripture references marked NEB are from *The New English Bible* © The Delegates of the Oxford University Press and The Syndics of the Cambridge University Press, 1961, 1970.

Scripture references marked NLT are from *The Holy Bible, New Living Translation*, copyright © 1996, 2004. Used by permission of Tyndale House Publishers, Inc., Wheaton, IL, 60189. All rights reserved.

Scripture references marked REB are from The Revised English Bible. Copyright ©1989, 2002 by Oxford University Press and Cambridge University Press. Published by Oxford University Press.

All emphases in Scripture quotations have been added by the authors.

Trade paperback ISBN: 978-1-4335-3904-6
ePub ISBN: 978-1-4335-3907-7
PDF ISBN: 978-1-4335-3905-3
Mobipocket ISBN: 978-1-4335-3906-0

Library of Congress Cataloging-in-Publication Data

Names: Morgan, Christopher W., 1971– editor.
Title: The love of God / [edited by] Christopher W. Morgan.
Description: Wheaton : Crossway, 2016. | Series: Theology in community series | Includes bibliographical references and index.
Identifiers: LCCN 2016004783 (print) | LCCN 2016020759 (ebook) | ISBN 9781433539046 (tp) | ISBN 9781433539077 (epub) | ISBN 9781433539053 (pdf) | ISBN 9781433539060 (mobi)
Subjects: LCSH: God (Christianity)—Love.
Classification: LCC BT140 .L68 2016 (print) | LCC BT140 (ebook) | DDC 231/.6—dc23
LC record available at https://lccn.loc.gov/2016004783

Crossway is a publishing ministry of Good News Publishers.

VP 26 25 24 23 22 21 20 19 18 17 16
15 14 13 12 11 10 9 8 7 6 5 4 3 2 1

To the ones who have encouraged me most in the love of God:
my wife, Shelley,
and
my daughter, Chelsey

CONTENTS

LIST OF ABBREVIATIONS

ApOTC	Apollos Old Testament Commentary
AUS	American University Studies
AUSTR	American University Studies, Series 7: Theology and Religion
BECNT	Baker Exegetical Commentary on the New Testament
CTJ	*Calvin Theological Journal*
CTM	*Concordia Theological Monthly*
EvQ	*Evangelical Quarterly*
HALOT	*The Hebrew and Aramaic Lexicon of the Old Testament*
ICC	International Critical Commentary
IJST	*International Journal of Systematic Theology*
JETS	*Journal of the Evangelical Theological Society*
NAC	New American Commentary
NICNT	New International Commentary on the New Testament
NIDOTTE	*New International Dictionary of Old Testament Theology and Exegesis*
NIGTC	New International Greek Testament Commentary
NPNF [1 or 2]	*Nicene and Post-Nicene Fathers, Series [1 or 2]*
PNTC	Pelican New Testament Commentaries
RTR	*Reformed Theological Review*
SBLDS	Society of Biblical Literature Dissertation Series
SJT	*Scottish Journal of Theology*
TDNT	*Theological Dictionary of the New Testament*
Them	*Themelios*
TNTC	Tyndale New Testament Commentaries
TynBul	*Tyndale Bulletin*
WBC	Word Biblical Commentary
WCF	Westminster Confession of Faith
ZAW	*Zeitschrift für die alttestamentliche Wissenschaft*
ZECNT	Zondervan Exegetical Commentary on the New Testament

SERIES PREFACE

As the series name, Theology in Community, indicates, theology in community aims to promote clear thinking on and godly responses to historic and contemporary theological issues. The series examines issues central to the Christian faith, including traditional topics such as sin, the atonement, the church, and heaven, but also some which are more focused or contemporary, such as suffering and the goodness of God, the glory of God, the deity of Christ, and the kingdom of God. The series strives not only to follow a sound theological method but also to display it.

Chapters addressing the Old and New Testaments on the book's subject form the heart of each volume. Subsequent chapters synthesize the biblical teaching and link it to historical, philosophical, systematic, and pastoral concerns. Far from being mere collections of essays, the volumes are carefully crafted so that the voices of the various experts combine to proclaim a unified message.

Again, as the name suggests, theology *in community* also seeks to demonstrate that theology should be done in teams. The teachings of the Bible were forged in real-life situations by leaders in God's covenant communities. The biblical teachings addressed concerns of real people who needed the truth to guide their lives. Theology was formulated by the church and for the church. This series seeks to recapture that biblical reality. The volumes are written by scholars, from a variety of denominational backgrounds and life experiences with academic credentials and significant expertise across the spectrum of theological disciplines, who collaborate with each other. They write from a high view of Scripture with robust evangelical conviction and in a gracious manner. They are not detached academics but are personally involved in ministry, serving as teachers, pastors, and missionaries. The contributors to these volumes stand in continuity with the historic church, care about the global church, share life together with other believers in local churches, and aim to write for the good of the church to strengthen its leaders, particularly pastors, teachers, missionaries, lay leaders, students, and professors.

For the glory of God and the good of the church,
Christopher W. Morgan

PREFACE TO *THE LOVE OF GOD*

This volume has been designed to help readers grow in their grasp of what it means to confess that God is love. Don Carson begins by helping us think deeply about the difficult doctrine of God's love, especially ways people distort it. Because Scripture is our foundation, there are three chapters devoted to it. Ray Ortlund answers the question, "Is the God of the Old Testament a God of love?" Andreas Köstenberger tackles, "What does Jesus teach about the love of God?" Rob Plummer addresses the query, "What do the apostles teach about the love of God?"

Theological chapters follow. John Mahony replies to the question, "Love in the triune community?" Chris Morgan addresses, "How does the Trinity's love shape our love for one another?" Dan Strange answers negatively the interrogative, "Does the love of God require universalism?" Dan Ebert replies to, "How does God's love in Christ relate to Islam?" Jimmy Agan addresses, "How does God's love shape the Christian walk?" Mariam Kamell rounds out the volume by answering, "How does God's love inspire social justice?"

ACKNOWLEDGMENTS

I thank our Crossway team, including Justin Taylor, Allan Fisher, Jill Carter, Lydia Brownback, Amy Kruis, Angie Cheatham, and Janni Firestone for their industry and support;

pastor Elliott Pinegar, for skillfully editing the whole manuscript and compiling the bibliography and indexes;

professors Tony Chute, Greg Cochran, and Mark Ryan for reading selected chapters and making suggestions;

Christina Sanders, my administrative assistant, for her kind spirit and excellent assistance;

Gary McDonald, for his enthusiastic support of these volumes.

CONTRIBUTORS

C. D. "Jimmy" Agan III (PhD, Aberdeen University), professor of New Testament and director of homiletics, Covenant Theological Seminary

D. A. Carson (PhD, University of Cambridge), professor of New Testament, Trinity Evangelical Divinity School

Daniel J. Ebert IV (PhD, Trinity Evangelical Divinity School), senior vice president, Clearwater Christian College

Mariam J. Kamell (PhD, University of St. Andrews), assistant professor, New Testament Studies, Regent College

Andreas J. Köstenberger (PhD, Trinity Evangelical Divinity School), professor of New Testament and Greek, Southeastern Baptist Theological Seminary

John W. Mahony (ThD, Mid-America Baptist Theological Seminary), professor of theological and historical studies, Mid-America Baptist Theological Seminary

Christopher W. Morgan (PhD, Mid-America Baptist Theological Seminary), dean and professor of theology, School of Christian Ministries, California Baptist University

Raymond C. Ortlund Jr. (PhD, University of Aberdeen), pastor, Immanuel Church, Nashville, Tennessee

Robert L. Plummer (PhD, The Southern Baptist Theological Seminary), professor of New Testament interpretation, The Southern Baptist Theological Seminary

Daniel Strange (PhD, University of Bristol), academic vice principal and tutor in religion, culture, and public theology, Oak Hill College, London

1

DISTORTING THE LOVE OF GOD?

D. A. CARSON

> God is love. Everything we know about him teaches us that, and every encounter we have with him expresses it. God's love for us is deep and all-embracing, but it is not the warmhearted sentimentality that often goes by the name of love today. —Gerald Bray

Gerald Bray, in the quote above, is correct on two counts.[1] First, God is love, and this grand subject is a major theme of the Scriptures and of this book, which seeks to capture something of the Bible's content and ethos on the subject. Second, Scripture's presentation of God's love is far from the "warmhearted sentimentality" so commonly confused with love today. This book focuses on a positive presentation of God's love in Scripture, theology, and Christian living. Nevertheless, a correction of distortions of God's love is foundational and is the subject of this chapter. I will set the distortions over against the rich and nuanced biblical picture of the love of God.

Why the Doctrine of the Love of God Must Be Judged Difficult

There are at least five reasons that the doctrine of the love of God must be judged difficult.

1) If people believe in God at all today, the overwhelming majority hold that this God—however he, she, or it may be understood—is a loving being. But that is what makes the task of the Christian witness so daunting, for this widely disseminated belief in the love of God is set with

[1] Gerald Bray, *God Is Love: A Biblical and Systematic Theology* (Wheaton, IL: Crossway, 2012), 17.

increasing frequency in some matrix other than biblical theology. The result is that when informed Christians talk about the love of God, they mean something very different from what is meant in the surrounding culture. Worse, neither side may perceive that that is the case.

Consider some recent products of the film industry, that celluloid preserve that both reflects and shapes Western culture. For our purposes, science-fiction films may be divided into two kinds. Perhaps the more popular ones are the slam-bang, shoot-'em-up kind, such as *Independence Day* or the four-part Alien series, complete with loathsome evil. Obviously the aliens have to be nasty, or there would be no threat and therefore no targets and no fun. Rarely do these films set out to convey a cosmological message, still less a spiritual one.

The other sort of film in this class, trying to convey a message even as it seeks to entertain, almost always portrays the ultimate power as benevolent. On the border between the two kinds of films is the Star Wars series, with its treatment of the morally ambiguous Force, but even this series tilts toward the assumption of a final victory for the "light" side of the Force. *ET*, as Roy Anker has put it, is "a glowing-heart incarnation tale that climaxes in resurrection and ascension."[2] And in Jodie Foster's *Contact*, the unexplained intelligence is suffused with love, wisely provident, gently awesome.

Anker himself thinks this "indirection," as he calls it, is a great help to the Christian cause. Like the writings of J. R. R. Tolkien and C. S. Lewis, these films help people *indirectly* to appreciate the sheer goodness and love of God. I am not nearly so sanguine. Tolkien and Lewis still lived in a world shaped by the Judeo-Christian heritage. Their "indirection" was read by others in the culture who had also been shaped by that heritage, even though many of their readers were not Christians in any biblical sense.

But the worldview of *Contact* is monistic, naturalistic, and pluralistic (after all, the film was dedicated to Carl Sagan). It has far more connections with New Age, Pollyannaish optimism than anything substantive. Suddenly the Christian doctrine of the love of God becomes very difficult, for the entire framework in which it is set in Scripture has been replaced.

2) To put this another way, we live in a culture in which many other and complementary truths about God are widely *dis*believed. I do not think that what the Bible says about the love of God can long survive at

[2] Roy Anker, "Not Lost in Space," *Books and Culture* 3 (November/December 1997): 13.

the forefront of our thinking if it is abstracted from the sovereignty of God, the holiness of God, the wrath of God, the providence of God, or the personhood of God—to mention only a few nonnegotiable elements of basic Christianity.

The result, of course, is that the love of God in our culture has been purged of anything the culture finds uncomfortable. The love of God has been sanitized, democratized, and above all sentimentalized. This process has been going on for some time. My generation was taught to sing, "What the world needs now is love, sweet love," in which we robustly instruct the Almighty that we do not need another mountain (we have enough of them), but we could do with some more love. The hubris is staggering.

It has not always been so. In generations when almost everyone believed in the justice of God, people sometimes found it difficult to believe in the love of God. The preaching of the love of God came as wonderful good news. Nowadays, if you tell people that God loves them, they are unlikely to be surprised. Of course God loves me; he's like that, isn't he? Besides, why shouldn't he love me? I'm kind of cute, or at least as nice as the next person. I'm okay, you're okay, and God loves you and me.

Even in the mid-1980s, according to Andrew Greeley, three-quarters of his respondents in an important poll reported that they preferred to think of God as "friend" rather than as "king."[3] I wonder what the percentage would have been if the option had been "friend" or "judge." Today most people seem to have little difficulty believing in the love of God; they have far more difficulty believing in the justice of God, the wrath of God, and the noncontradictory truthfulness of an omniscient God. But is the biblical teaching on the love of God maintaining its shape when the meaning of "God" dissolves in mist?

We must not think that Christians are immune from these influences. In an important book, Marsha Witten surveys what is being preached in the Protestant pulpit.[4] Let us admit the limitations of her study. Her pool of sermons was drawn, on the one hand, from the Presbyterian Church (USA), scarcely a bastion of confessional evangelicalism; and, on the other, from churches belonging to the Southern Baptist Convention. Strikingly, on many of the crucial issues, there was only marginal statistical difference between these two ecclesiastical heritages. A more significant limitation was that the sermons she studied all focused on the

---

[3] Andrew M. Greeley, *Religious Change in America* (Cambridge, MA: Harvard University Press, 1989), 37.
[4] Martha G. Witten, *All Is Forgiven: The Secular Message in American Protestantism* (Princeton, NJ: Princeton University Press, 1993).

parable of the prodigal son (Luke 15). That is bound to slant sermons in a certain direction.

Nevertheless, her book abounds in lengthy quotations from these sermons, and they are immensely troubling. There is a powerful tendency to "present God through characterizations of his inner states, with an emphasis on his emotions, which closely resemble those of human beings. . . . God is more likely to 'feel' than to 'act,' to 'think' than to 'say.'"[5] Or again:

> The relatively weak notion of God's fearsome capabilities regarding judgment is underscored by an almost complete lack of discursive construction of anxiety around one's future state. As we have already seen, the sermons dramatize feelings of anxiety for listeners over many other (this-worldly) aspects of their removal from God, whether they are discussing in the vocabulary of sin or in other formulations. But even when directly referring to the unconverted, only two sermons press on fear of God's judgment by depicting anxiety over salvation, and each text does this only obliquely, as it makes the point indirectly on its way to other issues while buffering the audience from negative feelings. . . . The transcendent, majestic, awesome God of Luther and Calvin—whose image informed early Protestant visions of the relationship between human beings and the divine—has undergone a softening of demeanor through the American experience of Protestantism, with only minor exceptions. . . . Many of the sermons depict a God whose behavior is regular, patterned, and predictable; he is portrayed in terms of the consistency of his behavior, of the conformity of his actions to the single rule of "love."[6]

With such sentimentalizing of God multiplying in Protestant churches, it does not take much to see how difficult maintaining a *biblical* doctrine of the love of God can be.

3) Some elements of the larger and still developing patterns of postmodernism play into the problem with which we are dealing. Because of remarkable shifts in the West's epistemology, more and more people believe that the only heresy left is the view that there is such a thing as heresy. They hold that all religions are fundamentally the same and that, therefore, it is not only rude but profoundly ignorant and old-fashioned to try to win others to your beliefs since implicitly that is announcing that theirs are inferior.[7]

---

[5] Ibid., 40.

[6] Ibid., 50, 53, 135.

[7] I have discussed these matters at some length in D. A. Carson, *The Gagging of God: Christianity Confronts Pluralism* (Grand Rapids, MI: Zondervan, 1996).

This stance, fueled in the West, now reaches into many parts of the world. For example, in a recent book Caleb Oluremi Oladipo outlines *The Development of the Doctrine of the Holy Spirit in the Yoruba (African) Indigenous Church Movement.*[8] His concern is to show the interplay between Christian beliefs and Yoruba traditional religion on the indigenous church. After establishing "two distinct perspectives" that need not detain us here, Oladipo writes:

> These two paradigmic [*sic*] perspectives in the book are founded on a fundamental assertion that the nature of God is universal love. This assertion presupposes that while Western missionaries asserted that the nature of God is universal love, most missionaries have denied salvation to various portions of the world population, and in most cases they did so indiscriminately. The book points out the inconsistencies of such a view, and attempts to bring coherency between Christianity and other religions in general, and Yoruba Traditional Religion in particular.[9]

In short, the most energetic cultural tide, postmodernism, powerfully reinforces the most sentimental, syncretistic, and often pluralistic views of the love of God, with no other authority base than the postmodern epistemology itself. But that makes the articulation of a biblical doctrine of God and of a biblical doctrine of the love of God an extraordinarily difficult challenge.

4) The first three difficulties stem from developments in the culture that make grasping and articulating the doctrine of the love of God a considerable challenge. This fourth element is in certain respects more fundamental. In the cultural rush toward a sentimentalized, sometimes even nontheistic vision of the love of God, we Christians have sometimes been swept along to the extent that we have forgotten that *within Christian confessionalism* the doctrine of the love of God poses its difficulties. This side of two world wars; genocide in Russia, China, Germany, and Africa; mass starvation; Hitler and Pol Pot; endless disgusting corruptions at home and abroad—all in the twentieth century—is the love of God such an obvious doctrine? Of course, that is raising the difficulties from an experiential point of view. One may do the same thing from the perspective of systematic theology. Precisely how does one integrate what the Bible says about the love of God with what the Bible says about God's

---

[8] Caleb Oluremi Oladipo, *The Development of the Doctrine of the Holy Spirit in the Yoruba (African) Indigenous Church Movement*, AUSTR 185 (New York: Peter Lang, 1996).

[9] Ibid.

sovereignty, extending as it does even over the domain of evil? What does love mean in a being whom at least some texts treat as impassible? How is God's love tied to God's justice?

In other words, one of the most dangerous results of the impact of contemporary sentimentalized versions of love on the church is our widespread inability to think through the fundamental questions that alone enable us to maintain a doctrine of God in biblical proportion and balance. However glorious and privileged a task that may be, none of it is easy. We are dealing with God, and fatuous reductionisms are bound to be skewed and dangerous.

5) Finally, the doctrine of the love of God is sometimes portrayed within Christian circles as much easier and more obvious than it really is, and this is achieved by overlooking some of the distinctions the Bible itself introduces when it depicts the love of God. This is so important that it becomes my next major point.

Some Different Ways the Bible Speaks of the Love of God

I had better warn you that not all of the passages to which I refer actually use the word *love.* When I speak of the doctrine of the love of God, I include themes and texts that depict God's love without ever using the word, just as Jesus tells parables that depict grace without using that word.

With that warning to the fore, I draw your attention to five distinguishable ways the Bible speaks of the love of God. This is not an exhaustive list, but it is heuristically useful.

1) *The peculiar love of the Father for the Son and of the Son for the Father.* John's Gospel is especially rich in this theme. Twice we are told that the Father loves the Son, once with the verb *agapaō* (John 3:35), and once with *phileō* (5:20). Yet the Evangelist also insists that the world must learn that Jesus loves the Father (14:31). This intra-Trinitarian love of God not only marks off Christian monotheism from all other monotheisms but is bound up in surprising ways with revelation and redemption.

2) *God's providential love over all that he has made.* By and large the Bible veers away from using the word *love* in this connection, but the theme is not hard to find. God creates everything, and before there is a whiff of sin, he pronounces all that he has made to be "good" (Genesis 1). This is the product of a *loving* Creator. The Lord Jesus depicts a world in which God clothes the grass of the fields with the glory of wildflowers seen by no human being, perhaps, but seen by God. The lion roars and hauls down its prey, but it is God who feeds the animal. The birds of the

air find food, but that is the result of God's loving providence; and not a sparrow falls from the sky apart from the sanction of the Almighty (Matthew 6). If this were not a benevolent providence, a *loving* providence, then the moral lesson that Jesus drives home, viz., that this God can be trusted to provide for his own people, would be incoherent.

3) *God's salvific stance toward his fallen world.* God so loved *the world* that he gave his Son (John 3:16). I know that some try to take *kosmos* ("world") here to refer to the elect. But that really will not do. All the evidence of the usage of the word in John's Gospel is against the suggestion. True, *world* in John does not so much refer to bigness as to badness. In John's vocabulary, *world* is primarily the moral order in willful and culpable rebellion against God. In John 3:16 God's love in sending the Lord Jesus is to be admired not because it is extended to so big a thing as the world, but to so bad a thing; not to so many people, as to such wicked people. Nevertheless, elsewhere John can speak of "the *whole* world" (1 John 2:2),[10] thus bringing bigness and badness together. More importantly, in Johannine theology the disciples themselves once belonged to the world but were drawn out of it (e.g., John 15:19). On this axis, God's love for the world cannot be collapsed into his love for the elect.

The same lesson is learned from many passages and themes in Scripture. However much God stands in judgment over the world, he also presents himself as the God who invites and commands all human beings to repent. He orders his people to carry the gospel to the farthest corner of the world, proclaiming it to men and women everywhere. To rebels the sovereign Lord calls out, "As surely as I live . . . I take no pleasure in the death of the wicked, but rather that they turn from their ways and live. Turn! Turn from your evil ways! Why will you die, people of Israel?" (Ezek. 33:11).[11]

4) *God's particular, effective, selecting love toward his elect.* The elect may be the entire nation of Israel or the church as a body or individuals. In each case, God sets his affection on his chosen ones in a way in which he does not set his affection on others. The people of Israel are told, "The LORD did not set his affection on you and choose you because you were more numerous than other peoples, for you were the fewest of all peoples. But it was because the LORD loved you and kept the oath he swore to your

[10] Scripture quotations in this chapter are taken from The Holy Bible, New International Version®, NIV®. Copyright © 1973, 1978, 1984, 2011 by Biblica, Inc.™ Used by permission. All rights reserved worldwide.

[11] The force of this utterance is not diminished by observing that it is addressed to the house of Israel, for not all in the house of Israel are finally saved; in Ezekiel's day, many die in judgment.

ancestors that he brought you out with a mighty hand and redeemed you from the land of slavery, from the power of Pharaoh king of Egypt" (Deut. 7:7–8; cf. 4:37). Again: "To the Lord your God belong the heavens, even the highest heavens, the earth and everything in it. Yet the Lord set his affection on your ancestors and loved them, and he chose you, their descendants, above all the nations—as it is today" (10:14–15).

The striking thing about these passages is that when Israel is contrasted with the universe or with other nations, the distinguishing feature has nothing of personal or national merit; it is nothing other than the love of God. In the very nature of the case, then, God's love is directed toward Israel in these passages in a way in which it is *not* directed toward other nations.

Obviously, this way of speaking of the love of God is unlike the other three ways of speaking of God's love that we have looked at so far. This discriminating feature of God's love surfaces frequently. "I have loved Jacob, but Esau I have hated" (Mal. 1:2–3), God declares. Allow all the room you like for the Semitic nature of this contrast, observing that the absolute form can be a way of articulating absolute preference; yet the fact is that God's love in such passages is peculiarly directed toward the elect.

Similarly, in the New Testament: Christ "loved the church" (Eph. 5:25). Repeatedly the New Testament texts tell us that the love of God or the love of Christ is directed toward those who constitute the church.

5) *Finally, God's love is sometimes said to be directed toward his own people in a provisional or conditional way—conditioned, that is, on obedience.* It is part of the relational structure of knowing God; it does not have to do with how we become true followers of the living God but with our relationship with him once we do know him. "Keep yourselves in God's love," Jude exhorts his readers (v. 21), leaving the unmistakable impression that someone might *not* keep himself or herself in the love of God. Clearly this is not God's providential love; it is pretty difficult to escape that. Nor is this God's yearning love, reflecting his salvific stance toward our fallen race. Nor is it his eternal, elective love. If words mean anything, one does not, as we shall see, walk away from that love either.

Jude is not the only one who speaks in such terms. The Lord Jesus commands his disciples to remain in his love (John 15:9) and adds, "If you keep my commands, you will remain in my love, just as I have kept my Father's commands and remain in his love" (v. 10). To draw a feeble analogy: although there is a sense in which my love for my children is immutable, so help me God, regardless of what they do, there is another sense in which they know well enough that they must remain in my love. If for no good reason my teenagers do not get home by the time I have prescribed, the least they will experience is a bawling out, and they may come under some restrictive sanctions. There is no use reminding them that I am doing this because I love them. That is true, but the manifestation of my love for them when I ground them and when I take them out for a meal or attend one of their concerts or take my son fishing or my daughter on an excursion of some sort is rather different in the two cases. Only the latter will feel much more like remaining in my love than falling under my wrath.

Nor is this a phenomenon of the new covenant alone. The Decalogue declares God to be the one who shows his love to a "thousand generations *of those who love me and keep my commandments*" (Ex. 20:6). Yes, "the LORD is compassionate and gracious, slow to anger, abounding in love" (Ps. 103:8). In this context, his love is *set over against* his wrath. Unlike some other texts, his people live under his love *or* under his wrath, in function of their covenantal faithfulness: "He will not *always* accuse, nor will he harbor his anger forever; he does not treat us as our sins deserve or repay us according to our iniquities. For as high as the heavens are above the earth, so great is his love *for those who fear him. . . .* As a father has compassion on his children, so the LORD has compassion *on those who fear him. . . .* But from everlasting to everlasting the LORD's love is *with those who fear him . . . with those who keep his covenant and remember to obey his precepts*" (vv. 9–11, 13, 17–18). This is the language of relationship between God and the covenant community.

Three Preliminary Observations on These Distinctive Ways of Talking about the Love of God

In concluding this chapter, it will be useful to draw some strands together.

1) It is easy to see what will happen if any one of these five biblical ways of talking about the love of God is absolutized and made exclusive, or made the controlling grid by which the other ways of talking about the love of God are relativized.

If we begin with the intra-Trinitarian love of God and use that as the model for all of God's loving relationships, we shall fail to observe the distinctions that must be maintained. The love of the Father for the Son and the love of the Son for the Father are expressed in a relationship of perfection, untarnished by sin on either side. However much the intra-Trinitarian love serves as a model of the love to be exchanged between

Jesus and his followers, there is no sense in which the love of the Father redeems the Son, or the love of the Son is expressed in a relationship of forgiveness granted and received. As precious, indeed as properly awesome, as the intra-Trinitarian love of God is, an exclusive focus in this direction takes too little account of how God manifests himself toward his rebellious image bearers in wrath, in love, in the cross.

If the love of God is nothing more than his providential ordering of everything, we are not far from a beneficent if somewhat mysterious "force." It would be easy to integrate that kind of stance into pantheism or some other form of monism. Green ecology may thereby be strengthened but not the grand storyline that takes us from creation to new creation to new heaven and new earth by way of the cross and resurrection of our Master.

If the love of God is exclusively portrayed as an inviting, yearning, sinner-seeking, rather lovesick passion, we may strengthen the hands of Arminians, semi-Pelagians, Pelagians, and those more interested in God's inner emotional life than in his justice and glory, but the cost will be massive. There is some truth in this picture of God, some glorious truth. Made absolute, however, it not only treats complementary texts as if they were not there, but it steals God's sovereignty from him and our security from us. It espouses a theology of grace rather different from Paul's theology of grace and at its worst ends up with a God so insipid he can neither intervene to save us nor deploy his chastening rod against us. His love is too "unconditional" for that. This is a world far removed from the pages of Scripture.

If the love of God refers exclusively to his love for the elect, it is easy to drift toward a simple and absolute bifurcation: God loves the elect and hates the reprobate. Rightly positioned, there is truth in this assertion; stripped of complementary biblical truths, that same assertion has engendered hyper-Calvinism. I use the term advisedly, referring to groups within the Reformed tradition that have forbidden the free offer of the gospel. Spurgeon fought them in his day.[12] Their number is not great in America today, but their echoes are found in young Reformed ministers who know it is right to offer the gospel freely but who have no idea how to do it without contravening some element in their conception of Reformed theology.[13]

[12] See Iain H. Murray, *Spurgeon and Hyper-Calvinism* (Edinburgh: Banner of Truth, 1995).

[13] There are echoes as well in R. K. McGregor Wright, *No Place for Sovereignty* (Downers Grove, IL: InterVarsity Press, 1996).

If the love of God is construed entirely within the kind of discourse that ties God's love to our obedience (e.g., "Keep yourselves in God's love," Jude 21), the dangers threatening us change once again. True, in a church characterized rather more by personal preference and antinomianism than godly fear of the Lord, such passages surely have something to say to us. But divorced from complementary biblical utterances about the love of God, such texts may drive us backward toward merit theology, endless fretting about whether we have been good enough today to enjoy the love of God—to be free from all the paroxysms of guilt from which the cross alone may free us.

In short, we need *all* of what Scripture says on this subject, or the doctrinal and pastoral ramifications will prove disastrous.

2) We must not view these ways of talking about the love of God as independent, compartmentalized *loves* of God. It will not help to begin talking too often about God's providential love, his elective love, his intra-Trinitarian love, and so forth, as if each were hermetically sealed off from the others. Nor can we allow any one of these ways of talking about the love of God to be diminished by the others, even as we cannot, on scriptural evidence, allow any one of them to domesticate all the others. God is God, and he is one. Not only must we gratefully acknowledge that God in the perfection of his wisdom has thought it best to provide us with these various ways of talking of his love if we are to think of him aright, but we must hold these truths together and learn to integrate them in biblical proportion and balance. We must apply them to our lives and the lives of those to whom we minister with insight and sensitivity shaped by the way these truths function in Scripture.

3) Within the framework established so far, we may well ask ourselves how well certain evangelical clichés stand up.

a) "God's love is unconditional." Doubtless that is true in the fourth sense, with respect to God's elective love. But it is certainly not true in the fifth sense: God's discipline of his children means that he may turn upon us with the divine equivalent of the "wrath" of a parent on a wayward teenager. Indeed, to cite the cliché "God's love is unconditional" to a Christian who is drifting toward sin may convey the wrong impression and do a lot of damage. Such Christians need to be told that they will remain in God's love only if they do what he says. Obviously, then, it is pastorally important to know what passages and themes to apply to which people at any given time.

b) "God loves everyone exactly the same way." That is certainly true in passages belonging to the second category, in the domain of providence. After all, God sends his sunshine and his rain upon the just and the unjust alike. But it is certainly not true in passages belonging to the fourth category, the domain of election.

To sum up: Christian faithfulness entails our responsibility to grow in our grasp of what it means to confess that God is love.

2

IS THE GOD OF THE OLD TESTAMENT A GOD OF LOVE?

RAYMOND C. ORTLUND JR.

This study is prompted, in part, by a popular misconception of the Old Testament, which might seem to be validated by the New Testament. Think, for example, of the teaching of Jesus in Matthew 5:21–48, which has been construed by some to correct the Old Testament with a more gracious ethic. But the passage is better understood as the Lord's removing the overlay of oral tradition wrongly laid upon the Old Testament: "You have *heard* that it was *said* . . ." Still, the notion that the Old Testament underemphasizes the love of God requires an answer. My thesis is that the Old Testament presents the love of God with glorious clarity, fully worthy to be the voice preparing the way for the love of Jesus in the New Testament. By "love of God" I mean the benevolence of God in a large sense, the various manifestations of his care for his people.

I will make my case in three steps. First, I will highlight the vocabulary of divine love in the Old Testament. Second, I will exegete briefly several passages in the Old Testament conspicuous for their representations of divine love. Third, I will survey the plotline of the Old Testament as a story of divine love. These evidences argue for the love of God as an unmistakably clear teaching of the Old Testament, consistent with the New Testament.

Vocabulary

It would be a loss not to consider the vocabulary for the love of God in the Old Testament as a suggestive starting point. It is not obvious where to delimit the Old Testament's vocabulary for divine love. Some words are central. Other words are contiguous. The central words cluster around the roots *'hb*, *hsd*, and *rhm*. The contiguous words have to do with choosing, forgiving, delighting in, and so forth, which are functions of love. Our interest here is the essential vocabulary of love—as opposed to hatred, wrath, vengeance, and so forth.

'hb

The Old Testament presents human analogies for divine love in the special favor Abraham felt for his heir Isaac (Gen. 22:2), in the romantic longings of Jacob for Rachel, which so swept him away that his years of service for her sped by like days (29:20), and in the sense of personal identification and loyalty Jonathan felt toward David, so profound that they committed themselves to a covenant as friends and allies together (1 Sam. 18:3). However much human love falls short of the divine, the Old Testament nevertheless uses such language to describe the love of God as well. Here is a representative sample:

> Behold, to the Lord your God belong heaven and the heaven of heavens, the earth with all that is in it. Yet the Lord set his heart in *love* on your fathers and chose their offspring after them, you above all peoples, as you are this day. (Deut. 10:14–15)[1]

> In all their affliction he was afflicted,
> and the angel of his presence saved them;
> in his *love* and in his pity he redeemed them;[2]
> he lifted them up and carried them all the days of old. (Isa. 63:9)

> I have *loved* you with an everlasting *love*;[3]
> therefore I have continued my faithfulness to you. (Jer. 31:3)

> The Lord *loves* justice;
> he will not forsake his saints.[4]

---

[1] Election in the OT is not like a computer-driven mailing that chooses a name from an impersonal database and then sends out an advertisement or a political solicitation. Election is an act of personal love, God setting his heart on his people.

[2] Franz Delitzsch, *Biblical Commentary on the Prophecies of Isaiah* (Grand Rapids, MI: Eerdmans, 1969), 2:455, glosses "pity" as "his forgiving gentleness."

[3] Matthew Henry comments, "From everlasting in the counsels of it, to everlasting in the continuance and consequences of it, . . . no attractive can be more powerful," in *Matthew Henry's Commentary on the Whole Bible* (McLean, VA: MacDonald, n.d.), 4:598.

[4] The love of God is no compromise of his principles. It is love that prompts him to adhere to his principles, which are to be admired for their loving character. He will not forsake his saints, for it would be wrong to abandon them.

They are preserved forever,
 but the children of the wicked shall be cut off. (Ps. 37:28)

On the holy mount stands the city he founded;
 the LORD *loves* the gates of Zion
 more than all the dwelling places of Jacob. (Ps. 87:1–2)[5]

My son, do not despise the LORD's discipline
 or be weary of his reproof,
for the LORD reproves him whom he *loves*,
 as a father the son in whom he delights. (Prov. 3:11–12)[6]

The LORD *loves* him;
 he shall perform his purpose on Babylon,
 and his arm shall be against the Chaldeans. (Isa. 48:14)[7]

Those uses of the verb *'hb* establish the sense clearly enough. But it is worth noting as well that the etymology of the Hebrew word has been traced to the Arabic *hbb*, "to breathe, to pant (with eager desire)."[8]

hsd

The word *hsd* is rendered variously but compatibly in the English versions.[9] The definition "loyalty," with an emphasis on rights and obligations in the relationship, seemed for some decades to establish a consensus among scholars.[10] But the inadequacy of this proposal became apparent. The sense "lovingkindness" has been convincingly reasserted,[11] validating the tradition of the English versions. For example:

"In overflowing anger for a moment
 I hid my face from you,
but with *everlasting love* I will have compassion on you,"[12]
 says the LORD, your Redeemer. (Isa. 54:8)

[5] The biblical gospel is pervaded with selective particularities, with "not there but here." This outlook might offend the modern mind. But according to Scripture, the love of God is both "sufficient and inscrutable," as articulated by Derek Kidner, *Psalms 73–150* (Downers Grove, IL: InterVarsity, 1975), 314.

[6] When we suffer, we can be tempted to despise and resist the Lord's discipline, or grow despairingly weary and quit. But the OT teaches us to see in our sufferings the very proof of the Father's loving delight in us.

[7] Strikingly, the "him" whom God "loves" is Cyrus, the Persian warlord. God is not repulsed by his own surprising strategies for world redemption, which include using evil people like Cyrus. God is unembarrassed by himself. With this startling assurance, we can trust him with the buffetings and perplexities of our lives.

[8] D. Winton Thomas, "The Root 'love' in Hebrew," *ZAW* 57 (1939): 57–64.

[9] We observe "mercy" in the KJV ("his mercy endureth forever," Psalm 136); "love" in the JB, NEB, NIV, and REB; "lovingkindness" in the NASB; and "steadfast love" in the RSV, NRSV, and ESV.

[10] Nelson Glueck, *HESED in the Bible* (Cincinnati: Hebrew Union College Press, 1967), 102.

[11] Francis I. Anderson, "Yahweh, the Kind and Sensitive God," in *God Who Is Rich in Mercy*, ed. D. B. Knox (Grand Rapids, MI: Baker, 1986), 41–88.

[12] The contrast is asymmetrical. His anger burned for a moment; his love flows forever in endless compassion.

I will recount the *steadfast love* of the LORD,
the praises of the LORD,
according to all that the LORD has granted us,
and the great goodness to the house of Israel
that he has granted them according to his compassion,
according to the abundance of his *steadfast love*. (Isa. 63:7)[13]

Who is a God like you, pardoning iniquity
and passing over transgression
for the remnant of his inheritance?
He does not retain his anger forever,
because he delights in *steadfast love*.[14]
He will again have compassion on us;
he will tread our iniquities underfoot.
You will cast all our sins
into the depths of the sea. (Mic. 7:18–19)

Those citations have special clarifying value because they dovetail the noun *hsd* with the concepts of compassion, goodness, and forgiveness. This kind of *hsd* goes beyond loyalty to covenant obligations, a beautiful concept vulnerable to the hairsplitting technicalities of the legalistic mind. In contrast to such temptations, these uses of *hsd* suggest overflowing kindness as the personally heartfelt flavor of God's steadfast love.

rhm

The lexicon of Koehler and Baumgartner introduces the noun *rehem* by proposing "probably a primary noun, of which the verb *rhm* is denominative," noting the Arabic cognate *rahuma*, "to be soft."[15] This Hebrew noun means "womb," as in:

Did not He who made me in my mother's belly make him?
Did not One form us both in the *womb*? (Job 31:15 *JPS Tanakh*)

The word group seems to connote a mentality of maternal gentleness and caring tenderness:

[13] The verse is enclosed within two plural uses of *hsd*, summarizing the import of the whole, with the plurality suggesting "every possible aspect and display of the Lord's 'ever-unfailing-love,'" according to J. Alec Motyer, *The Prophecy of Isaiah* (Downers Grove, IL: InterVarsity Press, 1993), 513.

[14] The prophet celebrates God's steadfast love as a mark of his incomparability ("Who is a God like you?"). God's steadfast love that forgives is not a reluctant concession on his part; it is his heartfelt delight. "What other god of the ancient Near East forgave and saved his people and so continued to live in history? [The other gods] are all dead. Israel's forgiving God, by contrast, is praised today around the world," according to Bruce K. Waltke in *The Minor Prophets*, ed. Thomas Edward McComiskey (Grand Rapids, MI: Baker, 1993), 2:762.

[15] Ludwig Koehler and Walter Baumgartner, *HALOT*, s.v. *rehem*.

> Foreigners shall build up your walls,
> and their kings shall minister to you;
> for in my wrath I struck you,
> but in my favor I *have had mercy* on you. (Isa. 60:10)[16]
>
> Is Ephraim my dear son?
> Is he my darling child?
> For as often as I speak against him,
> I do remember him still.
> Therefore my heart yearns for him;
> I will *surely have mercy* on him, declares the Lord. (Jer. 31:20)[17]
>
> Now I will restore the fortunes of Jacob and *have mercy* on the whole house of Israel, and I will be jealous for my holy name. (Ezek. 39:25)[18]

To sum up: the Old Testament deploys vocabulary that clearly and even vividly bears witness to the love of God, such that the strong assertions of divine love in the New Testament are no shock to the attentive reader.

Passages

Exodus 34:5–7

> The Lord descended in the cloud and stood with him there, and proclaimed the name of the Lord. The Lord passed before him and proclaimed, "The Lord, the Lord, a God merciful and gracious, slow to anger, and abounding in steadfast love and faithfulness, keeping steadfast love for thousands, forgiving iniquity and transgression and sin, but who will by no means clear the guilty, visiting the iniquity of the fathers on the children and the children's children, to the third and the fourth generation." (Ex. 34:5–7)

After the nation's shocking apostasy to the golden calf, Moses prays, "Please show me your glory" (33:18). The Lord answers, "I will make all my goodness pass before you and will proclaim before you my name 'The Lord'" (v. 19). The display of God's glory, then, in Exodus 34:5–7 can

[16] The Jews' restored fortunes are not a stroke of good luck but the decisive intervention of God. It is "in my favor" that God has mercy. That is, with *rasôn*, with a will, with pleasure—the opposite of "in my wrath." His mercies are indeed tender, but they are not weak wishful thinking.

[17] Not induced by human misery but arising from deep within his own yearnings for his chosen son Ephraim, God's heartfelt sympathy forms within him a strong resolve ("surely") to act in mercy.

[18] God's mercy in restoring the Jews from exile is compatible with his jealousy for his own holy name. The final ultimacy of God's self-vindication does not overrule or even diminish his mercy for his people; the ultimacy of his own vindication guarantees his mercy to his people. The Bible frees us from our fallacious thought that God either stands up for himself or cares about us, but not both. The Bible asserts both, in their proper order, with God as ultimate, but even that to our benefit.

be summarized as "all my goodness."[19] But, paradoxically, the Lord also explains that he will reveal not all of himself, that is, not himself frontally with the full force of his face, but partly and indirectly, only his back (33:20–23). What Moses is given to see, therefore, is the back of God, so to speak, objectified with theological language of overflowing beauty.

The repeated divine name, "the LORD, the LORD" in 34:6, echoes the famous "I AM WHO I AM" of 3:14. The point is that God's definition of his own glorious love suffices. He need not refer to others to make sense of himself. He is who internally and unchangeably he is: "The greatest and best man in the world must say, *By the grace of God I am what I am*; but God says absolutely—and it is more than any creature, man or angel, can say—*I am that I am*."[20]

The implication is that the descriptive language that follows must be qualified in the mind of the reader. God is truly loving in the following ways, but his absolute self-referentiality cautions us against unfiltered transference of meanings from the human to the divine. Valid linguistic definitions must not limit our thoughts of God. To quote Hilary of Poitiers, "Our understanding of the [biblical] words is to be taken from the reasons why they were spoken, because the subject is not subordinated to the language but the language to the subject."[21] That is, we must not shrink God down to our thought categories; we must stretch our thought categories out to match the grandeur of God.

God then shows Moses his back through seven expressions displaying the glories of his love. Describing himself in the third person, the Lord is, first, a "God merciful and gracious." He is tenderhearted toward sinners, because his own grace is all the motivation he needs to be merciful, sympathetic, and compassionate: "As a father shows compassion to his children, so the LORD shows compassion to those who fear him" (Ps. 103:13). Next, he is "slow to anger." He is patient with backward sinners, not volatile or trigger-happy, giving us ample opportunity to see God and ourselves in a new way and to change: God "is patient toward you, not wishing that any should perish, but that all should reach repentance" (2 Pet. 3:9). Third, he is "abounding in steadfast love and faithfulness." His massively faithful love towers over our sins and weaknesses with an all-surpassing breadth and length and height and depth (Eph. 3:18–19).

[19] "All the words which the language contained to express the idea of grace in its varied manifestations to the sinner are crowded together here, to reveal the fact that in His inmost being God is love." C. F. Keil and F. Delitzsch, *Biblical Commentary on the Old Testament: Exodus* (Grand Rapids, MI: Eerdmans, 1972), 241.

[20] Henry, *Commentary*, 1:284.

[21] Hilary of Poitiers, *De Trinitate*, I4.14: "Non sermoni res sed rei est sermo subjectus."

Next, he is "keeping steadfast love for thousands." He guards and protects his steadfast love so that it reaches far, to thousands of generations and distant descendants, to the furthest extent of his promises and to the furthest extremity of their needs (Rom. 8:31–39). His love is unstinting, unmeasured, uninhibited, boundless, free, rugged: "Having loved his own who were in the world, he loved them to the end" (John 13:1). Fifth, he is "forgiving iniquity and transgression and sin." The whole range of human wrongdoing is covered by the all-sufficient love of God, including iniquity, that is, twisted perversity; and transgression, that is, defiant rebellion; and sin, that is, a bungled life: "He healed them all" (Matt. 12:15). Moreover, God's love is of such grandeur that he remains a morally serious person, for, sixth, he "will by no means clear the guilty." It is mistaken to see the text turning in a different direction here, as if the Lord were now revealing the "other side of God's nature."[22] We are still looking at God's back. As only the cross will later clarify, God's love and God's justice are compatible, not only logically in doctrine but also psychologically in God's own heart (Rom. 3:21–26). His love does not trivialize guilt but answers for that guilt. Last, he will visit "the iniquity of the fathers on the children . . . to the third and the fourth generation." The qualifying phrase "of those who hate me" (Ex. 20:5) is assumed rather than stated here. Our resistance will not wear God down, though we fight on from one generation to the next. But still, God is love (1 John 4:8). The Bible never says, "God is wrath." We must provoke him to wrath. But we need not provoke him to love, for that is his glorious name.

Exodus 34:6–7 is one of the most important passages in the Bible. Echoes of this text resonate throughout the rest of the Old Testament (e.g., Num. 14:18; Neh. 9:17; Ps. 86:15; Joel 2:13; Jonah 4:2). Only a massive love from God could preserve faithless Israel after their worship of the golden calf. But that is precisely the God he reveals himself to be.

Hosea 11:8–9

How can I give you up, O Ephraim?
  How can I hand you over, O Israel?
How can I make you like Admah?
  How can I treat you like Zeboiim?
My heart recoils within me;
  my compassion grows warm and tender.
I will not execute my burning anger;

[22] R. Alan Cole, *Exodus: An Introduction and Commentary* (Downers Grove, IL: InterVarsity, 1973), 228.

> I will not again destroy Ephraim;
> for I am God and not a man,
> the Holy One in your midst,
> and I will not come in wrath. (Hos. 11:8–9)

After Israel's egregious spiritual whoredoms, painfully exposed in chapters 1–3, the Lord's shuddering at the thought of the nation's total destruction and utter disappearance from history, with his aching longing for their restoration—he seems to be writhing in anguish—is breathtaking. His repeated "How can I?" reveals that his own character, and not theirs at all, is the only explanation for his restraint of severity and yearning for mercy. On Admah and Zeboiim, Genesis 10:19 and 14:8 and Deuteronomy 29:23 group them together with Sodom and Gomorrah—unsavory company, and ripe for irrevocable and complete divine judgment! It is not as though God hasn't the stomach for extreme wrath, as the historical realities of Admah and Zeboiim prove. But in Israel's case, given God's covenanted and indeed marital love for the chosen nation, he will not and indeed cannot utterly disown them.

What is striking about this passage is the personal and even emotional intensity with which God turns away from retribution toward compassion. It is not a coldly calculating decision. It pours out of his deepest being: "My heart recoils within me," that is, "I'm churning inside. Yes, I am offended by you. But at a deeper level, I can't bring myself to hand you over to what you deserve." The ESV's "My compassion grows warm and tender" seems too mild a translation of the Hebrew text. The NIV paraphrases the sense more clearly: "All my compassion is aroused," that is, stirred up to intensity (cf. Gen. 43:30; 1 Kings 3:26). God is deeply upset over his adulterous people but not with the emotion one expects: "I will not execute my burning anger." His anger does burn. But his love burns more fiercely, finally overruling his anger.

Even more strikingly, the divine attribute that finally explains God's astonishing love for the undeserving is not his grace but his holiness: "I am God and not a man, the Holy One in your midst, and I will not come in wrath." Given the many and extreme insults heaped upon God by his heartless people, human love would fail. Human offense would escalate to exasperation, venting itself in wrath. But God is God and not man, the Holy One. He is wonderfully other, and incomparable as such (Isa. 40:25). It is his perfect holiness that guarantees his extreme love. His holiness does not condone their evil, which truly deserves the judgment of Genesis

19; but God is so holy that he is moved to demonstrate a love no human being is capable of. This means that his love, flowing from his holiness, is not a compromise of principle but is itself a sacrosanct principle. The Holy One, who defines and vindicates himself with reference to himself only, is moved to decision by "those spontaneous emotional forces which are their own justification."[23]

The holiness of God would have struck terror in the hearts of God's people, for they had turned his holy land into their brothel. But the one who is God and not man is better in every respect than the simplistic categories of human intuition. Writing of the revelation of God's holiness to Moses in Exodus 3, which is foundational to subsequent revelations to Israel, Bruce Waltke captures the surprising character of divine holiness:

> The Eternal lowers himself into a bush amid the dirt and the rocks; he is present among the goats and sheep with dung hanging off their tails. Yet, his humility does not compromise his holiness, for none, not even Moses, may enter his presence with dirt on their shoes. This paradoxical scene, where God demands respect by being clean in the midst of dirt and dung, communicates the power of God's holiness to purify the surrounding impurities. This idea is intensified by the next paradoxical image, a purifying fire (i.e., God) dwells in a bush that is fit for kindling (i.e., Israel) without consuming it. This symbolic theophany also foreshadows God's grace to stay in the midst of his people after they commit adultery with a fertility deity on their wedding night with *I AM* (Exodus 20–34, esp. 32–34).[24]

"The power of God's holiness to purify the surrounding impurities" reappears in the New Testament. Jesus, the healthy one—"moved with pity"—touches the leper and is not infected by him; the leper is cleansed by Jesus (Mark 1:40–42). "God's holiness, then, which initially seems so forbidding and judgmental, is the means of our salvation."[25]

Hosea's vision of the saving love of God, invincibly secured by the surprising holiness of God, prepares the way for the gospel of the New Testament. "How can I give you up, O Ephraim?" leads us to "He who did not spare his own Son but gave him up for us all" (Rom. 8:32). The mystery of God's love mingled with God's holiness is not, for us, resolved at the cross; it is deepened at the cross, reducing us to wonder and gratitude.

[23] Walther Eichrodt, *Theology of the Old Testament*, trans. J. A. Baker (Philadelphia: Westminster, 1961), 1:250.
[24] Bruce K. Waltke, *An Old Testament Theology* (Grand Rapids, MI: Zondervan, 2007), 363.
[25] John M. Frame, *The Doctrine of God* (Phillipsburg, NJ: P&R, 2002), 29.

Zephaniah 3:17

The LORD your God is in your midst,
a mighty one who will save;
he will rejoice over you with gladness;
he will quiet you by his love;
he will exult over you with loud singing. (Zeph. 3:17)

Most of the prophecy of Zephaniah is "unrelieved in its stress on God's wrath, . . . with a white-hot fury almost unparalleled in Scripture."[26] In the immediate aftermath of such startling divine judgment, God here declares his love for his own in terms equally startling. The warrior who bares his sword over the nations on his day of wrath, distress and anguish, ruin and devastation, darkness and gloom, clouds and thick darkness, trumpet blast and battle cry (1:15–16)—that same warrior will draw near to his people with loving reassurances in the most extravagant terms. Truly, there is nothing small, simplistic, or predictable about him!

What then does Zephaniah reveal about the love of this fierce one? After the life-depleting miseries of God's people—the slack hands of 3:16 are hanging limp in exhaustion from the strain of his judgments—the Lord promises he will no longer be distant but will be actively present among his people, their all-sufficiency in all things. The ancient promises sworn by "the LORD your God" will finally come true, for he by grace declares himself to be their God. He will reveal himself to be a "mighty one who will save," that is, a powerful military hero (Ps. 24:8), not fighting against his people any longer but now fighting for them, intervening to save the day. He will rejoice over his people with a whole heart, feeling nothing toward them but approval, all his wrath having been spent. He will calm and reassure his people, not rebuking them but relieving their anxieties, satisfying their unresolved questions, wiping every tear from their eyes (Rev. 21:4). But, paradoxically, he will also exult loudly over his people with a "love that cannot be contained but bursts into elated singing."[27] The love of God is somehow able to lift gently the troubles of the mind and gush happily with volcanic exuberance, both at the same time. These apparently opposite experiences combine to suggest the totality of God's fully satisfying love for his people. To quote Matthew Henry: "Oh the condescensions of divine grace! The great God not only loves

[26] William Sanford LaSor, David Allan Hubbard, and Frederic William Bush, *Old Testament Survey: The Message, Form and Background of the Old Testament* (Grand Rapids, MI: Eerdmans, 1996), 315.
[27] J. Alec Motyer, in *An Exegetical and Expository Commentary on The Minor Prophets*, ed. Thomas Edward McComiskey (Grand Rapids, MI: Baker, 1998), 958.

his saints, but he loves to love them."[28] The vision of Zephaniah reveals the love of God as wholehearted, enthusiastic, not grudging, not holding back at all.

These three passages display the love of God with claims so clear and bold I dare say there is nothing in the New Testament to exceed them for beauty or force.

Survey

The Bible is not a hodgepodge of sweet, disconnected devotional thoughts. Reading the Bible is not like breaking open a fortune cookie so that a hopeful wish might parachute into our reality from out of nowhere. The Bible tells a story, one massive story, from cover to cover. As a coherent whole, the Bible provides its own interpretative clues. Sprinkled throughout the course of the Old Testament are atomically weighted verses and passages that summarize the entire plot. These texts are not limited to a specific situation but survey the broader ways of God evidenced throughout the history of Israel. The message thus conveyed is the love of God. An obvious example of such a text is Psalm 136. This psalm recounts the active involvement of God—from the creation to the exodus to the conquest of the land to the time of the psalm's composition—as a unified story with one consistent theme, stated 26 times: "His steadfast love endures forever." Or, put in the confident terms of the New Testament, "Who shall separate us from the love of Christ?" (Rom. 8:35). There is simply no end to his steadfast love, and Psalm 136 is saying that the biblical narrative proves it over and over again. Here are other examples of these summarizing texts, in canonical order:

> As for you, you meant evil against me, but God meant it for good. (Gen. 50:20)

This flash of insight explains Joseph's story in Genesis 37–50. But further, because the verse unveils the very ways of God, it pertains equally well to all of Genesis, from chapter 3 on. The key to redemptive history and the only hope of the world, then, is the overruling goodness of God. Human evil is real and active, but God's goodness is working down underneath the evil to reverse its impact. Thus, there are two levels of causation in all human events. The opposition, setbacks, failures, and betrayals fall out, at an observable level, through evil human intention. But at a deeper

[28] Henry, *Commentary*, 4:1387.

level, God is working all things according to the counsel of his own will for a triumphant good. What gives hope to God's people is the undergirding love of God, moving all things toward a life-giving outcome, even through real human evil.

> The LORD bless you and keep you; the LORD make his face to shine upon you and be gracious to you; the LORD lift up his countenance upon you and give you peace. (Num. 6:24–26)

The blessing of Aaron defines God's domestic policy, so to speak, toward his people, even within the framework of the Mosaic law. And that policy is complete and comprehensive blessing, a fullness of grace upon grace that leads to eternal shalom and is sealed infallibly by the threefold repetition of the divine name.

> You shall make response before the LORD your God, "A wandering Aramean was my father. And he went down into Egypt and sojourned there, few in number, and there he became a nation, great, mighty, and populous. And the Egyptians treated us harshly and humiliated us and laid on us hard labor. Then we cried to the LORD, the God of our fathers, and the LORD heard our voice and saw our affliction, our toil, and our oppression. And the LORD brought us out of Egypt with a mighty hand and an outstretched arm, with great deeds of terror, with signs and wonders. And he brought us into this place and gave us this land, a land flowing with milk and honey. And behold, now I bring the first of the fruit of the ground, which you, O LORD, have given me." And you shall set it down before the LORD your God and worship before the LORD your God. And you shall rejoice in all the good that the LORD your God has given to you and to your house, you, and the Levite, and the sojourner who is among you. (Deut. 26:5–11)

The Mosaic law commanded each harvest time to be set apart as a celebration of God's goodness, looking back to the remotest origins of Israel's history. Each season's firstfruits reminded the people, year after year, of what they were in fact experiencing—the same generous love of God that took them from their humble beginnings into the fullness of their present blessing in the land.

> The LORD gave to Israel all the land that he swore to give to their fathers. And they took possession of it, and they settled there. And the LORD gave them rest on every side just as he had sworn to their fathers. Not one of all their enemies had withstood them, for the LORD had given all

> their enemies into their hands. Not one word of all the good promises that the LORD had made to the house of Israel had failed; all came to pass. (Josh. 21:43–45)

"The theological heart of the book of Joshua"[29] asserts the faithfulness of God to all his "good promises" up to this time. Moreover, these verses create the presumption that the Lord will continue to fulfill faithfully his promises in the future, all the way to the final consummation of his kingdom purpose. The rugged, steady goodness of the Lord never fails.

> Whenever the LORD raised up judges for them, the LORD was with the judge, and he saved them from the hand of their enemies all the days of the judge. For the LORD was moved to pity by their groaning because of those who afflicted and oppressed them. (Judg. 2:18)

The purpose of this context, Judges 2:11–23, is to summarize the pattern of apostasy, misery, deliverance, and more apostasy evident throughout the book of Judges. The point of verse 18 is that God was repeatedly moved by Israel's misery, though that misery was deserved. They provoked him to wrath time after time, but deeper still was his heart ever moved to pity.

> The LORD is good to all,
> and his mercy is over all that he has made. . . .
> The LORD is righteous in all his ways
> and kind in all his works.
> The LORD is near to all who call on him,
> to all who call on him in truth. (Ps. 145:9, 17–18)

Representative of other such statements in Psalms, this view of God, marked by the repeated use of *all*, is a sweepingly comprehensive vision, extending beyond the boundaries of the covenanted people. Moreover, these verses stand within an acrostic psalm, structured to communicate, "I've said it all, from A to Z." Finally, Psalm 145 is the last of David's psalms in the Psalter, his final statement. The one assertion of divine wrath in Psalm 145 is, "All the wicked he will destroy" (v. 20). But even that final judgment is required by God's goodness. It is endless divine love that the wicked finally reject.

---

[29] Dale Ralph Davis, *No Falling Words* (Grand Rapids, MI: Baker, 1996), 157.

When he established the heavens, I was there;
when he drew a circle on the face of the deep,
when he made firm the skies above,
when he established the fountains of the deep,
when he assigned to the sea its limit,
so that the waters might not transgress his command,
when he marked out the foundations of the earth,
then I was beside him, like a master workman,[30]
and I was daily his delight,[31]
rejoicing before him always,
rejoicing in his inhabited world
and delighting in the children of man. (Prov. 8:27–31)

Speaking with the voice of Wisdom personified, the sage asserts the joyous nature of God's creation. Long before man was here to vandalize God's original design, Wisdom was here, suffusing created reality with a beauty and meaning to thrill the heart. The loving and wise goodness of God is not limited to Israel's history. It is the secret code to the very universe itself.

I will recount the steadfast love of the LORD,
the praises of the LORD,
according to all that the LORD has granted us,
and the great goodness to the house of Israel
that he has granted them according to his compassion,
according to the abundance of his steadfast love.
For he said, "Surely they are my people,
children who will not deal falsely."
And he became their Savior.
In all their affliction he was afflicted,
and the angel of his presence saved them;
in his love and in his pity he redeemed them;
he lifted them up and carried them all the days of old.
(Isa. 63:7–9)

Isaiah surveys the entire length of Israel's history, "all the days of old," as a story of the love of God. Verse 7 begins and ends with the noun in the plural—literally, "I will recount *the steadfast loves* . . . the abundance of

[30] Bruce K. Waltke, *The Book of Proverbs: Chapters 1–15* (Grand Rapids, MI: Eerdmans, 2004), 417–22, argues that the sense is not "like a master workman" but "constantly." The parallelism favors his interpretation: "Then I was constantly beside him, / and I was daily his delight, / rejoicing before him always."

[31] The ESV marginal translation seems preferable, since the emphasis of vv. 30–31 is the joy of wisdom in the creation, not the Creator's joy in wisdom.

his steadfast loves"—the plural form suggesting "every possible aspect and display of the Lord's ever-unfailing love."[32]

> Thus says the LORD, the God of Israel, concerning this city of which you say, "It is given into the hand of the king of Babylon by sword, by famine, and by pestilence": Behold, I will gather them from all the countries to which I drove them in my anger and my wrath and in great indignation. I will bring them back to this place, and I will make them dwell in safety. And they shall be my people, and I will be their God. I will give them one heart and one way, that they may fear me forever, for their own good and the good of their children after them. I will make with them an everlasting covenant, that I will not turn away from doing good to them. And I will put the fear of me in their hearts, that they may not turn from me. I will rejoice in doing them good, and I will plant them in this land in faithfulness, with all my heart and all my soul. (Jer. 32:36–41)

Not only does the Old Testament look back to the past as a narrative of the love of God, it looks forward to the future as the same—but with a difference. After the ultimate discipline of the exile, the people of God will be restored so fully that even the heart condition that doomed them before will be remedied. Adam fell and suffered for it. Israel fell and suffered for it. But God also promises a new era of blessing so full, so all-providing, that it will never end.

Significantly, the Old Testament does not include analogous passages arguing the opposite—that the wrath of God is the deep insight disclosed through the history of Israel. His wrath is ominously real in the Old Testament's account of reality, but it is reluctantly unleashed upon his people and is not his final word to them:

> The Lord will not
> cast off forever,
> but, though he cause grief, he will have compassion
> according to the abundance of his steadfast love;[33]
> for he does not afflict from his heart
> or grieve the children of men. (Lam. 3:31–33)

> As I live, declares the Lord GOD, I have no pleasure in the death of the wicked, but that the wicked turn from his way and live; turn back, turn back from your evil ways, for why will you die, O house of Israel? (Ezek. 33:11)

[32] Motyer, *Prophecy of Isaiah*, 513.
[33] There is a Kethib-Qere variant here, the Qere, also witnessed to by the Vulgate, being the plural "steadfast loves."

Who is a God like you, pardoning iniquity
  and passing over transgression
  for the remnant of his inheritance?
He does not retain his anger forever,
  because he delights in steadfast love.
He will again have compassion on us;
  he will tread our iniquities underfoot.
You will cast all our sins
  into the depths of the sea.
  You will show faithfulness to Jacob
  and steadfast love to Abraham,
as you have sworn to our fathers
  from the days of old. (Mic. 7:18–20)

Finally, the apostle Paul in the New Testament validates this reading of the Old Testament story. He makes clear in Galatians 3:7–29 that the only authentic hermeneutic that can do justice to the unfolding narrative of the Old Testament works with the logic of grace and promise, not law and judgment. Is there law in the Old Testament? Yes, but "it was added" (v. 19) as a sidebar to the already-established record of grace and promise, until Christ came. Paul's point in Galatians 3 is to establish the only properly privileged explanatory lens through which to perceive the Old Testament, according to the Old Testament itself. That hermeneutical key is God's love for the undeserving, received through Christ with the empty hands of faith:

> The Bible speaks with one mind and one message. That one message is justification by faith alone. God's plan of salvation, the covenant of grace, runs from Abraham right through to Christ: "The Scripture . . . preached the gospel beforehand to Abraham" (Gal. 3:8). What God said to Abraham was nothing less than a proclamation of the gospel. Christians sometimes sing about "the old, old story of Jesus and his love." The story is older than some people realize. It goes back at least to the days of Abraham. Indeed, it goes all the way back to Adam and Eve (Gen. 3:15), who were the first to hear it. Ultimately, the good news of the Old Testament is the good news about Jesus Christ.[34]

Conclusion

The New Testament builds upon the Old Testament, obviously. But as far as the love of God is concerned, that canonical development is not

[34] Philip Graham Ryken, *Galatians*, Reformed Expository Commentary (Phillipsburg, NJ: P&R, 2005), 101.

from lesser to greater or even from ambiguous to clear. The New Testament does identify Jesus as the person and his advent as the time of Old Testament fulfillment (1 Pet. 1:10–11). The ultimate expression of God's love is the cross of Jesus. But it is not as though the New Testament is thereby changing the subject. The careful reader of the Old Testament is fully prepared for the New Testament's absorption with the love of God at the cross of Jesus. The vocabulary of divine love in the Old Testament is not lacking in its usefulness for proclaiming the good news. The God who revealed his glory to Moses in Exodus 34 became flesh, and we beheld his glory in Jesus, full of grace and truth (John 1:14). The God who revealed his holy love in Hosea 11, whose heart recoiled within him, was in agony in the garden of Gethsemane (Luke 22:44). The God who revealed the full magnitude of his love in Zephaniah 3, singing for joy over his people, also rejoiced over the divine bounty freely given to the undeserving (Luke 10:21). Indeed, the entire plot of the Old Testament, marked by key verses along the way and illuminated by apostolic commentary in Galatians 3, tells the story of, above all else, "God's pursuing, faithful, wounded, angry, overruling, transforming, triumphant *love*."[35]

Therefore, the misrepresentation of the Old Testament as a volume overshadowed with divine gloom, requiring the correction of the radiant New Testament, must be forever set aside.

[35] Raymond C. Ortlund Jr., *Whoredom: God's Unfaithful Wife in Biblical Theology* (Downers Grove, IL: InterVarsity, 1996), 173; emphasis original.

3

WHAT DOES JESUS TEACH ABOUT THE LOVE OF GOD?

ANDREAS J. KÖSTENBERGER

One of the challenges one faces when discussing Jesus and the love of God is that, at one level, virtually everything Jesus is and does could be subsumed under the rubric of love. If God is love (1 John 4:8), and if Jesus perfectly reveals the Father (John 1:1–3, 18), then is not everything Jesus says and does an expression of God's love? Conversely, does Jesus ever act in an unloving manner or teach anything contrary to God's character, which (among other attributes) is love?[1] This seems to be out of the question. If God is love, and if he loved the world in such a way that he gave Jesus, his one and only Son, as an expression of this love, then Jesus is the Son of God's love and is himself love due to his close association with God the Father. Nevertheless, while all of Jesus' teachings and actions proceed within the orbit of love, it will be instructive to investigate how Jesus specifically reveals God's love in his interaction with others.

In the present chapter, God's love in the Gospels will be examined first in the life of Jesus, specifically in his incarnation, compassionate life, sacrificial life and death, and establishment of a new relationship with his people.[2] Then God's love will be considered in Jesus' teachings, namely, his commands about loving God and loving others and his teachings on

[1] While God certainly *is* love, however, love is certainly not his only attribute. The same holds true for Jesus. John, for example, records Jesus' clearing of the temple (John 2:13–22) and speaks of the Father's having committed all judgment to the Son, issuing in a "resurrection of judgment" over against a "resurrection of life" (5:26–29). Elsewhere, the NT speaks of Jesus' role as judge (Acts 10:42; 17:31; cf. Rev. 2:5) and avenger (Rev. 6:10); his hatred of false doctrine (2:15); and the "wrath of the Lamb" (6:16–17). That said, space does not permit tracing out in the present essay the more severe expressions of God's love in and through Jesus.

[2] In the following discussion, I will assume the Gospels' historical reliability in portraying Jesus' actions and words. See Andreas J. Köstenberger, L. Scott Kellum, and Charles L. Quarles, *The Cradle, the Cross, and the Crown: An Introduction to the New Testament* (Nashville: B&H Academic, 2009), chaps. 3–7.

the Father's love for the Son, the Son's love for the Father, the love of the Father and the Son for others, the proper response to God's love, and opposites of proper love. There will also be treatments of the various recipients of God's love: lost sinners, those who see their need for Jesus and respond in faith, those who belong to the Father, those who respond to God's love with love and forgiveness, and specific individuals who receive God's love. Finally, there will be a brief discussion of those who reject God's love, followed by some concluding remarks.

The Expression of God's Love in Jesus

John's Gospel, commencing as it does with "the beginning" (1:1) and the eternal Son who comes to reveal the Father, reminds people that they don't start learning about God's love with Jesus' teachings or even his loving actions. Instead, God's love is expressed by and grounded in the Word's becoming flesh, that is, Jesus' incarnation (v. 14). After examining how God's love is revealed in Jesus' taking on flesh, there will be a discussion of Jesus' compassionate life, sacrificial life and death, and love in establishing a new relationship with his people.

God's Love in the Incarnation

The very act of God's revealing himself in Jesus constitutes an unparalleled act of love. This is particularly evident in John's Gospel, which stresses God's self-revelation in the Son (1:18; 14:9–10). God's revelation in his Son is highlighted throughout the Gospel as Jesus reveals his glory through the various signs he performs.[3] According to John, it is Jesus' purpose to reveal God's glory in everything he does and says, culminating in his death and resurrection. In this way, the fourth evangelist bears witness to the "perfect revelation of God's love for the world at the self-humiliation and divine exaltation of the Son."[4]

It is not that God loves his people just by sending Jesus to die for them; God loves his people by giving *himself* to them so that they may see his glory and one day share in it (John 17:24). Likewise, God displays his glory to his people so that they may share in his love, the love that characterizes the relationship between the Father and the Son (vv. 22–26). The connection between the revelation of God's glory and his love is evident

[3] See, e.g., John 2:11: "This, the first of his signs, Jesus did at Cana in Galilee, and *manifested his glory*. And his disciples believed in him"; John 11:4: "This illness does not lead to death. It is for the *glory of God*, so that the Son of God may *be glorified* through it."

[4] John 3:16; 13:1; see Andreas J. Köstenberger, *A Theology of John's Gospel and Letters: The Word, the Christ, the Son of God*, Biblical Theology of the New Testament (Grand Rapids, MI: Zondervan, 2009), 186.

in John's Gospel also when Jesus, having told his disciples that Lazarus's sickness will manifest the glory of the Son, delays going to see Lazarus, not only out of love for Mary and Martha but also owing to his desire for God's glory to be revealed in the ensuing miracle (11:4–6).[5]

God's Love in Jesus' Compassionate Life

One of the defining characteristics of Jesus' ministry is his care for the needy. Jesus is not simply an itinerant teacher who teaches a crowd of people and then moves on to another location without showing compassion toward those who came to hear him. Rather, he spends a great deal of time caring for a large number of individuals and healing all kinds of sickness, affliction, and spiritual oppression among the people who gather around him. Jesus' actions consistently display his deep, compassionate care for the needy, his heart for the lost, his kindness, and his love for children; he grieves with those who grieve, encourages those who doubt, and makes provision for the care of his mother subsequent to his passing.

Jesus' compassion for the needy. While the very act of incarnation represents a testimony to God's love, as God reveals himself to the world, the life of the Son is also full of love. As mentioned, it is difficult to narrow the discussion of God's love in Jesus' life, because everything he does and says is characterized by love. Therefore, the discussion below aims to sketch in broad strokes the ways in which God's love is demonstrated in and through Jesus' life and specific actions rather than to serve as a comprehensive account of every loving act performed by Jesus. The focus will be on examples of Jesus' actions that particularly highlight God's love.

Matthew notes that Jesus' healing ministry represents the fulfillment of Isaiah's prediction regarding a coming gentle servant (Matt. 12:15–21; cf. Isa. 42:1–3). In his tender care for those who are suffering physically, Jesus shows himself to be the gentle servant who will not break a bruised reed or quench a smoldering wick.

The Gospels regularly show Jesus as acting with compassion. The Greek term for *compassion* speaks of a deep, "gut-level" care for people.[6] Jesus acts not simply out of a sense of duty; neither is he generically philanthropic. Instead, he is deeply concerned for the well-being of those to whom he ministers. What is more, Jesus' compassion and kindness are demonstrated even where the word *compassion* is not used, such as when

---

[5] Andreas J. Köstenberger, *John*, BECNT (Grand Rapids, MI: Baker Academic, 2004), 327–28.

[6] The word is *splanchnizomai*. See, e.g., Matt. 14:13–21 par. Mark 6:30–44; Matt. 15:32–39 par. Mark 8:1–10; Matt. 20:29–34; Mark 1:40–45; and Luke 7:11–17, on which see the discussion in the following paragraph.

he heals and forgives people at his arrest and crucifixion and in the many healings he performs throughout the course of his ministry.

The most common recipients of Jesus' compassion are those who are needy in a variety of ways. When two blind men cry out to him for mercy, Jesus responds with compassion and heals them (Matt. 20:29–34). Likewise, when a leper comes to him, begging to be clean, Jesus is filled with compassion and heals him (Mark 1:40–45). Even after Jesus withdraws to an isolated location to be by himself, a great crowd follows him, bringing the sick to him. Rather than responding with frustration, Jesus is filled with compassion and heals, teaches, and feeds the people (Matt. 14:13–21). When another great crowd comes to him, he is filled with compassion on account of their hunger and feeds them (15:32–39). Finally, when he encounters the funeral procession of the only son of a widow, he stops the procession, takes compassion on the woman, raises her son to life, and gives him back to her (Luke 7:11–17).

While all of Jesus' healing miracles should be considered acts of love and compassion, two other miracles that demonstrate his great love particularly stand out. The first is found in John 5:1–9, where Jesus heals a man who has been an invalid for thirty-eight years. In a rare occurrence, Jesus approaches the man and asks him if he wants to be healed, rather than waiting to be asked. Luke also records a unique healing miracle at the end of Jesus' life. After Peter cuts off the ear of the high priest's servant, who is among those coming to arrest Jesus, Jesus heals the man's ear (Luke 22:49–51). Luke records also a unique saying of Jesus from the cross, when Jesus prays for God to forgive those who are crucifying him (23:34). This last account, in particular, illustrates what it means for followers of Jesus to love their enemies.

Jesus' heart for the lost. All four Gospel narratives are focused ultimately on Jesus' death and resurrection as the culmination of his ministry.[7] Of course, Jesus' death not merely constitutes an example illustrating the principle of sacrificial love to be followed but also expresses God's great love for a lost and dying world (John 3:16). Importantly, Jesus' concern for the lost doesn't begin at his crucifixion; it rather is evident throughout his entire life as Jesus seeks out the lost in order to save them. He calls the disciples away from their familial encroachments and respective vocations to follow him, including a despised tax collector, Matthew (Levi). What is more, not only does Jesus call Matthew; he spends time with

[7] See Andreas Köstenberger and Justin Taylor (with Alexander Stewart), *The Final Days of Jesus: The Most Important Week of the Most Important Person Who Ever Lived* (Wheaton, IL: Crossway, 2014).

Matthew's sinful friends because they, too, need a savior (Matt. 9:9–13; see also 11:19; Luke 15:1–2). As Stanley Grenz notes, "The primary focus of Jesus' ministry and the primary audience for his message were not the privileged few of his day but the disadvantaged, the outcast, the 'sinners.'"[8]

It is not only those with physical needs who elicit Jesus' deep compassion but all those who are lost and in need of a savior. As Jesus travels, teaching the good news of the kingdom and healing the needy, he has compassion on the crowds on account of their helplessness and lack of a "shepherd" (Matt. 9:35–36; cf. Num. 27:17). What is more, Jesus urges his disciples to pray for more laborers to gather the waiting harvest (Matt. 9:37–38) and then sends them out as the first laborers to reach the lost (Matthew 10).

After healing a man who was born blind, Jesus seeks him out again so that the man can experience not just physical sight but spiritual illumination as well (John 9:35–41). Perhaps the most memorable statement about Jesus' care for the lost is found in the story of Zacchaeus, who has climbed a tree in order to see Jesus over the crowd. Jesus calls Zacchaeus to come down from the tree and then goes to his house. After Zacchaeus has repented of his sins, Jesus says to him, "Today salvation has come to this house, since he also is a son of Abraham. For the Son of Man came to seek and to save the lost" (Luke 19:1–10).[9] Jesus' desire to save the lost is seen also in his lament over Jerusalem, whose children he seeks to gather (Matt. 23:37–39).

Jesus' kindness. God's love is seen in Jesus in the kindness not only of his actions but also of his words. Occasionally, the authors of the Gospels draw the reader's attention to Jesus' kind words toward those who are in need both physically and spiritually, demonstrating the tenderness of God's love. Thus when Jesus forgives a paralytic's sins, he does so with tender words: "Take heart, my son; your sins are forgiven" (Matt. 9:2). Similarly, when a woman who has been suffering for years from a discharge of blood touches the hem of his garment to be healed, Jesus turns to her and says, "Take heart, daughter; your faith has made you well" (vv. 20–22).

Jesus' love for children. The Gospels demonstrate consistently that God's love is not bound by ethnicity, social status, economics, or gender. Neither is his love constrained by age. The Synoptic Gospels all record how Jesus, despite the best efforts of his disciples to prevent him from

[8] Stanley J. Grenz, *Theology for the Community of God* (Nashville: Broadman, 1994), 374.

[9] See the discussion in Darrell L. Bock, *Luke 9:41–24:53*, BECNT (Grand Rapids, MI: Baker Academic, 1996) 1520–22.

doing so, takes time to welcome and bless little children whose parents have brought them to him (Matt. 19:13–15; cf. Mark 10:13–15; Luke 18:15–17).

Jesus' weeping. One of the most concrete manifestations of God's love in Jesus is that he weeps. What is more, while it may not be surprising that Jesus weeps over the death of Lazarus, a close friend (John 11:35–36), it is remarkable that he weeps over Jerusalem (Luke 19:41–44), which he had earlier described as a "city that kills the prophets and stones those who are sent to it" (13:34–35).

Jesus' help of the doubting. Jesus' love is seen also after his resurrection when he encourages those who doubt. Having been raised from the dead, vindicated and exalted by God, Jesus does not now sneer at those who still struggle to understand what has taken place. Luke recounts a story of the risen Jesus appearing to his disciples and asking them, "Why are you troubled, and why do doubts arise in your hearts?" He encourages them to touch him to see that it is really he, and when some still disbelieve, Jesus asks them for something to eat. They give him a piece of broiled fish, and he eats it in front of them (Luke 24:36–43; see John 20:19–23). In a similar scene, Jesus invites Thomas to put his hands in Jesus' wounds and urges him to believe (John 20:24–29).

Jesus' care for his mother. The hours leading up to Jesus' trial, scourging, and sacrificial death are hours of love (John 13:1–15).[10] This love continues to be palpable in the hours of Jesus' agony as he sees his mother and makes provision for her care (19:26–27). In honoring his mother, Jesus demonstrates his love for both God and his mother in caring for her in the hour of her need.[11] Jesus' expression of concern for his mother is remarkable at a time when he himself is in dire need. He exhibits love by putting concern for others above concern for his own well-being.[12]

God's Love in Jesus' Sacrificial Life and Death

At the center of all four Gospels is the crucifixion of Jesus Christ. The Gospels make clear that Jesus' death was not an accident; nor, as mentioned, does its significance consist simply in his sacrificial lifestyle. Rather, Jesus' death is a death for the world, an expression of God's love for a world that is spiritually lost and hardened in rebellion against its Creator and King.

[10] See Köstenberger, *Theology of John's Gospel*, chap. 13: "John's Love Ethic," which makes the point that the foot washing constitutes an anticipation of the cross.

[11] See Köstenberger, *John*, 548–49; D. A. Carson, *The Gospel according to John*, PNTC (Grand Rapids, MI: Eerdmans, 1991), 618.

[12] Cf. Paul's words in Phil. 2:1–11.

At the same time, Jesus' sacrificial death doesn't stand on its own; it is the culmination of a sacrificial, self-giving life that includes his birth, identification with sinners in order to save them, love of his own to the end, and death in obedience to the will of the Father.

Jesus is born to save sinners. From the announcement of Jesus' conception, his life is identified by God as a life that would bring salvation to his people. This is underscored by the meaning behind his name, Jesus, which reflects the Hebrew *yehōšûa*, "Yahweh is salvation," or *yēšûa*, "Yahweh saves," indicating what the child was born to do.[13] As the Gospel narratives progress, it becomes clear gradually that the salvation this child was born to bring would be accomplished through his substitutionary death.[14]

Jesus identifies with sinners in order to save them. Jesus doesn't live a life separated from sinners but rather moves among them freely. Jesus' identification with sinners commences with his baptism by John the Baptist (Matt. 3:13–17; cf. Mark 1:9–11; Luke 3:21–22). His baptism, in turn, points ahead to his entire ministry, which has as its ultimate goal bringing glory to God by saving sinners (Luke 4:16–21; 19:1–10; John 4:31–38). Jesus is a light in the land of darkness (Matt. 4:12–17), a light that the world largely rejects (John 1:9–11; cf. Matt. 23:37–39; Luke 13:34–35). But despite the attempts of the darkness to extinguish his light by killing him, it is his very purpose to die and in this way save his people (John 3:16–21, 35–36; 6:35–59; 10:7–18; 12:31–36, 44–50).

Jesus loves his own to the end. As Jesus approaches the cross, he doesn't turn inward and isolate himself from those around him. Rather, even before he pours himself out for the world, he expends himself for those closest to him, serving them and loving them to the fullest extent. Jesus never stops loving his close followers and never holds back his love, even washing the feet of the one who would betray him (John 13:1–20). In fact, the love exhibited by Jesus at the foot washing serves as an anticipatory glimpse of the same love Jesus displays at the cross. Before Jesus goes to the cross to die, he shows his followers what will lead him to go to the cross in the first place—his great love for the people God had made.[15]

Jesus suffers and dies for sinners, doing the will of the Father while being forsaken by him. At the end of Jesus' earthly life, when, in the hor-

[13] Matt. 1:21; cf. Luke 2:11. D. A. Carson, "Matthew," in *Expositor's Bible Commentary*, rev. ed. (Grand Rapids, MI: Zondervan, 2010), 101.
[14] See, e.g., the progression in the "lifted up sayings" in John 3:14; 8:28; and 12:32.
[15] Köstenberger, *Theology of John's Gospel*, 518.

ror and the glory of the cross, he is lifted up to draw all people to himself, Jesus prays Psalm 22, "My God, my God, why have you forsaken me?" (Matt. 27:46; cf. Mark 15:34). These words illustrate what it means for God to so love the world that he gave his one and only Son to die (John 3:16). It is through the cross that Jesus glorifies God and makes his love known to the world.[16]

All of Jesus' acts of compassion—healings, exorcisms, raising the dead to life—find their meaning and lasting value at the cross, where Jesus gives his life as a ransom for many (Mark 10:45). However, the cross reveals not merely Jesus' love for the world; more importantly, it displays his love for the Father, as Jesus perfectly accomplishes the Father's will by laying down his life in order to take it up again (John 10:17–18; see Matt. 26:39; Mark 14:36; Luke 22:42). Jesus, the sent Son, left his heavenly glory and entered the spiritual darkness of this sinful world, even though it would cost him his life (Matt. 21:33–44; cf. Mark 12:1–12; Luke 20:9–18).

God's Love in Jesus' Establishment of a New Relationship with His People

While Jesus' life inexorably moves toward his death, that death has a very particular purpose. His life and death are directed toward redeeming a people for himself, establishing a new relationship with them on the basis of his life, death, and resurrection. The Gospels show Jesus fulfilling the law and establishing a new covenant, extending his kingdom to a new people, bringing them into the orbit of God's eternal love, and preserving this people for himself.

Jesus fulfills the law and establishes a new covenant. Jesus' life and sacrificial death have as their purpose forgiveness, but not forgiveness in a generic sense. Rather, his sacrifice was sacrifice *for a people.* Just as God brought a people out of slavery in Egypt and established a covenant with them, constituting them as his people (Exodus 12–24), so Jesus during his life on earth begins to gather a people for himself (John 10:16; 11:49–52). At two places in particular the Gospels focus on Jesus' fulfilling the law and establishing a new covenant.

The first is at the Mount of Transfiguration (Matt. 17:1–5; cf. Mark

[16] Francis Moloney, *Love in the Gospel of John: An Exegetical, Theological, and Literary Study* (Grand Rapids, MI: Baker Academic, 2013), 95. But see D. A. Carson's review of Moloney's book in *JETS* 57 (2014): 429–31, who writes that the "weakest point [of Moloney's work] is its treatment of the cross. Moloney is surely right to say that the cross is the high point of God's self-disclosure in Christ Jesus as the loving God. . . . Unfortunately, he does not work out *why* or *in what way* the cross displays divine love," 431. Carson adds that, like J. Terence Forestell, *The Word of the Cross: Salvation as Revelation in the Fourth Gospel* (Rome: Biblical Institute Press, 1974), "the theme of revelation—in Moloney's case, the revelation of divine love—is developed in so exclusive a fashion that there is no space for Johannine atonement theology." Ibid.

9:2–8; Luke 9:28–36). Here Jesus is glorified and speaks with Moses (type of the end-time prophet) and Elijah (type of Jesus' forerunner). Yet when Peter suggests making three tabernacles, one for each of them, God's glory covers the mountain and the divine voice urges Jesus' terrified followers to listen to Jesus, God's beloved Son. In Christ, God is doing something new.[17]

Then, as the crucifixion looms, Jesus shares a Passover meal with his disciples. As he celebrates this meal—remembering God's great works of deliverance and establishment of his covenant with his people, celebrated yearly according to God's command for fifteen hundred years—Jesus does something astonishing. He takes the unleavened bread, meant to remind the Israelites of their hasty escape from Egypt, the bread of their affliction (Ex. 12:39; Deut. 16:3), and tells his disciples that the bread represents his body, giving it to them to eat and saying, "Do this in remembrance of me" (Luke 22:19; see Matt. 26:26; Mark 14:22).[18] Again, as Jesus takes one of the Passover cups, he tells the disciples that it represents the cup of the "new covenant in my blood" (Luke 22:20; see Matt. 26:27–28; Mark 14:23–24). God's love in Jesus is not simply offering forgiveness; it is gathering a new people for himself.

The kingdom is extended to a new people. One of the themes that pervades all four Gospels is that the coming kingdom will not be enjoyed exclusively, primarily, or even at all by those who stake an exclusive claim to it, namely the Jewish people. Instead, Jesus warns the self-righteous that their religious heritage is not sufficient for entrance into the kingdom. What is needed are faith, repentance, and bearing fruit (Matt. 4:17; cf. 8:5–13; 21:33–46; Mark 1:14–15). Remarkably, a reversal will take place: Jesus' new messianic community will include not only (some) Jews, but all kinds of people (Matt. 8:11–12; Luke 13:22–30).[19] The inheritance will belong not to those born of Abraham by way of natural, ethnic descent (John 8:39–59) but to those born from above, from the Spirit (3:1–8), born on account of divine rather than human initiative (1:12–13).

Jesus brings others into God's eternal love. The clearest expression that this work of bringing together a people is an act of love is found in John's Gospel, in Jesus' High Priestly Prayer (John 17:1–26). Here Jesus speaks

[17] Carson, "Matthew," 437–39.

[18] See Andreas J. Köstenberger, "Was the Last Supper a Passover Meal?" in *The Lord's Supper: Remembering and Proclaiming Christ until He Comes*, ed. Thomas R. Schreiner and Matthew R. Crawford, NAC Studies in Bible and Theology 10 (Nashville: B&H Academic, 2010), 6–30.

[19] See also the parable of the wicked tenants (Matt. 21:33–46 par. Mark 12:1–12; Luke 20:9–19) and the parable of the wedding feast (Matt. 22:1–14 par. Luke 14:15–24).

of bringing his disciples, both present and future, into the love and glory shared between Father and Son (vv. 22–26). As Francis Moloney writes, "The love that has existed from all time between God and the Word, between the Father and the Son, has burst into the human story. Jesus has made it known so that others might be swept into that same relationship."[20]

God's love in Jesus' preservation of his people. The love of God for his people is such that no one or nothing can snatch them out of his hand. In the aftermath of the feeding of the five thousand, Jesus affirms, "All that the Father gives me will come to me, and whoever comes to me I will never cast out. . . . This is the will of him who sent me, that I should lose nothing of all that he has given me, but raise it up on the last day" (John 6:37, 39). The preservation theme is highlighted in John's Gospel most poignantly in chapter 10, where Jesus calls himself the "good shepherd." He is not like hirelings who run away in the face of danger, nor is he like thieves and robbers who use the flock to enrich themselves. Rather, he lays down his life for the sheep (John 10:7–18).[21] As the Good Shepherd, Jesus gives his sheep eternal life, and no one will be able to take them away from him, for they were given to him by the Father (vv. 25–30). The only exception is Judas, the betrayer, in keeping with God's sovereign plan (17:12).

As Jesus' earthly ministry draws to a close and he prepares to leave his followers, he assures them that his departure is not permanent; he will return to take them with him at a later time (John 14:1–4). It is a powerful testimony to Jesus' love and care for his disciples that as he makes his way toward Gethsemane—having just told Peter of his impending denial—he tells his followers, "Let not your hearts be troubled" (v. 1). He further assures them that while they will not be able to follow him now, he will not leave them as orphans but send the Spirit and give them peace (vv. 15–28). Jesus' final words to his disciples as recorded in the Gospel of Matthew also testify to this great comfort, with the promise that Jesus will always be with his followers (Matt. 28:20).

Jesus' Teachings on Love

Jesus' teaching that the two most important commandments are to love God and to love others (Matt. 22:34–40; cf. 19:19; Mark 12:28–34; Luke 10:25–28) is arguably one of his most notable pronouncements—not just on love but on any subject. In teaching that love represents the fulfillment

[20] Moloney, *Love*, 56–57.

[21] Köstenberger, *John*, 304–6.

of the law, Jesus makes clear that love holds the central place in the life of a Christian. In fact, the natural consequence of turning to Jesus and following him is that such a person will love God and others.[22] In addition to the "great commandment," Jesus teaches also about the Father's love for the Son, the Son's love for the Father, the love of both the Father and the Son for others, the proper response to God's love, and various opposites of proper love.

Loving God

Jesus' teaching on what it means to love God highlights three themes: the relationship between loving God and obedience, the connection between loving God and receiving Jesus, and the importance of devotion to Jesus.

Loving God means obedience. The Gospel of John, in particular, elaborates on what it means to love God, with Jesus teaching his disciples that their love for God is demonstrated in obedience to God (John 14:15–24; 15:1–17), just as he demonstrates his love for the Father by obeying him (14:31). The fact that Jesus presents his followers' love for God as the most important commandment cannot be missed or overstated. Leon Morris makes the point well, noting, "This puts love for God squarely at the heart of real religion: Nothing is more important than loving God. This love brooks no rival, and Jesus points to slavery to illustrate his point."[23] Believers have one master, God (Matt. 6:24; cf. Luke 16:13).

Loving God means receiving the Son. For John, the ultimate example of obeying God and therefore demonstrating love for him is receiving the Son (John 5:42–43). The fact that Jesus can encapsulate what God requires of people as believing in the one the Father sent is truly remarkable and highly significant (6:29). The foundational piece of evidence that demonstrates whether a person knows, loves, and obeys God is how he relates to his Son.[24] All four Gospels make clear the essence of the relationship between the Father and the Son: the Father loves the Son.[25] This is exemplified particularly in the accounts of Jesus' baptism and the

[22] Darrell L. Bock, *Jesus according to Scripture: Restoring the Portrait from the Gospels* (Grand Rapids, MI: Baker Academic, 2002), 634. See also Karl Barth, *Church Dogmatics*, vol. 1, pt. 2, §18.2, 371–72, who writes, "The Christian life begins with love. It also ends with love, so far as it has an end as human life in time. . . . There is no higher or better being or doing in which we can leave it behind us. As Christians, we are continually asked about love, and in all that we can ever do or not do, it is the decisive question."

[23] Leon Morris, "Love," in *Dictionary of Jesus and the Gospels*, ed. Joel B. Green, Scot McKnight, and I. Howard Marshall (Downers Grove, IL: InterVarsity, 1992), 494. The entry by E. E. Popkes, "Love, Love Command" in the 2nd edition of *Dictionary of Jesus and the Gospels*, ed. Joel B. Green, Jeannine K. Brown, and Nicholas Perrin (Downers Grove, IL: InterVarsity, 2013), 535–40, is limited essentially to Jesus' love command and the theology of God's love in Johannine literature.

[24] Köstenberger, *John*, 208.

[25] See the section below on the Father's love for the Son.

transfiguration, in both of which the divine voice attests to the Father's love for his "beloved Son" (Mark 1:11; 9:7).

The reality that the Father loves the Son is set forth not just as information for readers but also as a call to love the Son.[26] People's attitude toward Jesus should be the same as the Father's disposition toward him. It is no wonder, then, to find that Jesus says it is impossible for a person to remain in the Father's love and to love him if one rejects the Son (John 5:23). There can be no obedience to God's commands given through Jesus without accepting Jesus in faith as the divine Son sent by the Father.[27] Just as no one can come to the Father apart from the Son (14:6), so no one can love the Father without loving the Son.

Loving God means being devoted to the Son. While love for God involves obedience and faith, it is characterized also by devotion. This is evident in Jesus' affirmation of Mary, who has chosen to sit at his feet and to listen to him. Jesus affirms that she has chosen the "good portion" (Luke 10:38–42). And when Mary demonstrates her lavish devotion to Jesus by anointing his feet with expensive perfume, Jesus commends her love (Matt. 26:6–13; cf. Mark 14:3–9; John 12:1–8).[28] These are essential reminders that love for God requires obedience but also that a certain kind of obedience is required. Similarly, loving God demands believing in the Son and receiving him, but, again, it is a certain kind of belief and reception that are required, a belief and reception that flow from devotion to the Father and, in a unique way, to the Son.[29] Ultimately, these three elements are inseparable. To claim to love God while not obeying him, or while not receiving the Son, or while not being devoted to the Son, is not to love God.

Loving Others

Given that Jesus teaches that the second greatest commandment is to love others as oneself, it should come as no surprise that he regularly teaches about what it means to carry out this command. He teaches about the object of our love; the relationship between love and obedience, love and forgiveness, and loving others and loving God; and how our love is to be like God's love.

---

[26] James A. Brooks, *Mark*, NAC (Nashville: Broadman, 1991), 43.

[27] Fernando F. Segovia, *Love Relationships in the Johannine Tradition: Agapē/Agapan in I John and the Fourth Gospel*, SBLDS 58 (Chico, CA: Scholars Press, 1982), 146–49. Segovia, however, argues that love in John's Gospel does not go beyond faith, which overstates the evidence.

[28] Cf. the similar but distinct account in Luke 7:36–50.

[29] Köstenberger, *John*, 116–17, 261; Barth, *Church Dogmatics* vol. 4, pt. 2, §68.3, 796–97.

The object of love. If the second-greatest command is to love others as ourselves (Matt. 19:19; Luke 10:27), it may seem reasonable to ask who these "others" are. At the same time, it is hard to think of any way to ask that question without expressing some sort of desire to limit whom a person should love. When Jesus is questioned about who is the "neighbor" one should love, he responds by telling the parable of the good Samaritan (Luke 10:30–36). In this penetrating story, Jesus cuts to the heart of the issue and transforms the question from "Who is my neighbor?" to "Am I a neighbor? Do I show mercy to others?" As Darrell Bock observes, "Love does not figure out how to get out of loving; it just loves."[30] When Christians do this, they reflect God's character rather than acting like sinners.[31]

Jesus also makes abundantly clear that love extends far beyond those with whom one is comfortable. Indeed, Christians' love for others ought to extend even to their enemies. It is God's love for his enemies, his care for the righteous and unrighteous alike, that forms the basis for people's love toward those who hate them. Were Christians to do otherwise, they would be no different from the world (Matt. 5:38–48; cf. Luke 6:27–30, 32–35).

But while people's neighbors are indeed any whom they can help (Luke 10:29–37), including their enemies, they also include those closest to them, and they, too, must not be neglected. What is more, Jesus reminds his followers to love the "little ones" (Matt. 18:10), that is, the humble, those who seem insignificant, for they are those whom the Father delights to save.[32] It is precisely in caring for brothers and sisters in difficult situations that Christians display their love for Jesus (25:31–46). Love for one another is not only the necessary reflection of love for Jesus, but also the demonstration to the world that a person belongs to Jesus. Just as Jesus shows the world his love by obeying the Father completely, even by dying on the cross, so believers show the world that they obey the Father completely by loving one another, an action that involves serving one another sacrificially and laying down their lives for one another (John 13:13–20). Indeed, love is arguably the premier mark of what it means to be a disciple of Jesus (vv. 34–35).[33]

Loving others and obedience. Just as our love for God is displayed through obedience, loving others is never contrary to the law but rather

[30] Bock, *Jesus*, 256.
[31] Ibid., 137–38.
[32] Carson, "Matthew," 451, 454–55; Craig Blomberg, *Matthew*, NAC (Nashville: Broadman, 1992), 274.
[33] Köstenberger, *John*, 423. See Francis A. Schaeffer, *The Mark of a Christian*, 2nd ed. (Downers Grove, IL: InterVarsity, 2006).

fulfills it. This is expressed memorably in the Golden Rule, where Jesus tells people to do to others as they would have others do to them (Matt. 7:12; Luke 6:31). The same truth is expressed in Jesus' teaching about the Sabbath, where he makes clear that the Pharisees have grossly misunderstood what it means to keep the Sabbath (Matt. 12:9–14; cf. Mark 3:1–6; Luke 6:6–11; 13:10–17). In elevating love to the essence and fulfillment of the law, Jesus reminds people not only that loving others is an essential part of obeying God but also that it is the law that teaches them what it means to love others.[34] The Pharisees fail on both accounts. They do not understand the core of the law and so fail to grasp what it means to truly love.

The relationship between forgiveness and love. Forgiveness is another important aspect of Jesus' teaching on love. In his teaching on forgiveness, Jesus often makes a connection between the forgiveness that people receive from God and that which they extend to others (Matt. 5:21–26; Mark 11:25; Luke 12:57–59).[35] It is a wicked person who, having experienced forgiveness and mercy, withholds it from others (Matt. 18:21–35). In Matthew's account of the Lord's Prayer, Jesus says that those who fail to forgive others will not be forgiven by God (6:12–15). This is not an instance of having to earn one's forgiveness, but rather an essential recognition that *forgiven* people are *forgiving* people.[36] As John Stott observes, "Once our eyes have been opened to see the enormity of our offense against God, the injuries which others have done to us appear by comparison extremely trifling. If, on the other hand, we have an exaggerated view of the offense of others, it proves that we have minimized our own."[37] A similar point is made in Luke's Gospel, where a sinful woman anoints Jesus' feet. The Pharisee hosting Jesus is outraged, but Jesus' response is that those who are forgiven are the ones who love (Luke 7:36–50). Jesus not only commands people to forgive others; he also instructs them to seek forgiveness when they are in the wrong (Matt. 5:21–26).

How love for others relates to love for God. Jesus' parable about the sheep and the goats, related in Matthew 25:31–46, highlights again the supreme importance of love in the lives of Jesus' followers. This parable puts in vivid detail Jesus' teaching that love fulfills the law. Here the object of our love is the "least of these my brothers." The language of "brother"

[34] See Carson, "Matthew," 224.

[35] Bock argues that the context of the Lucan account implies that Jesus is speaking of the relationship between people and God; Bock, *Luke 9:51–24:53*, 1200; see also Carson, "Matthew," 183.

[36] Carson, "Matthew," 207. See also Matt. 18:15–35; Luke 17:3–4; John 20:23.

[37] John R. W. Stott, *The Message of the Sermon on the Mount* (Downers Grove, IL: InterVarsity, 1985), 149–50.

in Matthew is used normally to refer to a fellow believer.[38] To ignore the needs of brothers and sisters in Christ is tantamount to not acting as a brother and sister in Christ. Just as James and John would later assert in their respective letters, so Jesus emphatically states that those who fail to love their brothers and sisters neither know nor love God.[39]

Our love is to be like God's love. It should come as no surprise that Jesus points to both himself and the Father as examples of what it means to love. God, who is kind not only to his children but also to those who are ungrateful and evil, is the supreme model of showing mercy and love toward enemies (Matt. 5:44–46; Luke 6:35–36). Jesus, who humbled himself to serve others, even to the point of dying for them, shows what it means to love God and others (John 13:1–20; 15:12–17). Here in the Son of God, the Word made flesh, is the new point of reference that makes his command to love others a new command (13:31–35).[40]

The newness of the command stems, first, from the concrete model given to Jesus' followers as to what true love looks like: "just as I have loved you." Second, the newness is found in the intensity of love in the community of faith, which points the world to God.[41] This love to which believers are called, modeled on Jesus' love for them and the world, is the foundation for believers' love of those in the world. As Darrell Bock notes, "In a sense, the great commissions of Matthew and Luke are impossible without the great incarnation of community love that is to mark the disciples as Jesus' disciples, modeling his very life and response to them."[42]

The Father's Love for the Son

While it is common and correct to think about the great love the Father has for the world (John 3:16), it is also essential to understand how much the Father loves the Son. John highlights this theme in his Gospel (see, e.g., 3:35). Indeed, it is possible to understand how great God's love is for people only when a person understands the greatness of the Father's love for the Son (15:9; 17:22–25).[43] The Synoptics, as mentioned, highlight this special relationship between Father and Son in particular at Jesus' baptism (Matt. 3:17; cf. Mark 1:11; Luke 3:22) and the Mount of Transfiguration (Matt. 17:5; cf. Mark 9:7; Luke 9:35), where the Father

---

[38] Carson, "Matthew," 182, 582–84; Blomberg, *Matthew*, 377–78.
[39] See James 2:14–17; 1 John 2:9–11; 3:10–18.
[40] Köstenberger, *Theology of John's Gospel*, 518.
[41] Bock, *Jesus*, 498.
[42] Ibid.
[43] D. A. Carson, *The Difficult Doctrine of the Love of God* (Wheaton, IL: Crossway, 2000), 35; Moloney, *Love*, 59–60.

calls Jesus his "beloved Son" with whom he is pleased. The language highlights not only the unique relationship between Father and Son but also the particular role Jesus has in accomplishing the Father's mission as the suffering servant. Jesus is the beloved, obedient Son.[44] While the Synoptics demonstrate this relationship from the Father's perspective, John relates teaching from Jesus about the same relationship, emphasizing Jesus' teachings about the Father's love for the Son in three areas.

First, Jesus teaches that the Father's love for the Son is related to the Son's obedience to the Father (John 10:17–18; 15:10). The Son has always obeyed the Father and has done so perfectly; this is what it means for him to be "the Son." While the Son's love for the Father does not begin at the cross, it is there that the Son's perfect obedience climaxes.[45]

Second, Jesus teaches that the Father shows everything he does to his obedient Son, holding nothing back. This perfect unity of Father and Son—the Father revealing his plans to the Son, and the Son obeying his Father's will—is a demonstration of the Father's love for the Son as well as the Son's love for the Father (John 5:19–47).[46]

Finally, Jesus teaches that the Father shows his love for the Son by sharing his glory (John 17:24). Again, the perfect unity between Father and Son of giving and receiving, delegating and obeying, opens the Christian's eyes to understand what it means to enter into the love of Father and Son.

The Son's Love for the Father

In the same way that the Father loves the Son, who obeys him completely and does his work, so also the Son loves the Father. In fact, Jesus makes clear that the demonstration of his love consists in his perfect obedience to the Father (John 5:19–47; 15:1–17; cf. 4:34; 6:38; 8:29, 55). But Jesus' love is not just a private display of love between himself and his Father. Rather, he tells his followers that it is an outward display for the world to see in order that they might know that the Son loves the Father (14:31).[47] Jesus therefore presents himself as an example not only of what it means to love others, namely, to lay down one's life for them (13:1–20), but also of what it means to love God, to obey him wholeheartedly.[48]

---

[44] James Moffatt, *Love in the New Testament* (New York: Richard R. Smith, 1930), 76–77; Carson, "Matthew," 137–38.

[45] Köstenberger, *John*, 307; Carson, *John*, 388.

[46] Köstenberger, *John*, 186–87.

[47] Moloney, *Love*, 183.

[48] Bock, *Jesus*, 508.

The Love of Father and Son for Others

The Gospels speak about the love of God in both specific and general terms. On the one hand, Jesus teaches about God's love for his people and children. On the other hand, Jesus regularly teaches about God's love for the lost and dying world. Both expressions of God's love need to be understood and balanced with each other.

God's love for his children. As discussed above, it is in Jesus that a person learns what it means to love God, but Jesus also teaches what it means to enjoy God's love. Jesus is the Son who perfectly obeys the Father and therefore remains in his love. He shows believers that they, too, are called to this obedience to remain in and enjoy the love of both Father and Son (John 15:9–10). The Gospels repeatedly stress Jesus' teaching about God's fatherly love for his children. He is the perfect Father who gives good gifts to his children (Matt. 7:7–11; Luke 11:5–13; John 1:12); he is the Father who cares for them by preventing this age from running its course, with a plan to cut it short for their good (Matt. 24:22; cf. Mark 13:20).[49] Most amazingly, he is the glorious God who shares his glory with his children, testifying to the world of his great love for them (John 17:22–25).

God's love for the lost. Of course, there would be no hope of experiencing God's fatherly love if it were not for the astonishing fact that he loved sinners before they were his children. The Gospel of John teaches that it was to a world lost in darkness, a world at enmity with him, that God sent his Son. And it is only when a person understands how great God's love is for the Son and how great each person's sin and lostness are that he begins to grasp what it means for God to love the world by sending his Son (John 1:9–13; 3:16–21).[50]

For this reason it is not surprising to find Jesus not only demonstrating this love in his life and death but also deliberately teaching his disciples and the crowds about God's great love for the lost. And while the culmination of the Father's love for the lost world is the sending of the Son, it is not his only expression of love. Indeed, Jesus teaches that the facts that the sun continues to shine and rain continues to fall in spite of the world's sinfulness are a testimony to God's love (Matt. 5:44–46).

Jesus further testifies to God's love for the lost by pointing to his own life and mission as that of one who came to heal the sick and to seek and save the lost (Matt. 9:10–13; Mark 2:13–17; Luke 5:27–32; cf. 15:1–32;

---

[49] Carson, "Matthew," 564–65.

[50] Köstenberger, *John*, 128–29; Carson, *John*, 205.

19:10). The parables of the lost sheep, the lost coin, and especially of the lost son show God to be the heavenly Father who seeks out and rejoices in the salvation of those who are lost (Luke 15). They present, in Darrell Bock's words, "heaven's view of the sinner regained."[51] So there is nothing incidental about Jesus' seeking out sinners; it is the very purpose of his mission, the reason he was sent by the Father.[52]

The Proper Response to God's Love

While Jesus presents himself as the perfect demonstration of what it means to love God, he also sets forth in his teachings what it looks like to respond to God's gracious love. There is no better place to start than by accepting Jesus' call to come to him and learn from him, to be his disciple (Matt. 11:25–30; Luke 10:38–42). The call of Jesus issued to the disciples is the paradigm for the readers of the Gospels to follow as well (Matt. 4:18–22; Mark 1:16–20; Luke 5:1–11; John 1:35–51). There can be no proper response to God's love that does not begin with following Jesus (Matt. 8:18–22; cf. Luke 9:57–62).

What is more, Jesus teaches that following him involves not just *learning* from him but also being *sent* by him to carry on his task of making disciples and saving the lost (Matthew 10; 28:18–20; Mark 5:14–20; Luke 8:37–39; 24:44–49). This is what it means to follow in the loving obedience of the Son, just as Jesus teaches that he sends his disciples in the same way he was sent by the Father (John 20:21).[53] The call to follow Jesus involves following him in his suffering, loving him more than anything else, even one's life (Matt. 16:24–27; cf. Mark 8:34–38).[54]

Being sent by Jesus involves making disciples, proclaiming the gospel,[55] and calling people to repentance, but it also entails serving and loving just as Jesus himself served and loved (Matt. 20:20–28; Mark 10:35–45; Luke 22:24–30; John 13:1–20, 31–35; 21:15–19). God's love transforms people into disciples, fishers of people, and servants. It transforms them also into worshipers (John 4:21–24). Jesus teaches that those who come to know the Father do not remain unaffected by his love but

[51] Bock, *Luke 9:51–24:53*, 1294.

[52] Leon Morris, *Testaments of Love: A Study of Love in the Bible* (Grand Rapids, MI: Eerdmans, 1981), 148–49.

[53] See on this Andreas J. Köstenberger, *The Missions of Jesus and the Disciples according to the Fourth Gospel* (Grand Rapids, MI: Eerdmans, 1998).

[54] See also Jesus' question to Peter in John 21:15: "Do you love me more than these?" (though it is disputed whether by "these" Jesus was referring to Peter's greater love for him than for these *other disciples*, or for these *fish*, or whether he was inquiring whether Peter loved him more than these other disciples loved him. See Köstenberger, *John*, 597).

[55] The proclamation of the gospel involves proclaiming God's love for the world in Jesus and calling the lost to enter into a relationship with the Father and the Son. See Köstenberger, *Theology of John's Gospel*, 519.

respond to it with love themselves, with a love that is expressed in adoration, even one that is lavish (Matt. 26:6–13; Mark 14:3–9; John 12:1–8; cf. Luke 7:36–50).

Jesus teaches his disciples that in following him they should seek his kingdom rather than their own, trusting that he will meet all their needs (Matt. 6:25–34; 10:26–33; Luke 12:4–9, 22–32). Jesus teaches his followers also that their response to being called to follow him is to be faithful managers of what God entrusted to them (Matt. 25:14–30; cf. Luke 19:11–27), being people who show mercy (Luke 6:32–36) and are filled with joy (John 16:16–24).

Opposites of Proper Love

As this essay nears its conclusion, it may be helpful to take a brief look at Jesus' other teachings and compare them to his teachings on love, determining the opposites of proper love. Jesus is quite clear that love for God harbors no equals, certainly not with money. If people love God truly and rightly, they will tolerate and submit to no other master, no other idol to whom they give their affection, worship, or trust (Matt. 6:24; cf. Luke 16:13). While Jesus normally provides positive instruction on how to love others, telling his followers how to treat them and serve them, he also issues a warning, teaching that love for the "little ones," those who appear to be of little significance, entails never causing these "little ones" to sin (Matt. 18:5–9; cf. Mark 9:42–47; Luke 17:1–2).

Jesus ties his teaching about not causing others to sin to his teaching on humility, suggesting that the two are related. It is only a proud, self-seeking individual who causes another to sin, and so pride and arrogance are opposed to true love (Matt. 18:1–4; Mark 9:33–37; Luke 9:46–48; cf. Matt. 23:1–12). Nothing could be more unloving toward fellow believers in Christ than pointing them away from their greatest good and only source of true and lasting joy. Likewise, Jesus makes clear that it is impossible for people to serve their brothers and sisters in Christ lovingly when they are interested in serving themselves (Luke 22:24–27; John 13:12–17). Jesus' teaching on lack of forgiveness and on anger, as well as retaliation, reminds his followers that one of the costs of following Jesus is putting aside grievances toward others in order to forgive them, as well as seeking their forgiveness rather than harm in pursuit of retribution (Matt. 5:21–26, 38–42). Those who harbor anger and resentment do not love their brothers and sisters.

The Recipients of Jesus' Love

The introduction to John's Gospel testifies that while God sent his Son into the world as a light into the darkness, he was not received by the world at large (John 1:9–11). The glorious reality that God so loves the world that he sent his Son to die does not mean that the entire world reciprocates God's love. Throughout the course of Jesus' life, he teaches about the recipients of his love. His love is for those who are lost, see their need for forgiveness and respond in faith, belong to the Father, and respond to God's love and forgiveness with love and forgiveness toward others. What is more, Jesus shows that God's love is not simply extended in a generic or communal manner but is directed toward individuals. Finally, Jesus also teaches his followers what it looks like to reject God's love.

Those Who Are Lost, Oppressed, Blind, Sick, Sinners

It is important to remember that what the recipients of God's love have in common is that they know they are lost. God sent his Son to seek those who are lost and held captive, to die for a rebellious world, and to save sinners (Luke 19:1–10; John 3:16). Jesus expresses this emphatically when he tells the Pharisees that he came to call sinners, not the righteous (Matt. 9:9–13; cf. Mark 2:13–17; Luke 5:27–32). There is no place for pride among believers in thinking that they merit God's love or in looking at the lost and trying to determine who among them might merit God's favor. None of them does, and so they are precisely those to whom the good news should be proclaimed (Luke 4:16–30).

Those Who See Their Need for Him and Respond in Faith

Yet while God's love is poured out on the world, it is not received by everyone (John 1:9–11). Rather, it is only those who see their great need for God, for salvation and a savior, who enjoy being the objects of his love. Jesus' teaching regarding those who are truly blessed, memorialized in the Beatitudes of the Sermon on the Mount, highlights that it is precisely those who see themselves as needy and wanting who will receive what they truly need (Matt. 5:3–12; cf. Luke 6:20–23).

This is captured poignantly in a scene narrated toward the end of Luke's Gospel, when Jesus is reviled by one of the two men who are crucified along with him. The other criminal, however, rebukes the first, saying, "'Do you not fear God, since you are under the same sentence of condemnation? And we indeed justly, for we are receiving the due reward of our deeds; but this man has done nothing wrong.' And he said, 'Jesus, remember me when you come into your kingdom'" (Luke 23:40–42). It is sinners such as this who will be with Jesus in paradise (v. 43).

In the parable of the prodigal son, it is the younger son who, despite his profligate lifestyle, is welcomed with open arms by his loving father when he repents and comes to him in need and with a contrite spirit (15:11–32). In the parable of the Pharisee and the tax collector, it is not the self-righteous individual who is forgiven but the humble sinner who cries out for mercy (18:9–14).

John, in particular, highlights this aspect of Jesus' teaching, recording on multiple occasions Jesus' insistence that he is the source of people's greatest need: true and lasting life. He is the one who gives living water (John 4:10–14; 7:37–39); he is the one who is himself the "bread of life" (6:35–40). But in order to have this life, people must come to him. And in coming to him for life, people find themselves the recipients not simply of life, but of love, for whoever loves the Son also has the love of the Father (3:35–36; 16:25–28; cf. 1:12).

Those Who Belong to the Father

There is another glorious truth that lies behind this. Faith in Jesus is not something that people bear the ultimate burden of producing, either in themselves or in others. Rather, God is calling a people to himself, and those whom he calls will receive his love and never be separated from it (Luke 2:14; John 6:37, 44; 15:16; 17:9).[56] Jesus' call to come to him for rest is a call that is understood not by the wise but by the little children to whom God reveals himself (Matt. 11:25–30). There is immeasurable comfort and joy in knowing that God has chosen, called, and set his affection upon his followers. Saved sinners did not search for him, but he pursued them (cf. Luke 19:1–10).

Those Who Respond with Love and Forgiveness

Those who have been called by God and have trusted in Jesus Christ are changed irrevocably and wonderfully. As the recipients of God's love and forgiveness, they are called now to be those who forgive. A failure to forgive and love is evidence that people do not understand God's love for them

[56] According to Darrell Bock, "those with whom he is pleased" serves as a virtual technical phrase referring to God's elect. In the context, it is a reference to those who will trust in Jesus Christ. Darrell L. Bock, *Luke 1:1–9:50* (Grand Rapids, MI: Baker Academic, 1994), 220–21.

and may not have truly received his love and forgiveness (Matt. 6:14–15; 18:21–35; Mark 11:25–26; Luke 7:36–50).

Individuals

The Gospels are a great source of encouragement in recognizing that God's love is not abstract. It is not a love that filters down from a distant God but one that is intimately personal. This is seen most conspicuously in the fact that God sent his Son to die for the world,[57] but it is seen also in a wonderful way in the very personal nature of Jesus' love for those around him. John especially highlights this aspect of God's love in Jesus. John speaks of Jesus, as he serves his disciples and prepares to go to the cross, as loving his own "to the end" or "to the fullest."[58] He also refers to himself as the "disciple whom Jesus loved" on multiple occasions (John 13:23; 19:26; 20:2; 21:7, 20).[59] Finally, he speaks of Jesus loving Lazarus, Mary, and Martha, even weeping over Lazarus's death, though he was about to raise him back to life (11:3, 5, 35–36). One can catch sight of this very personal nature of God's love also in Jesus' encounter with a rich young man, when Jesus looks at him and loves him (Mark 10:21).

Those Who Reject God's Love

Finally, the Gospels speak of those who refuse to receive God's love. Despite the glorious message of salvation in Jesus Christ, there are those who reject being gathered under Jesus' loving care (Matt. 23:37–39; Luke 13:34–35; cf. John 1:9–11), who refuse to come inside and celebrate God's forgiveness of sinners, like the older brother in the parable of the prodigal son (Luke 15:25–32). Those who refuse to believe in Jesus and reject him not only fail to receive the benefits of his earthly ministry (Matt. 13:53–58; cf. Mark 6:1–6), but far more severely find themselves living not as the recipients of God's love but as objects of his wrath (John 3:17–20, 35–36; 12:47–48). Tragically, those who reject God's love in Jesus reject the supreme act of love in human history, God's sending of his Son to die for humanity's sins. This is a tragedy of the highest order, since there can be no salvation for those who refuse to accept the only way of salvation God has provided.[60]

---

[57] Köstenberger, *John*, 129.
[58] Ibid., 402.
[59] On the phrase "the disciple whom Jesus loved" as an epithet of authorial modesty, see Andreas J. Köstenberger, "'I Suppose' (οἶμαι): The Conclusion of John's Gospel in Its Contemporary Literary and Historical Context," in *The New Testament in Its First Century Setting: Essays on Context and Backgrounds in Honour of B. W. Winter on His 65th Birthday*, ed. P. J. Williams, A. D. Clarke, P. M. Head, and D. Instone-Brewer (Grand Rapids, MI: Eerdmans, 2004), 72–88.
[60] Cf., e.g., Heb. 2:3; 6:6.

Conclusion

Scouring the Gospels for references to God's love in Jesus and organizing these references is the easy part. Yet Christians must be doers of God's Word and not hearers only. It is considerably more difficult to put Jesus' teaching on love into practice and emulate his example. At the same time, it is wonderful to rejoice in God's love and marvel at how amazing God's love really is.

Not only has God loved those who have rebelled against him; not only has he called them to receive his love by trusting in what Christ has done for them on the cross; he proceeds to call them to extend his love to others. Let us prayerfully strive to delight in this amazing love more and more each day, and let us resolve to make every effort to help others come to recognize God's love for them in Christ and share the good news with still others.[61]

[61] Many thanks are due Dave Phillips for his helpful input and research assistance with this chapter.

4

WHAT DO THE APOSTLES TEACH ABOUT THE LOVE OF GOD?

ROBERT L. PLUMMER

The human heart craves love. Nearly every chart-topping song celebrates or mourns some experience of love. Most people go about their days consumed with love—whether in the joys or in the disappointments of relationships. Sadly, Christians' thoughts about love often fail to be shaped by the Bible's teaching about the true origin and nature of love. Augustine, in praying to God, said, "You have made us for yourself, O Lord, and our hearts are restless until they rest in you."[1] If "God is love" (1 John 4:8), and his most fundamental demand is to love him completely (Matt. 22:37), then how can we begin to understand love without starting with the love of God?

The purpose of this chapter is to answer the question, what did the apostles teach about the love of God? In one sense, the teaching of the apostles underlies every word in the New Testament, so this chapter could be a comprehensive New Testament theology on the love of God. The scope of such a project far exceeds the space limitations of this chapter (or the abilities and experiences of the author!). In light of the previous chapter's emphasis on Jesus' teaching about the love of God, it seems wise to focus now on God's love from Acts to Revelation. Through commenting on select themes and texts from this portion of the biblical canon, I hope to guide the reader into a deeper understanding and appreciation of God's love. We will explore the apostles' understanding of God's love under three main headings: (1) looking back to the love of God, (2) living in the love of God, and (3) looking forward to the love of God.

[1] *Confessions*, 1.1–2 (*NPNF* 1:45).

Terminology: Love and Love of God

Nearly every American Christian has heard a sermon in which the preacher notes the presence of the word *agapē* (or some variation on it) in a biblical text and expounds on the gracious, unique love of God, as opposed to selfish love or simply natural affection.[2] While such conceptual distinctions are valid, the linguistic basis for them is lacking. In his *Exegetical Fallacies*, Don Carson helpfully points out that the verb *agapaō* is used also in the Septuagint to refer to Amnon's incestuous and rapacious lust for his half-sister, Tamar (2 Sam. 13:15).[3]

The *Greek-English Lexicon of the New Testament Based on Semantic Domains* deals a further blow to simplistic distinctions between different Greek words for *love*, commenting on *phileō* and *agapaō*:

> Though some persons have tried to assign certain significant differences of meaning between *agapaō, agapē,* and *phileō, philia* (25.33), it does not seem possible to insist upon a contrast of meaning in any and all contexts. For example, the usage in Jn 21.15–17 seems to reflect simply rhetorical alternation designed to avoid undue repetition. . . . It would be quite wrong . . . to assume that *phileō* and *philia* refer only to human love, while *agapaō* and *agapē* refer to divine love. Both sets of terms are used for the total range of loving relations between people, between people and God, and between God and Jesus Christ.[4]

Moisés Silva notes that the New Testament authors show a preference for *agapaō* possibly because the verb *phileō* was experiencing "semantic shift" in the Greek language at the time the New Testament was being written. While sometimes nearly synonymous with *agapaō*, in other contexts *phileō* conveyed the meaning "to kiss." To avoid ambiguity, one can understand why New Testament authors might prefer the word *agapaō*.[5]

So, as we begin this study, it is important to note the inherent ambiguity of the word *love* in English, an ambiguity shared by Greek words that underlie our English translations. Though it sounds somewhat circular, the only way to know what the word *love* (*agapē, philia,* or any other Greek word for love) means is by considering the context in which the word is used. At the outset, I propose this working definition of love: love

---

[2] For a thoughtful discussion of conceptual distinctions between different kinds of loves, see C. S. Lewis's classic text *The Four Loves* (New York: Harcourt Brace, 1960).

[3] D. A. Carson, *Exegetical Fallacies* (Grand Rapids, MI: Baker, 1984), 30.

[4] LN 1:294 (§25.43). Greek text has been transliterated in this quotation.

[5] Moisés Silva, *Biblical Words and Their Meaning: An Introduction to Lexical Semantics*, rev. ed. (Grand Rapids, MI: Zondervan, 1994), 96.

is a relational and practical concern for another, rooted in the nature or disposition of the one loving and resulting in tangible expressions of that concern.

Also, we need to make a brief note about the ambiguity of the expression "love of God" (*agapē tou theou*). Both the English and Greek phrases share the same ambiguity. Depending on the context, the phrase "love of God" could be referring to a person's (or persons') love for God, or to God's love for a person (or persons).[6] Other nuances are possible as well (such as "divine love" or "love that comes from God"). The two main options appear in chart 4.1.

Chart 4.1

The Ambiguous Phrase	Possible Meaning 1	Possible Meaning 2
Love of God	God's love for people	People's love for God
agapē tou theou	*theou* as subjective genitive	*theou* as objective genitive

While many different dimensions of the love of God could be considered, the one that will serve as the basis for our unfolding reflections in this chapter is the first meaning (*theou* as subjective genitive)—the love God has and shows for others. While we will consider many texts containing an explicit word for love in the Greek text, more important for our study is the *concept* of love, as delimited by the working definition above.

Looking Back to the Love of God

The apostolic writers did not consider themselves religious innovators. They believed they were reporting the final chapters of a saving story of God's love that went back to the creation of the world. Looking back over redemptive history, the New Testament authors pointed to specific interventions of God in history that showed his love. God created the world and everything in it—including the first man and woman (1 Tim. 2:13; 2 Pet. 3:5). It was God, as creator, who both enabled and established a relationship of care (i.e., love) with humans. Though we might not think of creation as an act of love, it is so, for without conscious existence, humans can neither know nor receive God's love. In Acts 17, in an evangelistic sermon in Athens, Paul appeals to God as a creator who made humans to experience a relationship of love with him. Paul says:

[6] That is, in the Greek expression *apagē tou theou*, the word *theou* functions as either a subjective or an objective genitive.

> The God who made the world and everything in it, being Lord of heaven and earth, does not live in temples made by man, nor is he served by human hands, as though he needed anything, since he himself gives to all mankind life and breath and everything. And he made from one man every nation of mankind to live on all the face of the earth, having determined allotted periods and the boundaries of their dwelling place, that they should seek God, and perhaps feel their way toward him and find him. Yet he is actually not far from each one of us, for "In him we live and move and have our being"; as even some of your own poets have said, "For we are indeed his offspring." (Acts 17:24–28)

In this text we observe God's love for all humans—not just in creating them but in sustaining them with life, food, and places to live. As all humans experience such "common grace" from God, it is a reminder that God does indeed love the entire mass of humanity in some way.[7] In providing ongoing rain and sun for the crops of persons in rebellion against him, God demonstrates a love even for his enemies—a love his people are called to imitate (Matt. 5:43–48). Yet the Bible also clearly affirms a unique, salvific, electing love experienced only by Christians (Eph. 1:4–5).

Although the New Testament authors certainly focus on the saving love of God in Christ, they do not deny the ongoing providential love of God whereby he provides food, clothing, and companionship (1 Tim. 6:8, 17). This experience of God's "common grace" is shared with nonbelievers, absent the gift of divine contentment in Christ.

Undoubtedly, however, the New Testament focuses on the effective, saving love God has for Christians. When Paul expounds on the "great love with which [God] loved us [Christians]," he writes:

> When we were dead in our trespasses, [God] made us alive together with Christ—by grace you have been saved—and raised us up with him and seated us with him in the heavenly places in Christ Jesus, so that in the coming ages he might show the immeasurable riches of his grace in kindness toward us in Christ Jesus (Eph. 2:4–7).

So according to this text, the *sine qua non* of God's saving love is the (1) regeneration of former spiritually dead transgressors, (2) uniting of those believers with Christ, (3) saving of those believers from the coming wrath of God's righteous judgment, (4) securing of believers' adoptive

[7] See D. A. Carson's helpful discussion of different dimensions of God's love in *The Difficult Doctrine of the Love of God* (Wheaton, IL: Crossway, 2000).

filial status in union with Christ, and (5) promise of eternal joy and peace in God's presence guaranteed by the finished work of Christ on the cross.

The love of God is experienced by his people primarily through being saved from his righteous wrath and living in that blessed sphere of his acceptance, looking forward to the coming bliss of living in his presence. Paul is not an innovator in describing God's love in this way. All the authors of the New Testament look back on history and see God as one who constantly communicates with his chosen people—revealing his concern for humans in their lost state and his plan to reconcile estranged and rebellious creatures to himself through his Son. In Hebrews 1:1–2 we read:

> Long ago, at many times and in many ways, God spoke to our fathers by the prophets, but in these last days he has spoken to us by his Son, whom he appointed the heir of all things, through whom also he created the world.

Though God had revealed his loving concern in the past—speaking to his people and revealing himself to them—the author of Hebrews tells us that history has now turned a significant corner. We see the climactic demonstration of God's love in his sending of his Son.

Paul speaks in a similar way about the sharp turn that has taken place in salvation history, employing the language of "mystery" (*mustērion*). For Paul, a mystery is something that was "hidden in plain view" in the Old Testament, but has now become clearly visible and known through the final, climactic revelatory work of God.[8] The Greek word *mustērion* ("mystery") occurs twenty-one times in Paul's letters and touches on multiple different dimensions of the way God's love is experienced in a new, climactic way by those whom he is saving. Chart 4.2 summarizes some different dimensions of God's love, now fully unveiled, in the saving work of Christ.

Chart 4.2

Pauline *mustērion* Text	**Climactic Dimension of God's Love**
Rom. 11:25–26	Gentiles are welcomed into God's family; Jews are temporarily hardened to the gospel, but eventually "all Israel will be saved."
Rom. 16:25	God's saving, redeeming love is now made known through the proclamation of the gospel of Christ.

[8] I am borrowing the language of something "hidden in plain view" from D. A. Carson. I believe I first heard him use this expression in a visiting lecture on Southern Seminary's campus.

Pauline *mustērion* Text	Climactic Dimension of God's Love
1 Cor. 15:51	At Christ's return, both living and dead believers will be given resurrection bodies and dwell together in joy with God forever.
Eph. 1:9	God unites all things under Christ's headship. Through Christ, in accordance with God's predestining love, believers have an eternal inheritance.
Eph. 5:32	Christ's self-sacrificing love for the church is pictured by a husband's sacrificial love for his wife.
1 Tim. 3:16	Jesus died, was raised, and ascended. Salvation in his name is now proclaimed throughout the world.

Paul tells us that this most important mystery has now been unveiled. God has "shown his hand." He has revealed in visible history the final, saving act long hinted at throughout his prior revelations. Much of the New Testament, then, is looking back on this sharp turn in salvation history, whereby history no longer is directed toward the end but skirts along the edge of the consummation of history.[9]

It is instructive that when writers of the New Testament speak of God's care for Christians (i.e., his love), they favor speaking of God's "rescue plan" for lost humans through his Son. God's love, then, as described by the New Testament writers, is not a sentimental or emotional state but is a divine saving activity on the behalf of helpless, lost persons. A sampling of the different ways New Testament authors look back on God's saving love in Christ is listed in chart 4.3.

Chart 4.3

Text	Historical Retrospective on God's Saving Love
Acts 2:23	Jesus died and was raised "according to the definite plan and foreknowledge of God."
Rom. 3:25	God the Father put forward Jesus as a "propitiation" (wrath averter) by means of his sacrificial death.
1 Cor. 2:2	The message Paul is compelled to proclaim is nothing other than "Jesus Christ and him crucified."
Eph. 1:4–5	God the Father's love is demonstrated through his predestining believers to be adopted as sons and daughters through Jesus Christ.
Heb. 10:12	Christ offered an effective, unrepeated sacrifice for sins.

[9]My language here is influenced by J. H. Newman, as quoted by I. Howard Marshall: "[The course of things] has (if I may so speak) altered its direction, as regards [Jesus'] second coming, and runs, not towards the end, but along it, and on the brink of it; and is at all times near that great event, which, did it run towards it, it would at once run into. Christ, then, is ever at our doors." I. Howard Marshall, *The Epistles of John*, NICNT (Grand Rapids, MI: Eerdmans, 1978), 149.

Text	Historical Retrospective on God's Saving Love
James 1:18	By God's loving, sovereign choice, we have been "brought . . . forth" (*apekuēsen*, "birthed") by the intermediate means of the "word of truth," thereby picturing the forthcoming renewal of all creation.
1 Pet. 1:3–4	Jesus' resurrection from the dead assures our hope in his saving promises.
1 John 4:10	God loved us through the sending of his Son as a propitiation for our sins.
Jude 1	Christians rightly understand themselves as ones effectually "called," "beloved," and guarded or "kept" for Jesus Christ.
Rev. 1:5–6	The primary way we know that Jesus "loves us" is that he "has freed us from our sins by his blood and made us a kingdom, priests to his God and Father."
Rev. 7:14	The redeemed in heaven rejoice because "they have washed their robes and made them white in the blood of the Lamb."

In chart 4.3, at least one text from every author represented by the canonical section of Acts to Revelation is included. In all these passages, we note (1) a historical, retrospective focus on God's work in planning and providing salvation; (2) the prominence of the person of Jesus in providing salvation; and (3) a repeated emphasis on the centrality of the *death* of Jesus in securing forgiveness.

In addition to looking backward to the death of Jesus as the central demonstration of God's love, it is instructive to note the Trinitarian nature of God's love. God the Father sent the Son. The Son died for his people. The Spirit vivifies dead sinners and sets them apart for God. One of the many places we see this Trinitarian dimension is 1 Peter 1:1–2. Peter writes that believers are "elect" (1) "according to the foreknowledge of God the Father," (2) "in the sanctification of the Spirit," and (3) "for obedience to Jesus Christ and for sprinkling with his blood." In other words, (1) Christians become part of God's elect people because they are foreknown (salvifically known/chosen in advance); (2) Christians are set apart (sanctified) as God's holy people by the regenerative work of the Holy Spirit; and (3) Christians are cleansed of their sins by Jesus' death on the cross and transferred from the category of "rebels" to that of obedient disciples.

In this first of three sections on the love of God, we have focused on God's love for his people from a retrospective ("looking back") dimension. Surveying the apostolic writings from Acts to Revelation, we noticed a consistent glance backward to God's love demonstrated historically and climactically in the life, death, and resurrection of God's Son. We also noted the consistent Trinitarian dimension of the apostles' retrospective reflections on the love of God.

With this first "retrospective" pattern in mind, let us conclude this section by a more detailed look at one particular text, Galatians 2:20:

> I have been crucified with Christ. It is no longer I who live, but Christ who lives in me. And the life I now live in the flesh I live by faith in the Son of God, who loved me and gave himself for me.

It is important to remember that this text is not a lightning bolt that fell from heaven suddenly to strike the pages of Christian devotional books. Rather, the words are an integral part of Paul's argument. Paul avers that humans, in their fallen condition, are incapable of obeying God's commands. Such human rebellion requires punishment. Furthermore, by his death Jesus has borne that "curse" we deserve for our constant and flagrant violation of God's holy standards (Gal. 3:10–14).

One way to speak of Jesus' death for us and our being united to him is to speak (shockingly!) of our being "crucified with Christ" (2:20). Of course, in a literalistic way, Paul was not crucified with Christ. Only Christ was nailed to the cross on which he was suspended. Paul, in fact, was not even a disciple of Christ at the time of Jesus' crucifixion. Yet Christ's death is so surely and completely for Paul (as it is for all followers of Jesus) that the apostle can speak of himself as being "crucified with Christ." Paul took a historical retrospective on the love of God, and as he looked back into the vista of history, he found Jesus dying on the cross at the center. And there, in Jesus' historical death, Paul located the historical punishment his personal sins required.

Paul goes on to speak about his current life being driven and empowered by the presence of Christ before again glancing back. Paul's current eye of faith does not stare mysteriously into the cosmos, but backward to the revealed historical person of the Son of God. (Note that even though this text does not mention the role of the Father and the Spirit, the distinct title for the second person of the triune God implies the activity of the other persons.) In his role as "Son of God" and "Christ," Jesus fulfills the messianic and representative service predicted of the suffering servant (Isaiah 53). In Jesus' death, Paul does not see a stoical philosophical transaction, but love! "He loved me," Paul cries! "He loved me, and gave himself for me!" (cf. John 15:13). Indeed, unless a person looks back to the life and death of Jesus and there sees the love of God for himself or herself, that person has not come to know the love of God as taught in Scripture.

Living in the Love of God

Jesus predicted that his followers would be noticeably different from the broken world, which is in ongoing rebellion against God. In John 13:35, he said, "By this all people will know that you are my disciples, if you have love for one another." Elsewhere, Jesus compared his genuine disciples to trees that bear good fruit—not thistles or brambles. While false professors may claim to follow Jesus as Lord, their wicked behavior will belie their confessions (Matt. 7:15–23).

Jesus' parables also teach that one who experiences God's grace and forgiveness is constrained to extend that grace to others. In the parable of the unforgiving servant (Matt. 18:23–25), Jesus tells of a servant who was forgiven an unimaginably large debt by a king. Rather than being grateful and forgiving others, the servant threatens and imprisons a fellow servant for a very small debt. The king then calls the original servant to account, putting him in jail until he pays off his debt in full. Jesus warns, "So also my heavenly Father will do to every one of you, if you do not forgive your brother from your heart" (v. 35).

Indeed, it is no surprise that when Jesus is asked about the "great commandment" in God's law, he replies with the "double love command" (Matt. 22:36–40). That is, persons are to (1) love God with all their heart, soul, and mind, and (2) love their neighbors as themselves. These two injunctions are so inextricably connected that they can be thought of as two sides of the same coin. And, in fact, Jesus tells us that any other ethical teaching in the Scriptures can be understood as an elaboration or overflow of these two love commands. Or, in Jesus' explicit words: "On these two commandments depend all the Law and the Prophets" (v. 40).

If divine grace is really received, if God's love is genuinely known, then that reality will show up in the lives of God's people. This is a theme that reappears prominently from Acts to Revelation. The texts in chart 4.4 demonstrate this motif. As in chart 4.3, at least one text from each author in the canonical section of Acts to Revelation is represented:

Chart 4.4

Text	Experiencing God's Love Results in Transformed Living
Acts 2:44–47	Through his narrative, Luke shows how believers are transformed to love and sacrifice radically for other Christians.
Rom. 15:1–3	Just as "Christ did not please himself" (Rom. 15:3), so Christians are called to be concerned for the salvation and spiritual health of others in their community.

Text	Experiencing God's Love Results in Transformed Living
1 Cor. 8:11–13	A Christian should defer to others' needs for the sake of salvation and spiritual growth. If eating meat tempts other Christians to sin against their consciences, Paul says he will never eat meat again.
Eph. 5:25–32	The love that husbands have for their wives should mirror the sacrificial, cleansing love that Christ showed for the church in his atoning death.
Heb. 13:12–16	Jesus sacrificed himself to sanctify us with his blood. In a small way, Christians mirror that sacrifice through doing what is good and sharing with others.
James 2:14–26	If someone does not tangibly love other Christians who are in need, then that person's faith is "dead" and "useless." Simply a verbal affirmation with no accompanying deeds is a demonic faith.
2 Pet. 1:5–11	Whoever lacks godliness, brotherly affection, and love "is blind, having forgotten that he was cleansed from his former sins."
1 John 2:4–6	To claim to know God while not obeying his commands is to prove that one is a liar. A Christian's life should, in some ways, reflect the life of his Savior. A Christian should "walk in the same way in which [Jesus] walked."
1 John 4:7–8	A person who has been "born of God" and "knows God" demonstrates that reality through the loving of other Christians. Anyone who lacks such brotherly love shows that he or she does not know God, because God is, in his very nature, love.
2 John 5–6	The "commandment" the Christian community has had from its founding is to love one another. Indeed, it is impossible to know love only in the abstract—true love demonstrates itself through the keeping of God's commands.
Jude 1, 12	As persons "beloved in God," Christians now gather together at "love feasts" with one another. The heretics deny the loving Lord by their failure to live in holiness; they are "hidden reefs" at the love feasts.
Rev. 1:5–6	As persons who have been loved by Jesus and freed from our sins by his blood, we now live as priestly citizens of his kingdom.

Just as the "looking back to the love of God" (in the historical saving death of his Son) had a Trinitarian pattern, so texts related to believers' "living in the love of God" display a similar pattern. The Father's loving nature and his sending of the Son is a supernaturally constraining experience of love that enables (and demands!) believers to love others now (1 John 4:7–12). Whether relating to one's spouse (Eph. 5:25–33) or superior (6:5–8), it is the love of Christ that provides both the foundation and example of practical love. Finally, the Holy Spirit empowers God's people through gifts and spiritual fruit whereby they love and build up the church (1 Corinthians 12–14).

One dimension of Christians' overflowing and responsive love is the practical concern they have for the eternal souls of non-Christians around them. The Bible teaches clearly that Jesus will separate all persons in eternity—welcoming some to eternal joy and sending others to eternal punishment (Matt. 25:46). There is no chance to respond to God's offer of forgiveness after death, for "it is appointed for man to die once, and after that comes judgment" (Heb. 9:27).

The Protestant evangelical tradition is rich with reflection on the urgency and imperative of love that demands we take the gospel to others. Leonard Ravenhill tells the moving story of a minister sharing the gospel with infamous English criminal Charlie Peace as he was headed to his execution. Peace demanded, "Do you really believe in such a place called hell?" The minister responded, "Yes." Peace replied, "Sir, if I believed what you and the church of God say that you believe, even if England were covered with broken glass from coast to coast, I would walk over it, if need be, on hands and knees, and think it worthwhile living, just to save one soul from an eternal hell like that!"[10]

American evangelical Christians often abstractly agree with the urgency of rescuing sinners from hell—and even take short-term mission trips to share the gospel overseas—while neglecting the spiritual state of the neighbors who live right beside them. David Thomas aptly observes, "That feeling which induces man to cross seas, and to traverse islands and continents, to offer blessings which he has never presented to his own neighbors, who stand in equal need, is the simpering sentiment of a morbid and diseased mind, not the manly love of a true heart."[11]

One should understand that Christian love expressed toward those who are in a state of spiritual death is nothing other than the love of the heavenly Father sounding forth from his children (1 Thess. 1:8). It is the "good works" that he has prepared in advance for us to do, and in fact, in which he himself is working (Eph. 2:8–10). In explaining why God currently delays the day of judgment, Peter states, "The Lord is not slow to fulfill his promise as some count slowness, but is patient toward you, not wishing that any should perish, but that all should reach repentance" (2 Pet. 3:9). Paul tells us that God our Savior "desires all people to be saved and to come to the knowledge of the truth" (1 Tim. 2:4). The method God

---

[10] Leonard Ravenhill, *Why Revival Tarries* (Minneapolis: Bethany Fellowship, 1959), 19, cited by Ravi Zacharias at http://www.rzim.org/just-thinking/reading-the-fingerprints-on-your-soul/.

[11] David Thomas, *The Genius of the Gospel: A Homiletical Commentary on the Gospel of St. Matthew* (London: Dickinson & Higham, 1873), 151, as cited in Robert Duncan Culver, *A Greater Commission: A Theology of World Missions* (Chicago: Moody, 1984), 14.

has instituted for delivering this life-giving gospel to a perishing world is the proclamation of his servants (Rom. 10:14–17). We can move forward sharing the gospel in confidence because the electing and regenerating work of God ensures that all those appointed for eternal life will believe (Acts 13:48).

Martin Luther's companion Philip Melanchthon (1497–1560) famously once remarked, "To know Christ is to know his benefits."[12] In other words, we do not know Christ primarily in some abstract, ethereal pneumatic or gnostic contemplation. Rather, we know Christ in looking with faith upon his death for us and knowing propositionally and experientially that our sins are forgiven through him—that we are welcomed as righteous into God's presence through Christ. When we know these "saving benefits" of Christ, we are then compelled by that experience of love (and the Spirit's leading) to hold out God's life-giving message to others (Phil. 2:15–16).[13]

The apostle Paul speaks of the controlling or compelling experience of God's love in Christ that propelled him outward as a minister of reconciliation to a world estranged in its sin. Paul writes:

> The love of Christ controls us, because we have concluded this: that one has died for all, therefore all have died; and he died for all, that those who live might no longer live for themselves but for him who for their sake died and was raised. From now on, therefore, we regard no one according to the flesh. Even though we once regarded Christ according to the flesh, we regard him thus no longer. Therefore, if anyone is in Christ, he is a new creation. The old has passed away; behold, the new has come. All this is from God, who through Christ reconciled us to himself and gave us the ministry of reconciliation; that is, in Christ God was reconciling the world to himself, not counting their trespasses against them, and entrusting to us the message of reconciliation. Therefore, we are ambassadors for Christ, God making his appeal through us. We implore you on behalf of Christ, be reconciled to God. For our sake he made him to be sin who knew no sin, so that in him we might become the righteousness of God. (2 Cor. 5:14–21)

To the extent we are constrained by the love of God, to that extent we will see ourselves as joyful ambassadors—extending God's "olive branch" in Christ to his enemies. Like Paul, we will plead with neighbors, coworkers,

[12] *The Loci Communes of Philip Melanchthon*, trans. Charles Leander Hill (Boston: Meador, 1944), 68.

[13] See my defense of this translation in Robert L. Plummer, *Paul's Understanding of the Church's Mission: Did the Apostle Paul Expect the Early Christian Communities to Evangelize?*, Paternoster Biblical Monographs (Milton Keynes, UK: Paternoster, 2006), 74–77.

and friends, "We implore you on behalf of Christ, be reconciled to God" (2 Cor. 5:20).

While affirming the propositional and historical dimensions of God's love lived out among his people (i.e., the obedience of Jesus' disciples), one should not deny the personal, experiential nature of God's love. Paul writes, "The [Holy] Spirit himself bears witness with our spirit that we are children of God" (Rom. 8:16). This is the Spirit who confirms to us experientially our adopted status and enables us to cry out with intimacy and authenticity, "Abba! Father!" (Rom. 8:15).

The apostle John speaks in a similar way when he explains that God's Spirit is the one who enables us to know that we really belong to God and that he indwells us. John writes, "By this we know that we abide in him and he in us, because he has given us of his Spirit" (1 John 4:13). Howard Marshall offers these helpful reflections on this verse:

> [John] states that we can know that God lives in us by the fact that he has given us the Spirit. . . . Our knowledge that we have this relationship with God arises from the fact that that he has given us a share in the Spirit. . . . But how do we know that we have received the Spirit? In our earlier discussion of this point (3:24 n.) we concluded that various experiences might be in mind, such as confidence in prayer, inward conviction that we are God's children, and charismatic gifts. It is possible that the last of these is particularly in mind here: possession of the Spirit may lead to prophecy or other forms of utterance, but these may need to be tested by their fidelity to the apostolic witness.[14]

So, whether we appeal to an inner sense of our filial status, the spiritual gifts God has given us, confidence in prayer, or some other confirming work of the Spirit, we should never relegate the experience of belonging to God to intellectual affirmation. Rather, any genuine knowledge and relationship with God will manifest itself in our practical life and "religious affections."[15]

In this chapter we are looking at the love of God (God's love for his people) from three different dimensions—retrospective (looking back), experiential (living in), and prospective (looking forward). We are finishing the discussion of the second of these three dimensions—"living in" the love of God. Let us consider one particular text in more detail as we close out this section. In Ephesians 3:14–19 Paul writes:

[14] Marshall, *Epistles of John*, 219.

[15] See Jonathan Edwards, *A Treatise Concerning Religious Affections* (Philadelphia: James Crissy, 1821).

> For this reason I bow my knees before the Father, from whom every family in heaven and on earth is named, that according to the riches of his glory he may grant you to be strengthened with power through his Spirit in your inner being, so that Christ may dwell in your hearts through faith—that you, being rooted and grounded in love, may have strength to comprehend with all the saints what is the breadth and length and height and depth, and to know the love of Christ that surpasses knowledge, that you may be filled with all the fullness of God.

In this Pauline prayer, we will focus on Paul's desire for believers to live in the ongoing experiential reality of God's love.

We begin by noting the Trinitarian dimension of the Christian's experience of love. Paul prays to the Father. It is God the *Father* who is petitioned in this prayer. But the prayer is for the power of the *Spirit* to so operate that *Christ* will dwell in believers' hearts by faith. Any claim to Christian vitality and experience that is not apostolically Trinitarian is suspect.

Second, we note that Paul is expecting a real, transforming experience to be brought about in the lives of genuine believers. And this experience is both "grounded in love" (retrospective) and knowing love (experiential). Though the historical death of Jesus on the cross establishes the objective, historical basis for Christians' knowledge of God's love, Paul knows that sterile historical knowledge is not enough. Christians need to know the love of Christ—the love of a personal Lord who continues to love and transform them through their failures, sins, and fears. In one sense, of course, Christ already indwells all believers. But in this prayer, Paul prays for Christ to take up full residence—taking out the old gaudy wallpaper of our prior sinful life, so to speak, and bringing about an "extreme home makeover" in the core of our being.[16] This is what it means to live in the love of God—not to remain in some state of mystical contemplation but to live rationally, emotionally, and mentally in the joyful experience of Christ's love and to be transformed to reflect that love to others. Does that describe your Christian life? Does that describe your prayer and desire for those around you?

Looking Forward to the Love of God

New Testament scholar George Ladd convinced American evangelicals that the "end time" kingdom hope in the New Testament is best under-

[16] My language is influenced here by D. A. Carson, *A Call to Spiritual Reformation: Priorities from Paul and His Prayers* (Grand Rapids, MI: Baker, 1992), 186.

stood as having both present and future dimensions.[17] That is, as we read the New Testament (and as we live life today), we see our end-time hope in the process of being unfolded under Christ's lordship while we still await the consummation of Christ's kingdom at his return. Jesus said that if he drove out demons by the Spirit of God (and he did), then the kingdom of God had arrived (Matt. 12:28). Yet, at the same time, the followers of Jesus are taught to long for the full realization of God's kingdom through our regular prayer to God, "Your kingdom come" (6:10; cf. 8:11). Thus, we have in the New Testament the tension between the "already" and the "not yet" of God's kingdom. God's saving rule is already present in the person and work of Jesus, but it is not yet fully and universally present in its final unchallenged manifestation.

We see a mirror of these already and not-yet dimensions of God's kingdom in Christians' experience of his love. God's love is already secured to Christians through the death of his Son. Christians already experience some of the joys and benefits of this love. Yet believers also look forward to the final, lasting, and fuller experience of God's love when Christ returns and consummates the kingdom. At that time, Christians will no longer know the brokenness, sadness, and moral failure that characterize so much of their present existence. Then the Lord himself will wipe every tear from our eyes (Rev. 21:4).

The chart below shows how Christians, as described by New Testament authors, are to look forward to a fuller experience of God's love. At least one text from every author in the canonical section of Acts to Revelation is represented in chart 4.5.

Chart 4.5

Text	Christians Look Forward to the Full Experience of God's Love
Acts 1:11	Jesus, who ascended bodily into heaven, will return in the same way—to gather his people to himself and fulfill all his promises.
1 Cor. 15:19–49	If it is only in this life that we have hope, then we are a foolish and self-deceived people, says Paul. In fact, Christ's physical resurrection is a precursor to the coming resurrection and eternal bliss of God's people. Though now we are a weak and failing people, we can be assured that we will one day "bear the image of the man of heaven."
Phil. 1:6	The "good work" God has begun in believers (regenerating them and adopting them) will assuredly be completed on that final day when Jesus returns.

[17] George E. Ladd, *A Theology of the New Testament*, rev. ed. (Grand Rapids, MI: Eerdmans, 1993), 54–67.

Text	Christians Look Forward to the Full Experience of God's Love
1 Thess. 4:13–5:11	We look forward to the bodily return of Christ, when the physical bodies of dead believers will be resurrected with eternal glory and Christians then alive will experience the transforming power of God. On that day, we will experience the fullness of being delivered from God's eschatological wrath through Christ.
2 Thess. 2:1–12	When Jesus returns, he will destroy our spiritual enemies with the "breath of his mouth" and will nullify them "by the appearance of his coming."
2 Tim. 4:8	When Christ, "the righteous judge," returns, he will crown believers eternally with his righteousness.
Heb. 11:13–16	This fallen world is not the final home of God's people. Rather, we seek an eternal homeland—a heavenly city, which God has prepared for us.
Heb. 12:26–29	God will "once more" shake the heavens and the earth—resulting in a final, secure settling of his people in his eternal glorious presence.
James 5:4–8	Though we experience injustice and mistreatment now, we can be assured that the Lord hears our cries for justice and will enable us to be patient "until the coming of the Lord."
1 Pet. 5:10	Though we suffer and are tempted now, our ultimate destiny is God's "eternal glory in Christ."
1 John 2:28–3:3	We look forward to Christ's second coming, when we will be changed to be "like him, because we shall see him as he is." This hope has a purifying influence on our lives now.
1 John 4:18	Knowing God's perfect love now enables us to realize that we are accepted fully by him in Christ, so we do not need to fear the coming judgment. Christ has borne the Father's righteous wrath for us.
Jude 21	As we remain in the realm of God's love, we wait for the final expression of God's mercy in the day of judgment at Christ's return—a mercy that results in eternal life.
Rev. 21:1–4	In the new heavens and the new earth, there will be no more death, crying, or pain. God will dwell with his people.

Just as "looking back to the love of God" and "living in the love of God" have a Trinitarian dimension, so "looking forward to the love of God" is clarified by considering the Trinitarian motifs in the New Testament. We are assured that the Father does indeed hear our cries for justice and for the consummation of his kingdom (Matt. 6:10; James 5:4–8). The Son has promised that he will return again to take us to be with him (John 14:1–3). Indeed, when he returns, we will see him "as he is" and be transformed to reflect his glorious presence (1 John 3:2). Until that day of consummation, the Spirit functions as a down payment in our lives—reminding us of the fullness to come and guaranteeing us of its certainty (2 Cor. 1:22; 5:5; Eph. 1:14).

New Testament scholars rightly remind modern Bible readers that the ultimate hope of Christians is not some disembodied, soulish experience in heaven but the resurrection of glorified bodes under the reign of Christ in the new heavens and the new earth (1 Thess. 4:13–5:11; Rev. 20:1–15). Yet knowing that the final resurrection may very well happen after his or her death, the Christian still longs joyfully to be present with the Lord after death in spirit. Paul said he desired to die and be present with Christ, which is "far better" than living in this sin-stained and broken world (Phil. 1:23). Elsewhere, Paul confidently affirms that to be absent from the body (in physical death) is to be present with the Lord (2 Cor. 5:8).

Sometimes Christians do not look forward to being with God in heaven or living joyfully with him in the eternal state because they misunderstand the metaphorical nature of some descriptions of heaven in the New Testament. In this regard, C. S. Lewis cautions:

> There is no need to be worried by facetious people who try to make the Christian hope of "Heaven" ridiculous by saying they do not want "to spend eternity playing harps." The answer to such people is that if they cannot understand books written for grown-ups, they should not talk about them. All the scriptural imagery (harps, crowns, gold, etc.) is, of course, a merely symbolical attempt to express the inexpressible. Musical instruments are mentioned because for many people (not all) music is the thing known in the present life which most strongly suggests ecstasy and infinity. Crowns are mentioned to suggest the fact that those who are united with God in eternity share His splendour and power and joy. Gold is mentioned to suggest the timelessness of Heaven (gold does not rust) and the preciousness of it. People who take these symbols literally might as well think that when Christ told us to be like doves, He meant that we were to lay eggs.[18]

So, as we are seeing in this chapter, for a full-orbed understanding of God's love, Christians must not only look back to God's historical intervention in Christ to save them (retrospective), but they must also live in the transforming sphere and experience of that love (experiential), while longing for the full consummation of that love in the new heavens and new earth (prospective).

[18] C. S. Lewis, *Mere Christianity* (New York: Macmillan, 1952), 106.

In concluding this section on the forward-looking aspect of experiencing God's love, it is fitting for us to consider one text in more detail. In Philippians 3:20–4:1 Paul writes,

> Our citizenship is in heaven, and from it we await a Savior, the Lord Jesus Christ, who will transform our lowly body to be like his glorious body, by the power that enables him even to subject all things to himself. Therefore, my brothers, whom I love and long for, my joy and crown, stand firm thus in the Lord, my beloved.

Paul begins this section by contrasting true believers with the earthly "enemies of the cross of Christ" (Phil. 3:18). Drawing upon a metaphor that would have been significant to the many residents of Philippi, Paul says that the ultimate home and loyalty of true followers of Christ is in heaven.[19] But, again, this heavenly belonging does not mean we are destined to an eternity of ethereal pneumatic existence. Rather, we look to heaven, from whence we await the return of our Savior, the Lord Jesus Christ. The one who loved us and gave himself up for us (Gal. 2:20) is certainly returning to us that we may be with him forever (John 14:1–3).

When Jesus appears, it will not simply be a gathering of our broken and sin-beset bodies to live with him. Paul says he will "transform our lowly body to be like his glorious body" (Phil. 3:21). This is the love of God we are longing for. God will not leave us in our broken, fallen, sin-sick condition forever. No! He will transform us to be sinless, free from every taint of evil, disease, and sadness. And this will happen in an instant. In 1 John 3:2 the apostle John comforts his readers with these words: "We know that when he appears we shall be like him, because we shall see him as he is." As one commentator has said, "Vision will beget likeness."[20] When we see Jesus, we shall be transformed to be like him. This is the church's beloved bridegroom—coming for us and giving us clean garments, which can never become stained or worn out (Rev. 21:2–3).

As careful readers, we should note the inferential use of *hōste* (translated "therefore," Phil. 4:1). In light of this wonderful consummation of divine love in God's presence, Paul says we can "stand firm" and live faithfully as disciples in a world filled with temptation and discouragement. Our hope in an eternal, tangible experience of God's love is a means God

[19] Craig Keener notes, "Citizens of Philippi, a Roman colony, were automatically citizens of Rome, sharing all the rights and privileges of Roman citizens even though most of them had never been there." Craig S. Keener, *The IVP Bible Background Commentary: New Testament* (Downers Grove, IL: InterVarsity, 1993), 564.

[20] Robert Law, *The Tests of Life: A Study of the First Epistle of St. John*, 3rd ed. (Edinburgh: T&T Clark, 1914), 335.

uses to encourage believers to persevere through difficulties. Paul elsewhere says the Holy Spirit is the down payment (*arrabōn*) of these future blessings (Eph. 1:14)—blessings we will receive when the Father sends back his Son for his people. (Again, note the consistent Trinitarian dimension to every perspective on God's love—retrospective, experiential, and prospective.)

Conclusion

In this chapter, which focused on the canonical section of Acts to Revelation, we have sought to trace three motifs that appear in describing God's love for his people: (1) The New Testament authors consistently look back to the historical intervention of God in his Son to save his people through the Son's atoning death on the cross. Though God is "in nature" love, the way we know and experience that love is by the saving benefits secured by his Son's death. (2) The New Testament authors expect those who know God's love to live transformed lives, empowered by God's indwelling Spirit. Persons who know God's love will love others and live in obedience under God's rule, using their spiritual gifts to build up the body of Christ. (3) The New Testament authors speak of God's love as already known, but not yet fully known. Christians look forward to the return of Christ, the resurrection of their bodies, and living in the new heavens and the new earth in perfect loving bliss with God forever.

We summarized these three motifs as (1) *retrospective*, or looking back to the love of God; (2) *experiential*, or living in the love of God; and (3) *prospective*, or looking forward to the love of God. Also, within each one of these themes, we noted the Trinitarian nature of the New Testament authors' teaching about God's love. A mature Christian knowledge and experience of God's love should include an integration of the three vantage points above within a distinctively Trinitarian perspective.

Finally, for a practical example, we will consider how this teaching on the love of God should be applied by a Christian mother with a rebellious teenage daughter.

Looking Back to the Love of God

The vicissitudes and challenges of this life can feel overwhelming. Yet Christians have an anchor for their soul in the certainty of God's love for them. A mother is not accepted before God on the basis of her parenting skills or the behavior of her daughter. The mother's acceptance and forgiveness is secured on the basis of Christ's perfect life and once-for-all sacrifice. With Paul, this mother can cry out, "[Jesus] loved me and gave himself for me" (Gal. 2:20). The Spirit has opened the mother's eyes to see how great the Father's love was in sending his Son. The distraught mother needs to cast all her anxiety on the Lord, for he has left no doubt about his love and acceptance of her.

Living in the Love of God

When this mother herself was a rebel against God, God did not leave her in her sin. Rather, he regenerated her by his Spirit and enabled her to see herself as a sinner and grasp by faith the finished work of Christ. Now, by the Spirit's enabling, this mother can extend that grace to her teenage daughter. It is looking back to the love of God that enables her to live in the love of God now. This mother, by the power of the Spirit, can live out Ephesians 4:32: "Be kind to one another, tenderhearted, forgiving one another, as God in Christ forgave you." This mother can love her daughter, discipline her daughter, forgive her daughter, not exasperate her daughter—manifesting the fruit of the Spirit. And knowing the power and love of the Spirit in her own life, the mother can pray with hope that the Spirit will grant repentance and life to her rebellious daughter as well.

Looking Forward to the Love of God

This mother can be encouraged that this broken and sad world is not the end of the story. The Spirit will enable her to persevere in trial. Jesus promises to be with her to the end of the age. The Father will keep his promise to send the Son again and dwell forever with his people. He will wipe every tear from her eyes (Rev. 21:4). In the new heavens and the new earth, all the grief and pain will be forgotten. And, even now, God the Father is using these trials to shape her more and more into the image of his Son. She is being prepared for her eternal dwelling (1 Pet. 1:4–9).

Chances are that few mothers with rebellious teenage daughters are reading this chapter. Yet I am confident that you, the reader, are facing or will face suffering, injustice, disappointment, and sadness in this life. What can carry you through these challenges? The love of God. As we reflect on and live in this great love God has for us in Christ, may we grow to be more loving people by the power of his Spirit, looking forward to an eternal love relationship with the triune God, in whom we will delight forever.

5

LOVE IN THE TRIUNE COMMUNITY?

JOHN W. MAHONY

Our fallen world is full of references to love. It is the theme of countless poems (e.g., Elizabeth Barrett Browning's "How Do I Love Thee?"), songs (e.g., Burt Bacharach's contrasting takes on love, "What the World Needs Now" and "I'll Never Fall in Love Again"), plays (e.g., William Shakespeare's *Romeo and Juliet*), works of art (e.g., Rembrandt's *Return of the Prodigal* and Gustav Klimt's *The Kiss*), novels (e.g., Jane Austen's *Pride and Prejudice* and Charlotte Brontë's *Jane Eyre*), and, of course, movies (e.g., *The Notebook*; *Titanic*; and *Casablanca*). Love has its own special day (Valentine's), literary genre (romance novel), and websites for finding one's "soul mate." The American culture's fascination with romance and relationships makes love a continuous topic of conversation and a lucrative form of revenue.

Popularity, however, doesn't guarantee understanding. In fact, the word *love* describes our feelings about things (e.g., foods, pets, places, cars), institutions (e.g., schools, churches, country), and persons (both divine and human). Further complicating matters are the fallen context in which we live and the skewed perspective as to what love is. For example, the popular song "What's Love Got to Do with It?" was written by Terry Britten and Graham Lyle and recorded by Tina Turner in 1984.[1] It is a cynical take on the casual use of the word *love* in human relationships, especially as a cover for abuse and pain. Consequently, love is a "secondhand emotion" and a "sweet old fashioned notion." Hey, "Who needs a heart when a heart can be broken?" Why pursue a relationship that inflicts so much pain and heartache? Why open oneself up to disappointment and

[1] http://www.metrolyrics.com/whats-love-got-to-do-with-it-lyrics-tina-turner.html.

rejection? Vulnerability and transparency are so dangerous, aren't they? Like so many songs about love before and after it, the focus is on the hurt that comes with this thing called love (George Strait's "All My Ex's Live in Texas").[2] The lesson is to be strong, guard your heart, and remain uninvolved. Yet, as God's image bearers, we can't seem to resist the tug to relate. Love holds out the promise of meaning and purpose in life. It is often the source of great human joy.

From a biblical perspective, however, love has everything to do with it! The biblical story is a love story on a cosmic scale, with historical precedents. In fact, the Bible affirms, "God is love" (1 John 4:8, 16).[3] He enjoys, defines, and displays true love. This is the real deal, not some "second-hand emotion." Issues, however, confront us regarding God's love. First, the love of God is multidirectional. For example, the persons of the Trinity love each other, humanity, and creation. Is this love the same in each context? Does the Father love his only Son in the same way and to the same degree he loves humans? Second, God's love is multidimensional. God's love for people includes grace, mercy, and patience (Eph. 2:4). Does love within the Trinity include grace or patience, or do these dimensions of God's love appear only in his relationship with sinners?

Third, in a fallen world, rejected human love causes deep emotional and psychological pain. Is God hurt by our rejection of his love? Is this what Paul means when he admonishes the Ephesians not to "grieve the Holy Spirit of God" (Eph. 4:30; cf. Isa. 63:10 and 54:6, which picture the Lord as a rejected wife)? Is he vulnerable to pain because of his great love for sinners, or is his grieving tied more to his honor? Is vulnerability a feature of intra-Trinitarian love?[4] Does vulnerability (placing oneself at another's disposal) mean God is limited in either his power or his knowledge, a claim made consistently by process theologians and free-will theists?

Fourth, we are commanded to love one another in the same way we have been loved by our Savior (John 13:34). The incarnation gives us tracings of what that love looks like (putting others above ourselves and serving them, John 13:1ff.). Is it possible, however, for humans to love unconditionally, endlessly giving themselves to serve others without de-

---

[2] Lewis Grizzard takes a more satirical approach to the subject of love in *If Love Were Oil, I'd Be About a Quart Low* (Atlanta: Peachtree, 1983).

[3] Scripture quotations in this chapter are from *The New American Standard Bible®*. Copyright © The Lockman Foundation 1960, 1962, 1963, 1968, 1971, 1972, 1973, 1975, 1977, 1995. Used by permission.

[4] John Sanders pursues the risk angle of vulnerability and the Godhead in *The God Who Risks: A Theology of Providence* (Downers Grove, IL: InterVarsity, 1998); see also William C. Placher, *Narratives of a Vulnerable God: Christ, Theology, and Scripture* (Louisville, KY: Westminster John Knox, 1994).

serving reciprocation, the way Jesus loves us, reflecting divine *agapē*, or is our love for God and each other simply a higher form of "need love" or *eros*?[5] Is there perhaps reciprocity in divine *agapē*? For example, Paul instructs husbands to "love your wives [*agapate*, present tense imperative of *agapaō*], just as Christ also loved [*ēgapēsen*, aorist tense of *agapaō*] the church" and notes further, "He who loves [*ho agapōn*] his own wife loves [*agapai*] himself" (Eph. 5:25, 28). Indeed, marital love is unconditional and sacrificial, but doesn't it also include need, desire, and depth of feeling? What would marriage be without mutual giving and response?

Perhaps *agapē* has more to do with ultimacy. For example, 1 John 2:15 warns us, "Do not love the world." John uses the verb *agapate*. Thus there seems to be an ultimacy or totality to the *agapaō* word group, an absoluteness of commitment and devotion. The context in which this finality is reflected perfectly is the Trinity. Thus the believer who loves the world does not love the Father (cf. Matt. 6:24: "No one can serve two masters; for either he will hate the one and love the other, or he will be devoted to one and despise the other"). There cannot be two ultimates.

The God of the Bible is love. He perpetually loves. He loves his Son (John 3:35). He loves sinners and sent his Son to die on behalf of them, even those who hate him and are in open rebellion against him (John 3:16; 1 John 3:16; 4:9–10). As new creatures in Christ, his children love each other and their non-Christian neighbors as an expression of his love and demonstration of who they have become as sharers in the divine nature (2 Pet. 1:4). Beyond this, every encounter with true love among humans is an encounter with God's love ("Love is from God," 1 John 4:7).[6] When we place "God is love" in the context of 1 John 4:7ff., we are affirming three mighty truths: the Trinity is love defined, the incarnation is the love of the Trinity displayed, and the salvation of the sinner is the love of the Trinity realized.

The apostle John admonishes believers to love one another. The congregation of faith is a community of love. We are chosen by a gracious Father, redeemed by a loving Savior, and sealed for the day of redemption by the Holy Spirit (Eph. 1:3–14). As we share a journey of faith with God's people, we are actually participating in triune love. More specifically, we are experientially sharing in the triune life (cf. John 17:3). We have

[5] C. S. Lewis made this clear distinction in *The Four Loves* (New York: Harcourt, Brace, 1960).

[6] Herman Hoeksema observes, "Love is always of God, that is, that wherever you may find love, even among men, its source is always in God," in Herman Hoeksema, *Reformed Dogmatics* (Grand Rapids, MI: Reformed Free, 1966), 106. Leo Tolstoy's short story *Where Love Is, God Is* is about Martin Avdeitch, a shoemaker who discovers that God inhabits his simple acts of kindness, manifesting his love personally.

become "partakers of the divine nature" and are, therefore, to add with diligence to our faith "moral excellence," and "in your moral excellence, knowledge, and in your knowledge, self-control, and in your self-control, perseverance, and in your perseverance, godliness, and in your godliness, brotherly kindness, and in your brotherly kindness, love" (2 Pet. 1:4–7).

Communion of the saints is therefore both horizontal (fellowship among believers) and vertical (fellowship with the Trinity). The love between members of Christ's body is intra-Trinitarian. It is the actual love of the Father for the Son, the Son for the Father, and the Holy Spirit for both. Furthermore, the characteristics of the love we are called by the apostle to share are made actual in and through us as we participate in the dynamic relationships within the Trinity. Our participation began when, through the new birth and effectual calling, we came alive spiritually. Now indwelt by the Holy Spirit, we have the triune God come to abide in us. Union with Christ is union with the divine family. The divine life in us reaches out to others who share this life, much like an electric lamp invites the flow of electricity when plugged into an electrical outlet. Accordingly, God's love is communitarian. He loves each of us because he loves all of us. And he (the Father) loves all of us because he loves his Son, who is our head. Our narcissistic fascination with personal affirmation is a warped reflection of intra-Trinitarian love. We experience God's love in its fullest expressions within the context of Christ's body and the experience of sharing the Bread of Life with the lost.

"God Is Love": Love Defined

As we approach John's assertion "God is love," perhaps it is best to follow the lead of others and begin with a lexical study of the word used here, *agapē*, and other pertinent terms,[7] tracing the development of the biblical idea from the Old Testament to the unique contributions of New Testament writers. Others have done that for us.[8]

However, as helpful as these are to the overall study of love, our goal is to discover John's meaning and, in so doing, to understand John's application to believers. The way to do this is to allow John's view of *theos* to define *agapē*; after all, *theos* is the subject of the sentence. David Wells ar-

[7] In John 5:20, however, the term used for the Father's love for the Son is *philei*, adding a touch of confusion to the mix.

[8] Anders Nygren, *Agape and Eros*, trans. A. G. Hebert (London: SPCK, 1932); Leon Morris, *Testaments of Love* (Grand Rapids, MI: Eerdmans, 1981); Ethelbert Stauffer, *Agapao*, in *TDNT* (Grand Rapids, MI: Eerdmans, 1964); Lewis, *Four Loves*; D. A. Carson, *The Difficult Doctrine of the Love of God* (Wheaton, IL: Crossway, 2000); D. A. Carson, *Exegetical Fallacies* (Grand Rapids, MI: Baker, 1984).

gues this point: "We must start with God himself if we are to learn about the nature of love. We must start above, not below. We must start with who he is and not with our sense as to who he is or what we want."[9] Biblically, the covenant Lord disclosed in the Old Testament (Ex. 34:6–7) and the Father as finally revealed in Christ define love for us. "God is love" means love is a person, a person who is also holy, eternal, all-knowing, unchanging, and self-existing. Love, the abstract concept and unseen quality of human interpersonal relationships, is actually a real person who speaks and acts in love and is "eternally moved to self-communication."[10]

Thus, John's declaration "God is love" affirms love as an essential feature of the divine nature. Attributes, however, are "not to be considered parts of him, but rather are perspectives on his whole being, that is, his essence. In that sense, God is 'simple.' He is also complex, but each attribute describes God's entire complexity, not just a part of it."[11] Thus, God is holy, only holy, all holy, while being simultaneously love, only love, all love. Thus, "each attribute has all the attributes: God's love is eternal, just, and wise."[12] In *Proslogion* XVIII, Anselm writes: "Life, wisdom, and all the rest are not parts of you, but all are one, and each of them is the whole of what you are and the whole of what the others are."[13]

When viewed within the context of God's simplicity (that is, he is not divisible or composed of parts and is one with each of his characteristics), God's love is one with him and the rest of his attributes. For example, God is eternal, without beginning or end, transcending time and yet embracing all time in his perfect existence (Ps. 90:2, 4; 2 Pet. 3:8). God therefore exists with every moment of time and space absolutely (cf. his omnipresence). Reflecting his unity or simplicity, God's love is eternal (Jer. 31:3; John 17:24). Consequently, "God's eternity is the same as his love, for his eternity is the eternal existence of a loving person, and his love is the love of that eternal person. That is to say, eternity and love are not abstract qualities that characterize many beings including God, and that exist in him alongside many other abstract qualities. Rather, they are God himself."[14] Thus his eternal foreordination of all things—and specifically the destiny of all people—is an expression of his love (Eph. 1:4–5). God is also omnipotent (Gen. 18:14). Yet his power is not arbitrary but serves

[9] David Wells, *God in the Whirlwind* (Wheaton, IL: Crossway, 2013), 85.
[10] A. H. Strong, *Systematic Theology* (Old Tappan, NJ: Revell, 1907), 263.
[11] John Frame, *The Doctrine of God* (Phillipsburg, NJ: P&R, 2002), 388.
[12] Ibid.
[13] http://www.fordham.edu/halsall/basis/anselm-proslogium.asp.
[14] Frame, *Doctrine of God*, 388.

the purposes of his love. The nature of God's love defines each of his attributes and is defined by them.

God in 1 John

The epistle of 1 John can be structured theologically according to two significant theological references it makes about God. In chapter 1, God is "Light" (1:5), and in 4:8 and 16 he is "love." By the metaphor of light, God is morally perfect, holy, righteous, and true. As love, God is gracious, kind, merciful, and patient. David Wells may have the best expression for the juxtaposition of these two descriptive metaphors: "holy-love."[15] The practical implication of holy-love for believers is reflected in our pursuit of God. Prompted by his love, we pursue his standard of morality and truth. A few of the particular expressions of this pursuit are listed in 1 John:

1) The Christian is serious about sin. (1:5–2:2; 3:4–10)
2) The Christian obeys God's commands (2:3–11). In particular, these include trusting Christ and loving other Christians. (3:23; 4:7–21; 2 John 4–6)
3) The Christian resists the world. (2:15–17)
4) The Christian knows the truth and exposes the teaching of the "antichrist." (2:18–27; 4:1–6; 2 John 7–11)
5) The Christian seeks personal purity while awaiting Christ's return. (2:28–3:3)

As noted in the second of these expressions, loving others is an indication of walking in the light. Consequently, "definitions of human love and morality cannot originate from human thinking apart from God, for it is only God himself who by his nature is qualified to define such foundational truth."[16]

Thus God's love is holy-love. To say with John that God is light and love means that God's love is holy and his holiness loving. There are things God hates (Prov. 6:16–19) because he loves. His love would be hatred if he dismissed sin or those practicing and promoting it in any way. On the other hand, his holiness is loving; he is patient and merciful yet remains righteous. Isaiah's encounter with the thrice-holy God was accompanied by overwhelming expressions of his love (Isaiah 6). Holiness created an awareness of his sinfulness before God and his distance from God, while

[15] Wells, *God in the Whirlwind*, 85ff., although he certainly wasn't the first to use this expression, as G. B. Stevens, P. T. Forsyth, and Donald Bloesch did previously.
[16] Karen H. Jobes, *1, 2, and 3 John*, ZECNT 19 (Grand Rapids, MI: Zondervan, 2014), 198.

love provided the cleansing he required. The Lord remained completely holy while demonstrating his mercy.

Biblically, this doesn't mean mercy trumps justice. The same confluence of holy love and loving holiness encountered by Isaiah occurred at the cross of Christ. Even in the most loving act of sending his Son to die for sinners, the Father was also satisfying his own holy demands (Rom. 3:21–26). Thus God's love is inseparable from his holiness. In 1 John 2:7–11, John unites light and love: "The one who says he is in the Light and yet hates his brother is in the darkness until now. The one who loves his brother abides in the Light and there is no cause for stumbling in him" (vv. 9–10). To be in the light is to act lovingly. It is strategic in the context of the church that we act lovingly toward those who engage in egregious sin; church discipline is the loving thing to do. "God's love is stern, for it expresses holiness in the lover and seeks holiness for the beloved. Scripture does not allow us to suppose that because God is love we may look to him to confer happiness on people who will not seek holiness, or to shield his loved ones from trouble when he knows that they need trouble to further their sanctification."[17]

Majoring on one attribute tends to cause us to redefine the rest, skewing the biblical portrait of the God of the Bible. Consequently, when love becomes supreme and interpreted as simple goodness, it then reinterprets or diminishes other divine qualities, especially God's justice. It even issues a mandate to God as to how he is to act toward humans. This directly affects the teaching of Scripture on final judgment, especially the unpopular scriptural teaching on hell. For example, popular pastor Rob Bell, in his recent book *Love Wins*, apparently embraces a form of universalism called "recapitulation." He declares: "Central to their [early church fathers Clement of Alexandria's and Origen's] trust that all would be reconciled was the belief that untold masses of people suffering forever doesn't [*sic*] bring God glory. Restoration brings God glory; eternal torment doesn't. Reconciliation brings God glory; endless anguish doesn't. Renewal and return cause God's greatness to shine through the universe; never-ending punishment doesn't."[18] From this perspective, love trumps wrath. Restoration brings more glory to the Lord than judgment. According to John, however, there is a perfect balance between justice and love in the triune God.

[17] J. I. Packer, *Knowing God* (Downers Grove, IL: IVP, 1994), 110.

[18] Rob Bell, *Love Wins: A Book about Heaven, Hell, and the Fate of Every Person Who Ever Lived* (New York: HarperOne, 2011), 108.

Love in 1 John

First John is an epistle of love.[19] God defines love, and Christ's followers put it on public display. John gives three separate treatments of love within the context of the major Johannine theological themes of light (1 John 2:7–11), life (3:14–15), and love (4:7ff.). In 2:7–11, John reminds his readers of the "new commandment" to love one another (John 13:34–35) as an indication that one is walking in the light. This, of course, is in contrast to the ones who walk in darkness and do not practice true love. In 1 John 3:11–22, regenerate people love others as an expression of their spiritual state ("We know that we have passed out of death into life, because we love the brethren. He who does not love abides in death," v. 14). Christ's death is the supreme expression of this kind of love (v. 16). When we come to 4:7–5:3, John turns his attention to a more detailed analysis of true love. Here he explores love in relation to God's nature. The requirement to love flows from the God Christians know and serve. Consequently, "the duty of love is based upon the essential nature of God, and upon the inward fellowship which every believer has with him by partaking of his Spirit."[20]

In John's expanded treatment of love (4:7–5:3), the apostle teaches several general things about God's love. First, love is an essential feature of God himself. Love moves from a purely abstract concept to a living personal existence in the Trinity. In Ephesians 2:4–5, Paul brings together God's mercy, love, and grace in the work of Christ for us: "God, being rich in mercy, because of His great love with which He loved us, even when we were dead in our transgressions, made us alive together with Christ (by grace you have been saved)." Every believer is a testimony of God's wonderful love. J. I. Packer declares, "'God is love' is the complete truth about God so far as the Christian is concerned."[21] In his recent contribution to systematic theology, Gerald Bray named his work *God Is Love* and proposed, "Everything we know about him teaches us that, and every encounter we have with him expresses it."[22]

Second, 1 John 4:7 teaches us the source of all love is the living God ("Love is from God"). The prepositional phrase *ek tou theou* means love "flows from him, as the one spring, and in such a way that the connexion with the source remains unbroken."[23] John focuses on the divine source

[19] A. B. Simpson, *Messages of Love, or, Christ in the Epistles of John* (Nyack, NY: Christian Alliance, c. 1900); Thaddeus Barnum, *Real Love: Where Bible and Life Meet* (Fishers, IN: Wesleyan, 2014).
[20] J. J. Lias, *An Exposition of the First Epistle of John* (Minneapolis: Klock & Klock, 1982), 304.
[21] Packer, *Knowing God*, 111.
[22] Gerald Bray, *God Is Love: A Biblical and Systematic Theology* (Wheaton, IL: Crossway, 2012), 17.
[23] B. F. Westcott, *The Epistles of St. John: The Greek Text* (Grand Rapids, MI: Eerdmans, 1966), 147.

of love not only to exhort his readers to love each other ("Let us love one another"), but also to assert a characteristic of the regenerate ("Everyone who loves is born of God [*ek tou theou*]"). Thus, love and regeneration originate in God. "*Agapē* [God's love] is grounded in God himself, and where it is found in man, it is a sign of regeneration."[24]

Third, John teaches the sacrificial nature of God's love. The Father sent "His only begotten Son into the world so that we might live through Him . . . [that he might] be the propitiation for our sins . . . [and] the Savior of the world" (4:9–10, 14). Stuart Townend, a contemporary Christian musician, expresses it well: "How deep the Father's love for us / How vast beyond all measure / That he should give his only Son / To make a wretch his treasure."[25] Christians throughout history have tried to express the inexpressible: "Amazing love! How can it be / That Thou, my God, shouldst die for me?" (Charles Wesley).

John details the depth of God's sacrifice. It cannot be measured but is revealed by the Son he gave. Robert Law writes: "Such is the Love of God to men; and what can be said of it, except that it is at once incredible that the fact should be so, and impossible that it should be otherwise? It is what never did, never could, flit within the horizon of man's most daring dream; it is that which, when it is revealed, shines with self-evidencing light. It needs no argument. Apologetic is superfluous."[26] The depth of the Father's love also appears in the goal he pursues ("that we might live"), the means he uses to reach his goal ("propitiation"), and the unworthy objects he seeks to save ("for our sins").

Fourth, the shared experience of the community of faith, the church, manifests and magnifies God's love. John affirms, "No one has seen God," but when we love one another, he "abides in us, and His love is perfected in us" (1 John 4:12). Practically speaking, then, "John asserts that whenever believers practice mutual love, God's love becomes visible in the lives of those in whom he abides. The love which he has implanted in the heart of the believer through the Holy Spirit (v. 13; Rom. 5:5) is thus visibly expressed and confirms the reality of God's indwelling presence."[27] Through his love, God abides with us and assures our hearts in the face of certain judgment (1 John 4:17–18).

[24] Victor Bartling, "We Love because He Loved Us First (1 John 4:7–21)," *CTM* 23/12 (December 1952): 871.
[25] http://www.stuarttownend.co.uk/song/how-deep-the-fathers-love-for-us.
[26] Robert Law, *The Tests of Life: A Study of the First Epistle of St. John* (Edinburgh: T&T Clark, 1909), 74.
[27] D. Edmund Hiebert, *The Epistles of John: An Expositional Commentary* (Greenville, SC: Bob Jones University Press, 1991), 205.

John's Theological Definition of Love

Exploring more deeply John's defining expression, we see "God is love" used twice in 1 John 4 (vv. 8, 16), with distinct applications. In 4:7–8 John issues an initial command to love others. His admonition to love places before believers a choice. The choice is to turn away from self and make ourselves available to serve others (cf. Matt. 16:24). Second, John's command is for a lifestyle of love. The present tense *agapōmen* highlights the apostle's desire that believers perpetually pursue love for others. A. T. Robertson notes: "Persistence in loving (present tense *agapōmen* indicative and *agapōn* participle) is proof that one 'has been begotten of him God' (*ek tou theou gegennētai* as in [1 John] 4:7) and is acquainted with God."[28] Third, John's command to love reflects mutuality in the body of Christ ("one another," v. 7). Finally, beyond its mutuality, the command is also inclusive. The immediate context is the community of believers, but the scope is much wider (cf. Luke 10:30–37; Rom. 13:8–10).

What is the source of this love among believers, and what shape is it to have? God is both its source ("Love is from God," v. 7) and its definition ("God is love," v. 8). The expressions "for love is from God" and "for God is love" are set off by the Greek word *hoti*, which indicates the reasons behind the command to love. Coming from God, true love has no boundaries or limitations. Much like a stream of water, it flows continuously through the believer (cf. John 7:37–39; Rom. 5:5). Furthermore, God defines the shared love of believers ("God is love")—it is sincere, sacrificial, spontaneous, and sanctifying.

John continues by asserting it is the nature of true believers to love because love is the nature of God. A believer is a new person with a new spiritual orientation (2 Cor. 5:17). Love then reflects their new birth ("born of God," 1 John 4:7, perfect tense—past act with ongoing results: "having been born out of God with its continuing results"), growing knowledge of God ("knows God," v. 7, present tense), and daily lifestyle ("everyone who loves," v. 7) seen in contrast with the unbeliever ("the one who does not love," v. 8). Love validates one's claim to the new birth and true knowledge of Christ. "The divine begetting preceded the love: love is an activity of the implanted eternal life, and is therefore a proof that the life is present."[29]

The other occurrence of the expression, in 1 John 4:16, is in the context of the believer's union with the triune Lord. Thus to abide in love is

[28] A. T. Robertson, *Word Pictures in the New Testament*, vol. 6, *The General Epistles and The Revelation of John*, (Nashville, TN: Broadman, 1933), 231–32.

[29] James Orr, quoted by Hiebert, *Epistles of John*, 197–98.

to abide in God and God in him/her (cf. John 15:9–10). In both instances the dogmatic affirmation ("God is love") is the basis for the practical or experiential (regeneration and shared life). The results are evident in the individual (confidence before God even "in the day of judgment," 1 John 4:17) and in the congregation (5:2).

Love and the Trinity

As we pursue the theology behind the expression "God is love," we need to ask first the identity of the one about whom John writes; to whom is John referring when he writes, "God is love"? Obviously, he is talking about the Father who sent the Son (1 John 4:9–10, 14). But the word *God* (*theos*) is used for three persons in the New Testament. The Father is God (John 5:18; 6:27, 46; 8:54; 20:17; 1 John 3:1), the Son is God (John 1:1–2; Rom. 9:5; Col. 1:15–20; Phil. 2:5–11), and the Holy Spirit is God (Acts 5:3–4). Furthermore, John emphasizes the relationship of the three persons, especially between the Father and the Son (John 5:17–31, 37–38, 43–47; 1 John 1:3; 2:24; 4:14). John also identifies the Spirit as the one who indwells believers, making their relationship with the Father real (1 John 3:24; 4:13). Beyond several references to the Father and the Son, there are references to the Holy Spirit (his work of regeneration in 4:7 and his mission on behalf of the Father in v. 13). Thus, it is evident that in the redemption of sinners, God the Father is love (he sent the Son); God the Son is love (he willingly died for us); and God the Holy Spirit is love (he applies Christ's finished work to believers and manifests divine love within the redeemed community).

However, the phrase "God is love" also applies within the Trinity in the way each divine person relates to the others. God's love is realized perfectly in the relationship of the Father and the Son. The Father loves the Son (John 3:35; 5:20; 10:17; 17:23–24), and the Son loves the Father (John 14:31; 15:10). The three divine persons perfectly live in, with, and for each other. In John 17 Jesus prays, "I do not ask on behalf of these alone, but for those also who believe in Me through their word; that they may all be one; even as You, Father, are in Me and I in You, that they also may be in Us, so that the world may believe that You sent Me" (vv. 20–21). His desire for us is that we share his intimacy with the Father and with himself. Jesus then outlines the purpose: "that the world may know that You sent Me, and loved them, even as You have loved Me," and "I desire that they also, whom You have given Me, be with Me where I am, so that they may see

My glory which You have given Me, for You loved Me before the foundation of the world" (vv. 23–24).

Just as each person is God, each person has the essential feature of love. He (one God/three persons) is a community of loving persons. "Hence the Three Persons of the Holy Trinity are united in the bond of perfectness, and live the life of infinitely perfect love."[30]

We know from divine revelation that each divine person has a specific role to play in relation to the other divine persons. In creation, for example, the Father willed it, the Son superintended the process (and still does, Col. 1:17), and the Spirit brought it into existence. Accordingly, our salvation is an action of the triune God. The Father chose us, the Son died for us, and the Spirit seals us (Eph. 1:3–14). Do these roles apply only to God's works, or are they eternal expressions of the loving relationship within the Godhead? Is the Son's submission to the Father's redemptive purpose only a feature of the incarnation, or is his serving the Father an expression of their eternal relationship of love? If this is the case, Trinitarian love is pure selflessness; they exist totally in and for each other. In this regard the community of believers relates to each other the same way the divine persons relate to each other in perfect mutuality.

Setting the Theological Grid

The Rahner Rule. We need to make several qualifiers regarding the Trinity and our focus on intra-Trinitarian love. The renewed interest in recent years upon the Trinity has produced a large amount of literature and a new sophistication in Trinitarian studies. These qualifiers are given in recognition of these excellent contributions. The first is the "Rahner Rule."[31] Named for Roman Catholic theologian Karl Rahner, it asserts that the economic or functional Trinity (the scriptural revelation of the relationship of the three divine persons in the completion and operation of creation and redemption) is a clear revelation of the ontological or essential Trinity (as to their interpersonal relationship). T. F. Torrance affirms the parallels between the ontological and economic Trinity with regard to love: "The love of God revealed to us in the economic Trinity is identical with the love of God in the ontological Trinity."[32] In other words, the

---

[30] Hoeksema, *Reformed Dogmatics*, 106.

[31] Ted Peters, *God as Trinity: Relationality and Temporality in Divine Life* (Louisville, KY: Westminster John Knox, 1993), 96–103.

[32] Alan Coppedge, *The God Who Is Triune: Revisioning the Christian Doctrine of God* (Downers Grove, IL: IVP Academic, 2007), 172, citing Thomas F. Torrance, *The Christian Doctrine of God: One Being Three Persons* (New York: Bloomsbury T&T Clark, 2001), 157n12.

divine persons relate to each other in the hiddenness of the divine community in the same way they are clearly seen in the works of creation and redemption. Father, Son, and Holy Spirit are eternal relationships based in love. Thus the Son's submission to the Father is an expression of their eternal relationship that transcends the period of the incarnation.[33] The incarnation did not cause the Son's submission; rather, his incarnation was an expression of his essential role as Son to the Father. Their separate and distinct roles are an expression of the essence of deity. The decision of the Son to endure humiliation is a visible manifestation of the true God and a graphic demonstration of the Son's love for the Father.[34] Fulfilling the will of another because of love is not a loss of identity or equality but a declaration of one's true self.

Adopting the Rahner Rule needs further clarification. One of the principal reasons for using the economic Trinity as a grid for understanding the essential nature of God is the character of the triune God. As we already noted, in 1 John 1 "God is Light." He is holy; he cannot be other than he is. For example, when Jesus prays to the Father, he is actually talking to his Father. The context for these conversations is the incarnate state, so the parallels with our conversations with our heavenly Father are evident. While we speak in time, he hears and responds in eternity. For many, this means that God is not personally "in" the conversation. But perhaps the eternal perspective, which embraces all moments of time perfectly, allows him to be in the conversation more intimately than we are. Although he is unchanged as he interacts with us, he genuinely responds. Perhaps his immutability embraces all change in us, which he (the triune person) shares in himself.[35] Can we then affirm that Jesus' praying to the Father reflects their eternal perfect conversation and communion?

The other reason for adopting the Rahner Rule is the nature of God's love. The highest and purest revelation of God's love is the coming of the

---

[33] Peters explains: "The threefold manner by which God relates to us is not 'merely a copy or an analogy' of God's internal threefold relatedness. Rather, it is that relationship proper." *God as Trinity*, 97.

[34] In Phil. 2:5–11, Paul traces Christ's humiliation and exaltation. His focus is upon the selflessness of Christ, specifically regarding his own deity; he did not view it as a "thing to be grasped" for his own advancement or personal possession or privilege. He emptied himself by taking on the "form" (*morphē*) of a servant. Donald G. Dawe writes: "The reality of God in Christ is not in some way scaled down to a level compatible with human existence. For Christ is Lord even in his humiliation. He is God equally in the hiddenness of the servant form as in his transcendent glory." "A Fresh Look at Kenotic Christologies," *SJT* 15 (December 1962): 348. The final and highest revelation of the triune God (Heb. 1:1–4) is the one who "did not come to be served, but to serve, and to give His life a ransom for many" (Mark 10:45). The glory of the Trinity shines through the humiliation of the Son. In this way he was permitting us to view the mystery of intra-Trinitarian life and love. The grand paradox of the incarnation is also on display: the path to glory is the path of humiliation.

[35] Steven B. Cowan and James S. Spiegel, *The Love of Wisdom* (Nashville: B&H, 2009), 292–94. Cowan and Spiegel propose something like this as a resolution to the problem of divine passibility versus divine impassibility and call it "divine omnipathos."

Son to die for sinners. There is no greater sacrifice. Among humankind, sacrifice for certain worthy persons occurs, but as Paul declares, "God demonstrates His own love toward us, in that while we were yet sinners, Christ died for us" (Rom. 5:8). In 1 John 4:9–10, the apostle acknowledges: "By this the love of God was manifested in us, that God has sent His only begotten Son into the world so that we might live through Him. In this is love, not that we loved God, but that He loved us and sent His Son to be the propitiation for our sins." The incredible love on display here arises from the majesty, the magnitude of the sacrifice, the magnanimous purpose of the one who sent the Son. Isn't this also a revelation of the actual interrelationships of the triune family?

By using the economic Trinity as the window upon the inner life of the divine community, we are affirming the clarity of God's revelation of himself through the acts of history as interpreted in Scripture. Michael Downey agrees: "All theology, indeed, all Christian faith and practice, has to start with the economic Trinity, with the naming of Father, Son and Spirit in the Scriptures. The answer to theology's single most important question—Who is God?—emerges by looking to God's grand economy of redemption through Word and Spirit in history, and then reads this back into the mystery of God as Love itself."[36]

On the other hand, we are not claiming that the revelation of God through creation and redemption exhausts the dynamic inner life of the triune God. After all, the covenant Lord is eternal, unchanging, and self-existing; all human speech in this regard is by analogy. While his actions in history are indeed his and make him truly known, we are left to speculate about how unchanging persons carry on a conversation or even express their devotion to each other. But the economic Trinitarian revelation tells us they do. Furthermore, the operation of the plan of redemption articulates for us his love, which is also eternal, unchanging, and self-existing or spontaneous. God's love for his children is contiguous with his very existence. Beyond this we cannot go but only fall down in awe and worship.

Personal nature of the triune God. The second qualification we need to propose is the personal nature of the Trinity. The God of the Bible is a person, in contrast to the impersonal deity of pantheism, the withdrawn god of deism, or the immanent "force" of panentheism/new age as depicted in *Star Wars*. He possesses all the features that define personhood, such as personal knowledge of himself and other persons (Ps. 139:1–2;

[36]Quoted in Roderick T. Leupp, *The Renewal of Trinitarian Theology* (Downers Grove, IL: IVP Academic, 2008), 51.

1 Cor. 2:10–11), personal communication to others about himself (Ex. 32:16; Isa. 46:9–10), and personal involvement with other persons (Ps. 75:6–7; Jer. 1:5). The prophet Isaiah sarcastically compares God, the living person, to the idols before whom the people were bowing; in the words of the living God: "You carry them, but I carry you!" (see Isa. 46:1–4).

Love itself is a quality of persons. "To love is to act intentionally, in sympathetic response to others (including God), to promote overall well-being."[37] Thus there is a paradox. God is sovereign and completely independent of his creation. He is in debt to no one, and no one can place him in a position of obligation (Rom. 11:35). Accordingly, God appears aloof, detached, and unconcerned. Love, on the other hand, is a relational quality. Thus the dual affirmation of Scripture is that God is, on the one hand, sovereign over all, needing nothing, and, on the other, completely personal and perfectly relating to every part of his creation.

The triune God has the capacity to relate to all persons and all his creation in an intimate, one-on-one way. Omniscience (his knowing everything actual and possible) and omnipresence (his being actually fully present everywhere, all the time) mean God doesn't get reports about his creatures; he is actually present with them in a completely personal way. Robert Reymond defines God's omnipresence: "God transcends all spatial limitations and is immediately present in every part of creation, or (what amounts to the same thing) that everything and everybody are immediately in his presence."[38] He lives our lives with us. Furthermore, his personal nature driven by perfect love exposes him to suffering, reflected clearly at the cross. While God is transcendent over creation and not bounded by it, he is also immanent in the creation and among all humankind (Job 37:6–13; Pss. 104:27–29; 139:16; Jer. 23:23–24). He is a loving, personal Sovereign who reigns over all and participates in the lives of all by serving them.

Personal also applies to the Trinity and is defined by them. The highest expression for individuation is "person." For example, each human is an individual expression of a particular set of defining characteristics. The same is true for individual dogs or rocks. But when we call someone a *person*, we are speaking of certain higher qualities (caring, loving, purposing). *Person* also identifies them as relating to other persons. Rocks are not persons, although I had a friend in college who had a pet rock and talked

[37] Thomas Jay Oord, *Defining Love: A Philosophical, Scientific, and Theological Engagement* (Grand Rapids, MI: Brazos, 2010), 15.
[38] Robert Reymond, *A New Systematic Theology of the Christian Faith*, 2nd ed. (Nashville: Thomas Nelson, 1998), 168.

to it as a person. The problem, of course, is reciprocation—the rock had nothing to offer but individual rock-ness. Consequently, there is a higher quality about God's image bearers called personhood, which grants us the capacity to maintain very close relationships with other image bearers.

The Trinity is a perfect relation of three persons possessing one essence or being (one set of unique attributes). "God is spirit" (John 4:24). He is eternal, unchanging, holy, and all-powerful. These qualities and many more refer to God's essence—who he is in himself. There is only one God, one divine being. Yet his essence is not separate from the Father, the Son, and the Holy Spirit. Biblically speaking, then, three persons are God; they are perfectly divine persons simultaneously. Each relates to the others as an individual person, perfectly possessing and reflecting the divine nature. Thus, while each is a person and completely distinct from the others, they are together one person. Godhood means personhood. Consequently, the Trinity is three persons who as individuals have all the attributes of deity and perfectly relate to each other as persons in order to constitute one person, the God of the Bible.[39] In fact, while personhood is the highest quality possessed by humans, and therefore the highest esteem we can give each other is to refer to others as persons ("She is a great person!"), "person" is the very least we can say about our Lord. He is three persons who are yet one person.

Social nature of the triune God. The third qualification we are using is the social nature of the Godhead. The challenge of process thinking in its various expressions, especially with its focus on becoming instead of being, requires us to be self-conscious about the grid we use to interpret the Bible. We must keep God's unchangeableness and personal involvement in the changing lives of humans in tension and balance. Jesus' interactions with the Father and the Holy Spirit recorded in the Gospels reveal a social Sovereign, an exalted King who expresses his sovereignty through serving others. The Father didn't simply send his Son to serve us—he came himself and brought the divine family with him (Eph. 1:3–14). Royce Gruenler calls this divine "disposability."[40] It is important also to see this divine social nature as eternally loving and sharing. The Trinity enjoys an eternal embrace, what Cornelius Plantinga calls a "zestful, wondrous community of divine light, love, joy, mutuality, and verve."[41] Thus

[39] We are not suggesting that the three coalesce into a fourth separate person but that the three are one person.
[40] Royce Gruenler, *The Trinity in the Gospel of John: A Thematic Commentary on the Fourth Gospel* (Grand Rapids, MI: Baker, 1986).
[41] Cornelius Plantinga, "The Threeness/Oneness Problem Of The Trinity," *CTJ* 23 (April 1988): 50.

the Trinity is more of a family in the way they relate to each other than a hierarchy of being (such as the distinction in natures between divine, angelic, human, and animal natures).

A question has been raised at this point: What is the nature and duration of Jesus' subordination to the Father? Jesus declared his Father greater than he (John 14:28), although he also affirmed he and the Father are one (10:30). In 1 Corinthians 11:3 Paul asserts, "God is the head of Christ" and alternately refers to Christ as the "image of the invisible God" (Col. 1:15). Thus the Bible affirms the full equality of the Son and the Father while also affirming the full submission of the Son to the Father. What is the nature of the Son's submission to the Father, given their full equality? The orthodox view (dating back to the early church councils of Nicaea, AD 325, and Chalcedon, AD 451) supports the eternal subordination of the Son. This has become a huge point of division among evangelical scholars.

The issue is the duration of Christ's subordination, or "authority-submission structure."[42] Is his submission to the Father eternal, or is it limited to the time of his incarnation? Royce Gruenler's social model of the Trinity limits subordination to the period of the incarnation and the divine economy of salvation. He explains: "The subordination of the Son and the Spirit to the Father is for the time of redemption only; hence Jesus' subordinationist language describes what have traditionally been called the 'modes of operation' that pertain to the accomplishment of the redemptive task." On the other hand, Jesus' assertions of equality with the Father "describe the necessary relation of the persons of the Trinity."[43]

It is beyond the scope of this writing to delve into this highly nuanced theological issue, but there are a couple of issues raised by this discussion applicable to the social model of the Trinity.[44] One is the nature of Jesus' submission to the Father. Was it merely a formal arrangement, or was it an eternal quality of their relationship as Father and Son, the one who sent and the one who was sent? Jesus delighted to do the will of the Father; it was his daily food (John 4:34). Driven by love, submission is more than a simple choice—it is an honor and a joy. For many feminist thinkers, the

---

[42] Bruce Ware, *Father, Son, and Holy Spirit* (Wheaton, IL: Crossway, 2005), 21.

[43] Gruenler, *Trinity in the Gospel of John*, xiv.

[44] Much has been written on both sides, but a comprehensive overview is Millard Erickson, *Who's Tampering with the Trinity?* (Grand Rapids, MI: Kregel, 2009). Kevin Giles and others see the eternal subordination of the Son to the Father as inherently dangerous to the equality of women, especially in ministry. Cf. Kevin Giles, *The Eternal Generation of the Son: Maintaining Orthodoxy in Trinitarian Theology* (Downers Grove, IL: IVP Academic, 2012); Kevin Giles, *The Trinity and Subordinationism: The Doctrine of God and the Contemporary Gender Debate* (Downers Grove, IL: InterVarsity, 2002); Kevin Giles, *Jesus and the Father: Modern Evangelicals Reinvent the Doctrine of the Trinity* (Grand Rapids, MI: Zondervan, 2006); and Kevin Giles, "The Evangelical Theological Society and the Doctrine of the Trinity," *EvQ* 80 (October 2008): 323–38.

term *subordination* sounds like oppressive patriarchy or even misogyny, a form of hate speech toward women. Sadly, it is that in many circles. But in the context of the Trinity, sonship is defined as absolute authority/equality expressed in the context of submission.

The other issue is authority. Is submission a loss of authority? If we embrace a social model of the Trinity, are we asserting that Jesus' authority, even as God, is different from the Father's, less than ultimate in some way? If there is an eternal submission by the Son to the Father, isn't the Father's authority somehow greater than the Son's? Hierarchical schemes demand positional priority among participants. So the Father's authority/will takes precedence. The issue is also clouded by the concept of the Father's eternal generation of the Son.[45] But does this raise questions about Jesus' deity?

Returning to the original question, is submission a loss of authority? The answer is negative from the perspective of the Trinity. The issue is not separate authorities of the divine persons but the single authority of the one true God. While each member of the Trinity has absolute authority as God, they exercise that authority in the social context of intra-Trinitarian love. The designations Father, Son, and Holy Spirit define the exercise of that single divine authority. The Father exercises that authority as initiator and leader, the Son exercises absolute authority as revealer and redeemer, and the Holy Spirit exercises that authority as the actual agent of creation and redemption. The exercise of divine authority among the three is mutual service and recognition. Stanley Grenz expresses it well:

> Jesus willingly submitted himself to the One he called "Abba." Thereby he reveals that the Son is subordinate to the Father within the eternal Trinity. At the same time the Father is dependent on the Son for his deity. In sending his Son into the world, the Father entrusted his own reign—indeed his own deity—to the Son (e.g. Luke 10:22). Likewise, the Father is dependent on the Son for his title as the Father. As Irenaeus pointed out in the second century, without the Son the Father is not the Father of the Son. Hence the subordination of the Son to the Father must be balanced by the subordination of the Father to the Son.[46]

[45] "The personal property of the Son is that he is eternally begotten of the Father (briefly called 'filiation'), and shares with the father in the spiration of the Spirit. The doctrine of the generation of the Son is suggested by the Biblical representation of the first and second persons of the Trinity as standing in the relation of Father and Son to each other. Not only do the names 'Father' and 'Son' suggest the generation of the latter by the former, but the Son is also repeatedly called 'the only-begotten,' John 1:14, 18; 3:16, 18; Heb. 11:17; 1 John 4:9." Louis Berkhof, *Systematic Theology* (Grand Rapids, MI: Eerdmans, 1941), 93. While a reasonable implication from Scripture, it does appear to reduce the Son's status as God.

[46] Stanley J. Grenz and Denise Muir Kjesbo, *Women in the Church: A Biblical Theology of Women in Ministry* (Downers Grove, IL: InterVarsity, 1995), 153–54.

Awareness of the social nature of the Trinity is critical for the community of believers. Father, Son, and Holy Spirit reflect a dynamic social context based upon love. The Trinity is not only a pattern for the church's life; it is that life. Mutual service among believers is the realization of the divine intra-Trinitarian relationship. Take the issue of mutual authority within the local body of believers. The exercise of biblically ordained authority among believers is mutual service (John 13). Pastors exercise authority under the authority of Christ and the congregation. Pastoral authority is loving servanthood. Thus the pastor is chief servant of all, exercising the authority of that position through service.[47]

Unity in diversity. The fourth qualification is the matter of intra-Trinitarian unity in diversity. God is unity (Deut. 6:5)—there is only one. However, three diverse persons are this oneness. In this case, complete diversity equals absolute unity. Love creates this oneness. The issue we are confronting is the distinctive role each divine person plays within that oneness. The Father's role is clear; he is the head of the Trinity, and as such he is the leader—"The buck stops here." The Son's function is to reveal the Father and execute his plan. The Holy Spirit then honors the Father and the Son by realizing the Father's decrees and applying the Son's finished work (Eph. 1:3–14). These roles are not revelatory concessions, accommodations to the limitations of the human context or language. Father, Son, and Holy Spirit reflect an eternal relationship of perfect oneness and complete diversity. Thus, in the context of the divine persons, there is no competition or loss of personhood among them. Each is fully divine, and therefore they individually retain the essential attributes of the one God. Consequently, each expresses that deity through the roles he performs. There is a divine order in the Trinity, but there is also absolute equality among the divine persons.

Another way to think of unity in diversity is the expression of love among human persons. Accordingly, when one person loves another, a threefold pattern emerges: A ←L→ B = R (the love between A and B equals a relationship [R]). Thus the three components (A, B, and L) create the relationship. Love is the unifying feature and basis of the relationship. Augustine, for example, saw this pattern and used love as an analogy for the Trinity. The writings of Richard of Saint Victor (*De Trinitate*) and Jonathan Edwards ("An Unpublished Essay on the Trinity") expand the

47 Corporate authority is often configured as a triangle or pyramid, with the CEO at the pinnacle running the operation from the top down. According to John 13, Jesus inverted the pyramid so that the pinnacle of leadership is at the bottom, from which everyone else is served.

Augustinian analogy. The Father is lover, the Son is the beloved, and love is the Holy Spirit. Accordingly, the analogy affirms unity in diversity; perfect love within the context of perfect persons. John's affirmation "God is love" defines each divine person (possessing perfect love) and gives us a possible insight into the intra-Trinitarian relationships.[48] The eternal Father loves the eternal Son. This means the Father and the Son eternally share and communicate themselves to each other. The dynamic within their relationship (L) is perfect love. Perfect love, however, cannot simply be a form of "energy" or a common disposition but is another eternal person, the Holy Spirit.

The unique union of the divine persons in our discussion of intra-Trinitarian love establishes divine unity in diversity. Jesus uses these expressions to describe it—"The Father is in Me, and I in the Father" (John 10:38); "I am in the Father and the Father is in Me" (14:10–11)—and prays in his intercessory prayer pray for believers' unity—"even as You, Father, are in Me and I in You" (17:21). The word for this union of the divine persons is *perichoresis*. They perfectly share all because they are one. Union also applies to the incarnation. Jesus is God-man, two natures in one person. Another use of union is Christ and the church. He is our head; we are his body. Union with the divine sets the stage for the interpenetration of triune love in Christ's church (14:23).

Characteristics of Intra-Trinitarian Love

Triune love contains a certain mix of notable characteristics that make the divine family a model for the church. These qualities also facilitate the shared experience of love within the community of faith. The grid to use is Christocentric: what the Father wants us to know about himself is revealed by and in Christ (John 14:8–9). Intra-Trinitarian love is known through Christ's relationship to the Father. The highest expression of this relationship is the incarnation and the cross.

The evening before he is arrested, Jesus opens his heart to the disciples (John 14–17) and in the process opens heaven for them to see the shared love of the Father and his Son (4:8–11). The various threads of his teaching in chapters 14–16 culminate with a prayer (chap. 17). As Jesus speaks intimately about the Father and with the Father, these features of their relationship and the love they share become obvious.

The first characteristic of triune love: complete devotion to the others.

[48] Augustine, *On the Trinity*, in *Basic Writings of Saint Augustine*, ed. Whitney J. Oates, 2 vols. (Grand Rapids, MI: Baker, 1980), 2:896ff.

The first and most notable is the complete devotion of the divine persons to each other. This means that love arises out of the Father, is directed toward the Son, who reciprocates perfectly, and is realized through the Holy Spirit. God's love is the dynamic within the social relationships of the divine family, not a static, fixed, abstract quality. Triune love is a continuous stream, perpetually giving, sharing, and flowing. I feel that many see love as a quantity; there is only so much to go around. But true love is not a quantity, like a fixed amount, but a quality. As any parent knows, whether you have one child or ten, each is loved. In fact, the more there are to love, the more the love rises to greet them. This is also true in ministry among God's people. The capacity to love seems endless. As a professor, I love my students, all of them, past and present. That number grows regularly. With each new school year, a new crop of student theologians is added to the family. It is as if the stream widens to include them all.

Intra-Trinitarian love is a perfect fountain of love. Their love knows no bounds; there are no limits to their sacrifice for the others. Theologians of prior generations identified this kind of loving devotion as involving both *complacentia* and *benevolentia*.[49] The first term denotes affection for another, a disposition reflecting fascination and admiration. The other, *benevolentia*, is pursuing the good or the best for the object of one's affection. Applying these distinctions to our love for God, William Ames notes: "The love which is satisfaction is that affection by which we approve of all that is in God and rest in his supreme goodness. The love which is good will is the affection which bids us yield ourselves wholly to God."[50]

If these distinctions represent the true nature of love and can be applied to the Trinity, then intra-Trinitarian love holds each member of the divine family in the highest possible regard, seeing in each other an infinite beauty, which prompts complete admiration. In this regard, intra-Trinitarian love is not simply self-centered, as some hold: "God's absolute and pure Self centeredness is expressed and manifest especially in his love."[51] While Hoeksema is correct that God is perfect and complete in himself, and therefore loves himself perfectly, his statement needs to be placed in intra-Trinitarian context. The Father's devotion to the Son is completely other-centered. God's pursuit of his own glory is actually the

[49] David Jones, *Biblical Christian Ethics* (Grand Rapids, MI: Baker, 1994), 44.

[50] Ibid. Quoted from William Ames, *The Marrow of Theology*, ed. and trans. John D. Eusden (Boston: Pilgrim, 1968), 251.

[51] Hoeksema, *Reformed Dogmatics*, 103.

Father's adoration of the Son and the Son's devotion to his Father. His delight in himself is the perfect delight of each member of the divine family in each other. As perfectly holy, God refuses to share his glory (Isa. 42:8; 48:11), but as perfectly loving, the Father is completely captivated by the Son, the Son with the Father, and the Holy Spirit with the Father and the Son.

In Jesus' prayer, devotion within the triune family is prominent. On the one hand, Jesus' intimacy and affection for the Father is evident. His use of "Father" (John 17:1, 5, 21, 24), "Holy Father" (v. 11), and "righteous Father" (v. 25) sets the tone of intimacy ("the address of a child to its parent"[52]) and reverence. He identifies his unique relationship with the Father by referring to himself as "Your Son" (v. 1). Furthermore, in his prologue to his Gospel, John articulates the intimacy and fascination within the triune family when he refers to Jesus as the "only begotten God who is in the bosom of the Father, He has explained Him" (1:18). The picture is one of intimacy. This closeness is reflected in John's use of *monogenēs theos*—"only begotten God" (NASB), "only God" (ESV), or "one and only Son, who is himself God" (NIV)—an expression clearly indicating Jesus' deity. The verse describes their intimacy in terms of "the bosom of the Father" (NASB), "in closest relationship with the Father" (NIV), or "near to the Father's heart" (NLT). Leon Morris proposes that the metaphor implies intimacy and "carries overtones of affection."[53]

John's statement also affirms that Jesus comes to reveal the Father ("He has explained Him"). He is devoted to spreading the wonder of his Father. And the Father reciprocates. At Jesus' baptism, the three divine persons appear, and the Father declares, "This is My beloved Son, in whom I am well-pleased" (Matt. 3:17). David Wells captures this loving devotion within the divine family:

> The generosity of love is everywhere seen in the relation between Father, Son, and Holy Spirit. The Father, for example, gave to the Son those who would be redeemed. They are those "beloved in God the Father," who are being "kept for Jesus Christ" (Jude 1). But the Son responded by saying, "they are yours" (John 17:9). The Father has given "all things" to the Son (John 3:35; 13:3), and yet, at the end of the ages, all things will be surrendered up to the Father by the Son, "that God may be all in all" (1 Cor. 15:28). The Son glorified the Father while on earth (John 17:4–5), and yet in heaven Christ will be in the center of worship, for that is where

[52] Leon Morris, *The Gospel according to John*, NICNT (Grand Rapids, MI: Eerdmans, 1971), 717.
[53] Ibid., 114.

> the Father wants him to be. Is this not the heart of love? It magnifies the other, wants the other to have the glory, and wherever possible gives to the other.[54]

Intra-Trinitarian devotion also desires the best for the other and wills only the best possible good. This is love in action, or *benevolentia.* It appears frequently in Jesus' intercessory prayer, especially as he reviews his life of obedience. He aggressively pursues the Father's honor. Using the incarnation as a pattern of intra-Trinitarian love, pursuing the Father's honor defines his sonship and is a window into the eternal relationships within the Godhead. Even in his petitions before the Father, his passion for the Father's glory shapes his requests. The purpose even of his own desire for the Father to glorify him is that the Father receive glory, "that the Son may glorify You" (John 17:1) To this end, the Father authorizes the Son to give eternal life to those the Father has given him (v. 2), a bestowal necessitating the work of the Holy Spirit.[55] Here is further indication of the communal life of the Trinity, expressed in the salvation of sinners.

The greatest expression of Christ's devotion to the Father's glory is accomplishing the task the Father gave him (vv. 4–5). He now asks the Father to restore the glory they shared in his preincarnate state. He has done his part; now it is the Father's role to accept it by honoring the Son, a reference to the resurrection and exaltation to the Father's right hand. The task he completes involves his "active obedience" (his life of obedience during the incarnation) and his "passive obedience" (his acceptance of the Father's wrath on our behalf on the cross). The extent of his devotion to the Father is measured by the price he pays to honor him. Frederick Dale Bruner summarizes Jesus' devotion to the Father's assignment in a paraphrase of John 17:4–5:

> Father, please help me to say and to do the right things this decisive Weekend; give me the strength and the wisdom to go through the trials and Cross just ahead so that I can make a full and clean atonement for the whole world's sins, as you and I so deeply want. And then especially, Father, please raise me up again after I am put to death in order definitively to conquer death and to show the world, decisively and comfortingly, that death has, in fact and not just in myth, been conquered in history. I want this Weekend to be everything you and I have hoped it

[54] Wells, *God in the Whirlwind*, 95.
[55] F. L. Godet, *Commentary on the Gospel of John*, vol. 2 (Grand Rapids, MI: Zondervan, 1969), 325.

would be for the world and for the Church, the bearer of our message to the world. Please help me and them.[56]

The second characteristic of triune love: mutuality. Here we make a transition from single-minded devotion to the second characteristic of intra-Trinitarian love: mutuality, the willingness within the divine family to serve each other, to be eternally at the disposal of the others.[57] Although it is common to think of this disposability as another term for Christ's subordination to the Father during the incarnation, it seems best to view Christ's subordination to the Father as a reflection of their eternal mutuality.

Jesus' prayer in John 17 reflects Father/Son mutuality. The entire prayer is a window into the depth of their relationship. One indication of this is Jesus' posture in prayer, "lifting up His eyes to heaven" (v. 1). Apparently this was his common practice. When he traveled through the Decapolis, he restored a man's hearing and speech, preceded by "looking up to heaven" (Mark 7:34). Before raising Lazarus, he "raised His eyes" (John 11:41). His posture reveals his attitude of dependence upon the Father and his focus upon pleasing him. He is self-conscious of his sonship, a relationship no other human has. Furthermore, Jesus is speaking to his Father about the work of redemption he is about to accomplish: "The hour has come" (17:1). Like colleagues with a shared task about which others are not aware, Jesus knows the Father's mind and will.

Mutuality is apparent also in the number of matters the Father and the Son share. First, they share glory (John 17:1, 5, 22, 24). Jesus' initial request of the Father is for mutual glorification: "Glorify Your Son, that the Son may glorify You" (v. 1). Four features of this shared glory appear in the prayer. One is its paradoxical nature. Biblically, the glory of God is the majesty of the divine nature, the visible display of God's wondrous character. Yet when Jesus asks the Father to "glorify" him, he includes the cross and the lowliness of the servant Messiah. Splendor appears in humiliation. "So lowly in means, so majestic in ends is our God."[58] Second is the reciprocal nature of the glory. When the Father honors the Son, the Father is honored. Third is the eternal quality of their shared glory: "Now, Father, glorify Me together with Yourself, with the glory which I had with You before the world was" (v. 5). Fourth is the relation of love

[56] Frederick Dale Bruner, *The Gospel of John: A Commentary* (Grand Rapids, MI: Eerdmans, 2012), 967.
[57] Gruenler, *Trinity in the Gospel of John*, 1–22.
[58] Bruner, *The Gospel of John*, 967.

to the shared glory. In 17:24 Jesus requests that believers be permitted to view his shared divine glory, "which You have given Me, for You loved Me before the foundation of the world." Shared love prompts a sharing of divine glory.

Triune mutuality also means shared possessions: "All things that are Mine are Yours, and Yours are Mine" (v. 10; cf. 16:15). Jesus' claim is remarkable. It is one thing to claim that all one possesses comes from the Father; that is true for all of us. On the other hand, to claim that all the Father possesses belongs to the Son is striking indeed. Marcus Rainsford explains:

> In the original, the word "all" is neuter, "all things that are mine, are thine." All things belonging to Me personally, essentially, and relatively, are Thine, father; and "thine are mine," all that belongs to Thee—Thy nature, Thy name, Thine eternity, Thy perfections, Thine attributes, Thy fullness, Thy dominion, all that Thou hast an interest in, Thy kingdom, Thy heavens, Thy throne, Thy people, Thy glory—"all thine are mine.'" "We are *mutually, equally,* and *alike* interested in them; for all things that are mine are thine, and all that are thine are mine."[59]

Jesus and the Father also share love for the redeemed. Jesus makes a clear reference here to the Father's elective purpose. The redeemed are the ones the Father has chosen (1 Cor. 1:27–28; Eph. 1:3–4; Col. 3:12; 1 Thess. 1:2–4; 1 Pet. 2:9) and given to the Son (John 17:2, 6, 24). Fulfilling the Father's will on their behalf, the Son out of love for the Father and his people grants them eternal life (v. 2) and manifests the Father's name to them (v. 6). While the language of ownership of people sounds dehumanizing, we need to remember that God is the Creator; he owns all things, including all humankind (Ps. 24:1–6). In this context, the elect are chosen by the Father and mutually shared with the Son, who gives his life to redeem them.

The fourth expression of mutuality between the Father and the Son is their shared mission. Jesus identifies himself as the one sent. The repeated phrase "You sent Me" (John 17:18, 21, 23; cf. 3:34; 4:34; 5:24, 30, 36; 6:44; 7:16; 8:26, 29, 42; 20:21) indicates his awareness of his mission to save. Yet the mission is the Father's. In 17:4 Jesus prays, "I glorified You on the earth, having accomplished the work which You have given Me to do." Most contend Jesus is speaking proleptically, looking ahead to the cross as

---

[59] Marcus Rainsford, *Our Lord Prays for His Own* (Grand Rapids, MI: Kregel, 1985), 157.

an accomplished work.[60] And the work he accomplishes is shared by the Father: "My Father is working until now, and I Myself am working" (5:17).

Finally, the Father and the Son have a shared message. The truth, which the Father seeks to share with us, comes through the Son: "God, after He spoke long ago to the fathers in the prophets in many portions and in many ways, in these last days has spoken to us in His Son, whom He appointed heir of all things, through whom also He made the world" (Heb. 1:1–2). In John 1, Jesus is the divine Word who becomes flesh to reveal the Father (vv. 1–2, 14, 18). Jesus speaks only as the Father directs him: "The words that I say to you I do not speak on My own initiative, but the Father abiding in Me does His works" (14:10).

According to Jesus' prayer in John 17, certainty concerning the divine origin of the Son is one of the effects of this shared word (v. 8). The other result is the Son's joy realized in believers (vv. 13–14), with the accompanying ridicule from unbelievers. But it is not only the Father's word through the Son. Jesus reminds the disciples: "If you continue in My word, then you are truly disciples of Mine" (8:31), and, "If anyone keeps My word he will never see death" (8:51). The promise of participating in the triune life is based upon Jesus' word: "Do you not believe that I am in the Father, and the Father is in Me? . . . If anyone loves Me, he will keep My word; and My Father will love him, and We will come to him and make Our abode with him" (14:10, 23). Finally, cleansing from sin ("You are already clean because of the word which I have spoken to you," 15:3) and answered prayer are based upon Jesus' word: "If you abide in Me, and My words abide in you, ask whatever you wish, and it will be done for you" (15:7).

Believers in community mirror triune mutuality. Paul uses the metaphor of the human body in 1 Corinthians 12 to picture this dynamic. As a body, the church is a unity in diversity: "Even as the body is one and yet has many members, and all the members of the body, though they are many, are one body, so also is Christ. For by one Spirit we were all baptized into one body, whether Jews or Greeks, whether slaves or free, and we were all made to drink of one Spirit" (1 Cor. 12:12–13). The body achieves unity in the midst of diversity through mutuality: "The eye cannot say to the hand, 'I have no need of you'; or again the head to the feet, 'I have no need of you'" (12:21). Paul then expands his application:

[60] D. A. Carson, *The Gospel according to John* (Grand Rapids, MI: Eerdmans, 1991), 557; cf. Morris, *Gospel according to John*, 720–21.

> On the contrary, it is much truer that the members of the body which seem to be weaker are necessary; and those members of the body which we deem less honorable, on these we bestow more abundant honor, and our less presentable members become much more presentable, whereas our more presentable members have no need of it. But God has so composed the body, giving more abundant honor to that member which lacked, so that there may be no division in the body, but that the members may have the same care for one another. And if one member suffers, all the members suffer with it; if one member is honored, all the members rejoice with it. (12:22–26)

The apostle concludes by introducing the modus operandi of Christ's body, which is love, a "still more excellent way" (12:31). Love generates true mutuality among God's people and reflects the triune community from which they receive their life and identity.

The third characteristic of triune love: transparency. The third quality of intra-Trinitarian love is transparency. Imagine knowing every thought, motive, and attitude of another toward you and you toward them. On the human level, transparency with others is rare. Hiddenness among people is evidence of the fall in Eden. Adam and Eve's first act after eating the forbidden fruit was to hide from each other and their Creator (Gen. 3:7–8). We continue that cover-up today. In a fallen world, total transparency can complicate a relationship, as when a wife asks: "How do I look in this dress?" Within the divine family, however, transparency is an eternal reality. We might say they have nothing to hide. They are completely sincere and honest. This reflects both God's holiness (perfect righteousness) and his love (perfect sharing). Both create the context through which three absolutely perfect persons exist in absolute transparency.

In a conversation Jesus has with his disciples, Philip makes a pointed request: "Show us the Father, and it is enough for us" (John 14:8). The conversation is precipitated by references to Jesus' departure and return to the Father (13:33–14:6). Gerald Borchert observes: "Practical Philip in the present context is portrayed as trying to make sense out of what must have seemed to him as Jesus' ethereal talk about himself and God. So he asked Jesus to get practical and show the disciples the Father. If Jesus did that, they could dispense with any further discussion on the subject."[61] Jesus' response to Philip grants us insight into divine transparency. He first indicates the nature of divine transparency: "He who has seen Me

[61] Gerald L. Borchert, *John 12–21*, NAC 25B (Nashville: Broadman, 2002), 112.

has seen the Father" (v. 9). Jesus is the "image of the invisible God" (Col. 1:15). If the Father were to pass before a supernatural revealing mirror, we would see the Son, yet he would still be the Father. The Father is not hiding behind the image of the Son but is perfectly reflected in the Son. The audacity of Jesus' claim tells us that divine transparency is absolute within the Trinity. In the case of Jesus' admission of ignorance about the time of his return to earth (Mark 13:32) and the Father's knowing something he doesn't, the issue is his voluntary relinquishing of his right to know for the sake of his redemptive mission, not a lack of transparency between them.

The second feature of divine transparency to appear from Jesus' conversation with Philip is its basis. Jesus affirms: "Do you not believe that I am in the Father, and the Father is in Me?" (John 14:10). Jesus refers to the union between himself and the Father, termed *perichoresis* (cf. 10:37–39; 17:20–21). They perfectly share all things with each other. In John 5:19–23, Jesus declares he does only what he sees the Father doing because the "Father loves the Son, and shows Him all things that He Himself is doing" (v. 20).

The third feature of transparency between the Father and the Son includes Jesus' words and works: "The words that I say to you I do not speak on My own initiative, but the Father abiding in Me does His works" (14:10). The transition in expression from "words" to "works" is striking. Jesus' works support his words. Both are testimonies of the Father. Thus, when Jesus invites his disciples to see the Father through him, he isn't asking them to notice the physical features of his human person but to listen to his words and take note of his works. The Father becomes visible through them. The voice of the Father is heard in Jesus' words; the Father's works are Jesus' works. The instruments of their transparency are Jesus' words and deeds.

Transparency in the triune context is related to three divine attributes. The first is omniscience. Hebrews 4:13 affirms that all things are open and visible to the Lord: "There is no creature hidden from His sight, but all things are open and laid bare to the eyes of Him with whom we have to do." Triune omniscience means that each member of the Trinity knows the others absolutely and exhaustively. An evidence of the deity of the Holy Spirit is his knowledge of the deep things of God (1 Cor. 2:10). The second attribute is truth—divine veracity. God cannot lie (Titus 1:2). Implicitly this means that he cannot embrace any falsehood ("Let God be found true, though every man be found a liar," Rom. 3:4) nor perpetuate falsehood. Furthermore, he is the "only true God" (John 17:3) and is worshiped "in spirit and truth" (4:24). Truth and transparency are associated like cause and effect. For example, recent scandals have people calling for transparency; the source of this transparency is truth or veracity. Jesus calls himself "the truth" (14:6). Truth prevails through transparency.

The third attribute tied to transparency is the overarching quality of holiness. God is righteous ("Righteous are You, O Lord, And upright are Your judgments," Ps. 119:137). Righteousness describes the rightness that exists in personal relationships. This is God's holiness in relation to persons. Moral fault cannot exist in God or any of his relations (James 1:13). Transparency, then, is the consequence of God's absolute moral purity. Paul describes him: "He who is the blessed and only Sovereign, the King of kings and Lord of lords, who alone possesses immortality and dwells in unapproachable light, whom no man has seen or can see. To Him be honor and eternal dominion! Amen" (1 Tim. 6:15–16).

It is in the context of God's absolute purity and transparency that God's love finds its highest expression. Louis Berkhof notes this connection: "Since God is absolutely good in himself, his love cannot find complete satisfaction in any object that falls short of absolute perfection."[62] Herman Hoeksema continues: "Briefly, love is that spiritual bond of perfect fellowship that subsists between ethically perfect, personal beings, who, because of their ethical perfection have their delight in, seek, and find one another. And, the love of God is the infinite and eternal bond of fellowship that is based upon the ethical perfection and holiness of the divine nature, and that subsists between the Three Persons of the Holy Trinity."[63]

Transparency was evident in the church in Jerusalem. Believers shared openly with each other so that they had "all things in common; and they began selling their property and possessions and were sharing them with all, as anyone might have need" (Acts 2:44b–45). The needs of the one became the need of the rest. They were completely open with each other, and "day by day continuing with one mind in the temple, and breaking bread from house to house, they were taking their meals together with gladness and sincerity of heart" (v. 46). In fact, the first divine correction in the early church occurred because Ananias and Sapphira failed to be transparent with the church (5:1–11).

Accordingly, sincerity was sought throughout the New Testament era. Paul pled transparency before the church in Corinth (2 Cor. 1:12ff.).

[62] Berkhof, *Systematic Theology*, 71.
[63] Hoeksema, *Reformed Dogmatics*, 107.

The church questioned his conduct in the matter of his itinerary; he told them he would visit them, but his plan had changed. Paul was concerned his apparent duplicity reflected badly on the gospel: "As God is faithful, our word to you is not yes and no" (2 Cor. 1:18). Integrity and transparency are strategic among believers: "We are not like many, peddling the word of God, but as from sincerity, but as from God, we speak in Christ in the sight of God" (2:17).

Transparency is a characteristic of the triune community and is critical in the church.

Scandals among God's people, whatever the period of Christian history, compel us to pursue transparency and accountability. The inability to know and address the wickedness of our own hearts poses the greater danger for the church (Jer. 17:9). The result of this lack of personal transparency is the same insincerity and hypocrisy that blinded the Pharisees of Jesus' day. He called them "blind guides" (Matt. 15:14). We handle the truth of God and therefore must reflect the openness of the triune God who gave it to us.

The fourth characteristic of triune love: unity. The fourth characteristic of intra-Trinitarian love is unity, reflected in the perfect oneness of the divine persons. Stanley Grenz explains: "Love, therefore, that is, the reciprocal self-dedication of the Trinitarian members, builds the unity of the one God."[64] Love promotes unity. In contrast, the one god of Islam promotes sameness, even uniformity, closing the door to the notion of true unity and, by implication, true love.[65] In the High Priestly Prayer of Jesus, he prays for himself (John 17:1–5), his immediate disciples (vv. 6–9), and future believers (vv. 20–26). A key feature of the final section of his intercession is unity within the Godhead, between believers and the Godhead, and among all believers.

In verse 20, Jesus requests that all succeeding generations of believers ("those also who believe in Me through their [original disciples'] word") might be one with the initial group of followers. His desire is that many across the ages will be united as one body. Their shared faith, both doctrinal and experiential, is the source of their oneness.

Beyond the oneness of the body of Christ horizontally, unity arises out of vertical union with the divine family. Within the Trinity there is perfect oneness. Unity in the Godhead is both ontological and functional. Ontological unity reflects the singularity of the divine nature, which each

[64] Stanley J. Grenz, *Theology for the Community of God* (Nashville: Broadman, 1994), 92.
[65] Michael Reeves, *Delighting in the Trinity* (Downers Grove, IL: InterVarsity, 2012), 104.

divine person possesses totally. This oneness is the exclusive quality of the Trinity, not shared with believers. Functional unity, on the other hand, exists among the divine persons as they carry out their individual roles/ functions, sometimes referred to as properties. For example, in the program of salvation for sinners, the Father elects, the Son dies to redeem, and the Holy Spirit applies Christ's finished work to believers (Eph. 1:3–14; 2 Thess. 2:13–14). They are one in all their works. Functional unity is a product of their ontological oneness and the dynamic of eternal love that defines their relationship. "This is why Jesus can pray that believers may be one in the same way the Father and the Son are one. The Father and the Son are one in two ways, and we can be one with the Trinity and with each other in one of those two ways, by sharing in their fellowship of love."[66]

The same functional unity within the Trinity is shared by believers, "even as You, Father, are in Me and I in You, that they also may be in Us" (John 17:21). The unity Jesus requests for believers comes from sharing the oneness in fellowship with the triune God. The word *kathōs* is a strong comparative, translated here "even as" (NASB) or "just as" (NIV, ESV, NLT). Believers are included in the life of the divine family through regeneration, the new birth. The dynamic that gives rise to the fellowship within the Trinity is love. The Father loves the Son, the Son loves the Father, the Father and the Son love the Holy Spirit, and the Spirit loves the Father and the Son. Richard of Saint Victor used the metaphor of love to interpret the relationships within the triune community. Accordingly, his "conception of the interior life of God demands a fully personal Trinity. By extension, the relationality within the divine life captured in Richard's theological model carries implications for a theological understanding of humans as the *imago dei* as well."[67]

Unity also arises from a shared glory. Jesus bestows on believers the glory he received from the Father, "that they may be one, just as We are" (John 17:22). In what way does the glory Christ received unite the body of Christ? In 17:1–5, Jesus asks the Father to glorify the Son (v. 1) and restore the glory he had in his preincarnate state (v. 5). He is referring to his humiliation at the cross and his exaltation begun with his resurrection. His preincarnate glory shines through the redemption he accomplished and continues to be magnified in the unification of believers in the task of sharing the gospel. Thus shared, glory unites believers with Christ in

[66] Donald Fairbairn, *Life in the Trinity* (Downers Grove, IL: IVP Academic, 2009), 36.

[67] John R. Franke, "God Is Love," in *Trinitarian Theology for the Church: Scripture, Community, Worship*, ed. Daniel J. Treier and David Lauber (Downers Grove, IL: IVP Academic, 2009), 110.

selfless service. Selfless love binds believers to Christ and to each other, so that "just as his true glory was to follow the path of lowly service culminating in the cross, so for them the true glory lay in the path of lowly service wherever it might lead them."[68] Vicarious sacrifice promotes unity and is vindicated by that unity.

The unity for which Jesus prays serves two purposes. The first is a testimony to the world about Jesus as the true one sent by the Father (vv. 21 and 23, "that the world may know that You sent Me"). The evangelistic component is clear: "that the world may know." The purpose of John's Gospel is to create and support belief (20:30–31). What message does the world get when the church is embroiled in schism and tribal skirmishes? Complicating this is the instant spread of reports about church struggles on the Internet through blogs and postings to social media. When God's people unite in love for Christ and each other, Jesus' prayer is answered and the world gets a clear picture of the God who loves them.

The other purpose of unity among believers given by Jesus is the testimony to the world about God's love: "that the world may know that You sent Me, and loved them, even as You have loved Me" (17:23). Royce Gruenler captures the meaning of Jesus' request:

> What it does intimate is a divine hospitality so generous that it images its own unity and interpersonal communion in the new society, and invites believers to share in its inner life. It is this unity in interpersonal fellowship that bears witness to the world and invites its belief that the Father has sent the Son. The way of the higher Family is to share what is received, so that there is perfect oneness in love. As (*kathōs*) the persons of the divine Family are one, so, Jesus prays, may the believing family become perfectly one. This is the highest witness of divine love and hospitality and disposability to the world.[69]

He concludes: "Jesus' prayer reveals that the goal of the divine Family is to bring the separated and fallen into a redeemed and unified family that reflects the relationship of the divine persons in their ultimate oneness."[70]

Conclusion

God is love. The incredible relational dynamic within the triune family is love. The Father is its source and defines it in terms of bringing many sons

[68] Morris, *Gospel according to John*, 734.
[69] Gruenler, *Trinity in the Gospel of John*, 128.
[70] Ibid., 129.

and daughters to glory (Heb. 2:10). Christ demonstrates its depth and wonder through his life, teaching, and death on the cross (1 John 4:9–10). The Holy Spirit makes it a feature of our everyday lives together as believers (Rom. 5:5).

Triune love is life-changing. Its complete devotion to the Lord and the neighbor puts an end to selfish, me-focused lifestyles. Its mutuality leads to sacrificial service, embracing the needs of others as our own. Its transparency produces intimacy and attachment that is morally good and unconditional. Finally, its unity builds bridges of joyful acceptance, especially across generational, cultural, and linguistic barriers.

When Paul breaks into praise at the end of Romans 8, triune love is his focus: "Who will separate us from the love of Christ?" (v. 35). Is it the Father? No, he loves us and sent the Son to die for us and chose us as his children (vv. 31–33). Is it the Son? No, he loves us, died for us, and now reigns and intercedes for us (v. 34). We live in the triumph of triune love, and that victory is apparent when God's loved ones, his extended family, gather to enjoy him and serve each other.

6

HOW DOES THE TRINITY'S LOVE SHAPE OUR LOVE FOR ONE ANOTHER?

CHRISTOPHER W. MORGAN

What first comes to your mind when you think of the church? Do you think first of love? Since you are reading a book on the love of God, hopefully some of you do. But past experience teaches that most do not.

That the church should be characterized primarily by love, however, is plain from Jesus' teaching on the greatest commandment (Matt. 22:34–40). Jesus clarifies the "great and first commandment" as "You shall love the Lord your God with all your heart and with all your soul and with all your mind" (22:37; cf. Deut. 6:5). The second "is like it: You shall love your neighbor as yourself" (Matt. 22:39; cf. Lev. 19:18). Jesus adds, "On these two commandments depend all the Law and the Prophets" (Matt. 22:40).

So the highest command is to love God fully, and the second highest command is "like" it: to love others as ourselves. But why are those two the highest commands? Because they summarize the Law and the Prophets. Why is this so? Why do the Law and the Prophets hang and depend on loving God and others?

It might be more helpful to view these as two questions. First, what is it about loving God that God so values? Why is that the central command for humans? With God's glory being the ultimate end of all creation and salvation history, our love for God would rightly highlight God's purpose of glorifying himself. Since he is the reason for the universe (Col. 1:16: "All things were created through him and for him"), it makes sense that his highest command to us (loving him) would be linked to his highest purpose (glorifying himself): God is glorified in and through our love for him.[1]

The second question makes less sense: why does God place such a premium on our love for others? How is this significant enough to be the second highest command, such that the Law and the Prophets hang on it, too? In other words, since God is the point of all things, loving and prizing him as the point seems fitting. But since humans are not, how does loving others become so important?

The question is massive, but one passage that helps us wrestle with these matters is 1 John 4:7–12. It does not answer the question fully, but it sheds much light on it and our consequent responsibility. Note the theological progression:

- God is love (4:8). Love is an attribute of God. God genuinely desires the good of others and gives of himself for their good.

- Love is from God (vv. 7–10). The God who is inherently loving loves us. God's love is especially displayed through the Father's sending his one and only Son into the world via the incarnation to be a propitiation for our sins (vv. 9–10).

- God's love enables our new life and love for God (vv. 7–10). In particular, God's love initiates our salvation (v. 10), gives rise to our new life/birth (vv. 7, 9), and leads to our love for God (vv. 7–12)—all through uniting us to Christ and his saving work.

John Mahony's essay in this volume skillfully unpacks these first three foundational ideas in 1 John 4:7–12. This essay will focus on two that flow from them:

- Our new life and love for God lead to our love for others (4:7–11).

- Our love for one another displays the invisible God and his love to the world (4:12).

Our New Life and Love for God Lead to Our Love for Others (1 John 4:7–11)

God is love. He seeks the good of others and eternally gives of himself for their good. His love is intrinsic, eternal, and interrelated to all his divine

[1] For a careful treatment of this see Jonathan Edwards, "The End for Which God Created the World," in John Piper, *God's Passion for His Glory: Living the Vision of Jonathan Edwards* (Wheaton, IL: Crossway, 1998), 125–251. See also John Piper, *Desiring God: Meditations of a Christian Hedonist* (Portland, OR: Multnomah, 1986).

attributes. It is expressed within the Trinity, as the Father loves the Son, the Son loves the Father, each love the Spirit, etc. This intrinsic love flows out to others as well, even us.

Indeed, the indwelling Spirit communicates God's love to us, particularly displayed in Christ's coming and saving work. The Spirit gives us new life, a new nature, and communicates God's love through us back to God. We love God because he loved us first. That we love God shows we are born of God, and that we love others shows we are born of God (4:7–8). Robert Yarbrough notes that God's love "gives rise to love in those whom God grants spiritual rebirth."[2] Jonathan Edwards explains: "When the Spirit, by His ordinary influences, bestows saving grace, He therein imparts Himself to the soul in His own holy nature.... By His producing this effect, the Spirit becomes an indwelling vital principle in the soul, and the subject becomes spiritual." Such divine grace reaches to the "very bottom of the heart. It consists in a new nature, and therefore it is lasting and enduring."[3]

The Spirit communicates God's love *to us*; the Spirit communicates God's love *through us back to God*; and the Spirit communicates God's love *through us toward others*. It should also be remembered that the same Spirit is communicating God's love *to others*; he is communicating God's love *through others back to God*; and he is communicating God's love *through others toward us*. We are a part of God's people, the church, the community characterized by love. As such, we not only give love—we receive it too. The love we give and the love we receive all ultimately flow from God's own love.

So what does it mean to love others? As we will see, our love flows from, tends to, reflects, and is defined by God's own love. Just as God genuinely seeks the good of others and gives himself for their good, as his people we too genuinely seek the good of others and give ourselves for their good.

Love's "diffusive nature," how it espouses the interests of others, is ably highlighted by Edwards: "Selfishness is a principle that contracts the heart and confines it to the self, while love enlarges it and extends it to others. By love, a man's self is so extended and enlarged that others, so far as they are beloved, do, as it were, become parts of himself so that, wherein their interest is promoted, he believes his own is promoted; and wherein theirs is injured, his is also injured." Even deeper is Christian love that neither

[2] Robert W. Yarbrough, *1–3 John*, BECNT (Grand Rapids, MI: Baker Academic, 2008), 235.
[3] Jonathan Edwards, *Charity and Its Fruits* (repr., Orlando: Soli Deo Gloria, 2005), 32–33, 257.

springs from itself nor tends toward itself but "delights in the honor and glory of God for His own sake, and not merely for the sake of self; and it seeks and delights in the good of men for their sake and for God's sake."[4]

Being aware of this understanding of love is important because we sometimes mistake love for sentimentality, syrupy feelings, or cultural niceness. Some mistakenly associate love with tolerance, accepting everyone and everything, as if love were incongruent with holiness or truth. Some assume love is merely "building relationships." Still others conclude that love is equated with actively doing something for others.

But each of these perceptions of love falls short. Having nice feelings for someone is fine, but love goes beyond sentimentality to desiring his or her good and actively giving of ourselves to help bring about that good. Love as open acceptance misunderstands that love seeks the good of others and therefore must oppose everything that hurts the person, whether they are aware of it or not. Even church leaders may find themselves substituting building relationships for love. If we are not careful, those relationships can be tools in which we seek our own good (or our own vision) and give of ourselves to help ourselves. It may be nice to win friends and influence people, but if it is not out of a genuine interest to help others, it is not love but the approach of Wall Street or our local country club. And while love certainly acts, as 1 Corinthians 13 and James 2:14–26 make clear, its action is rooted in a sincere desire to bless others, serve others, and help others find good.

Paul's celebrated teachings in 1 Corinthians 13 further clarify the meaning of love.[5] In this famous passage, Paul points to the highest ambitions of these believers, or what these church members could have considered the pinnacle of spirituality: to speak in the tongues of heaven, attain the deepest of knowledge, possess faith that led to miracles, sacrifice all their money to help the poor, or die a martyr's death for Christ. Paul strategically points to their highest spiritual aspirations and then turns the tables on them (vv. 1–3). Paul asserts that to reach our highest aspirations—in their case, to experience spiritual gifts beyond measure, to have faith that leads to miracles, to know truth as much as it can be known, to give all of our money to the poor, or to be willing to sacrifice our very lives

[4] Ibid., 151.

[5] Our understanding and comments in this section have been shaped by the following works on 1 Corinthians 13: Edwards, *Charity and Its Fruits*; D. A. Carson, *Showing the Spirit: A Theological Exposition of 1 Corinthians 12–14* (Grand Rapids, MI: Baker, 1987); Ajith Fernando, *Reclaiming Love: Radical Relationships in a Complex World* (Grand Rapids, MI: Zondervan, 2012); David E. Garland, *1 Corinthians*, BECNT (Grand Rapids, MI: Baker Academic, 2003); Michael Green, *To Corinth with Love* (Dallas: Word, 1988).

for the gospel—to reach all of these, but to do them without having love, is likened to being worthless: "I am nothing" (v. 2); "I gain nothing" (v. 3). Even "radical" spirituality/religion without love is worthless.

Then, in verses 4–7, Paul points them to true spirituality, which at its core is true Christian love. He does not so much define love as describe and personify it as a person who thinks and acts. And though the content of this passage is indeed suitable for wedding ceremonies and the like, Paul originally wrote this to address real-life problems of the Corinthian church. He warns that their approach to religion is warped, portrays love as what is "central, characteristic, and irreplaceable in biblical Christianity,"[6] and selects particular facets of love they needed to hear.

Indeed, from the rest of Corinthians, it is clear that the primary failure of the Corinthian church was its failure to love. Some were impatient and unkind, filled with jealous ambition and egos, and puffed up. They insisted on their own way and were argumentative and resentful. They even rejoiced in wrong rather than righteousness (chap. 5). Some in the church promoted themselves rather than seeking to promote the good of the overall body. Instead of humbly serving others, they humiliated others. Instead of transcending the social class system, they highlighted it. Instead of following Jesus' example of service, love, and sacrifice for the good of others, they used the symbol of his sacrifice for self-promotion! Instead of viewing their spiritual gifts as a God-given means to strengthen the church, they boasted of their superior knowledge and spirituality. As David Garland notes, "Although the gifts of the Spirit are conspicuous in their assembly, their lack of love is even more conspicuous."[7]

Paul describes love by its response to others in the church. He offers manifold descriptions:

- Patient: endures suffering and difficult people (6:7).
- Kind: tender; Paul often links kindness with forgiveness (Eph. 4:32).
- Not jealous/envious: wants the best for others, not wishing that the successes of others were only ours (1 Cor. 3:3).
- Not boasting/vainglorious: unpretentious, not promoting ourselves so others would praise us (1:17; 2:1).
- Not proud/puffed up (4:6, 18, 19; 5:2; 8:1): humble, not arrogant.
- Not indecent/shameful/rude (5:1–2): pure, not immoral.
- Not insisting on its own way (10:24, 33; cf. Phil. 2:3–4): generous, not self-seeking.

[6] Carson, *Showing the Spirit*, 66.
[7] Garland, *1 Corinthians*, 616–17.

- Not irritable: long-suffering, not given to fits of anger.
- Not resentful/keeping records of offenses: has a forgiving spirit, not easily offended (1 Cor. 6:7: "Why not . . . suffer wrong?").
- Not rejoicing over injustice: supporting justice, not wrongdoing.
- Rejoicing in the truth: delighting in and endorsing truth.
- Bearing all things: putting up with all things.
- Believing all things: generously trusting, not suspicious or cynical (does not mean gullible).
- Hoping all things: hoping for the best, not pessimistic about others.
- Enduring all things: persevering.

These descriptions show that the particular expressions of love vary to meet the needs of the context. In the context of frustrating circumstances and people, love appears as patience. In the context of the successes of others, love does not allow envy but rejoices with those who rejoice. In the context of our own successes, love restrains us from self-promotion and leads to humility. In the context of someone's sin against us, love appears as forgiveness and not keeping track of wrongs. The Bible depicts loving others as expressed also in sharing the gospel, caring for the poor, helping the marginalized, building the faith of others, promoting unity in the church, teaching truth, correcting error, urging repentance, etc. Sometimes the people we love receive it, appreciate it, return it, and even pass it on to others. Other times they misunderstand our love, reject it, or even despise it. But whether or not it is received, love shows up in a variety of forms and applications due to the wide range of circumstances we encounter.

These descriptions of love in 1 Corinthians 13 affirm the emphasis on love as desiring the good of others and giving of ourselves for their sake. In his sermon series on love, John Piper observes that viewing love this way dovetails well with Jesus' forceful commands of dying to self, such as in Luke 9:23: "If anyone would come after me, let him deny himself and take up his cross daily and follow me" (cf. Matt. 16:24; John 12:20–26). Piper detects how love is consistent with Jesus' teaching to give of ourselves, deny ourselves, die to all that is in us that needs to die, and follow Jesus' example of self-giving. Before there can be love, there must be death to self, Piper concludes:

> We began this series on love with a quote from Francis Schaeffer to the effect that when Christians differ there is a golden opportunity to show the world how we love each other. Differences are not the end

> of love; they are the occasion for love, which means an occasion for death. One of the reasons it's so easy to walk away from a difference instead of working it out is that you don't have to die. But what we have seen for two weeks is that before there will be revival there will be a dying in each of us; and before we see a great resurgence of love we will have to die. Being long-suffering means dying to the desire for an untroubled life. Having no jealousy means dying to the desire for unshared affection. Not boasting means dying to the desire to call attention to our successes. Not acting unbecomingly means dying to the desire to express our freedom offensively. Not seeking our own way means dying to the dominance of our own preferences. Not being easily provoked means dying to the need for no frustrations. Not taking account of wrongs means dying to the desire for revenge. Bearing all things and enduring all things means dying to the desire to run away from the pain of obedience.[8]

Thankfully, dying to self and self-giving are not the end, as Piper elaborates. Jesus teaches a reversal, an upside-down way of the kingdom in which those who promote their own life lose it, and those who give it for the sake of Christ and others find it (Luke 9:24–27; cf. Matt. 16:24–28; John 12:23–26). Edwards depicts the scenario vividly: "If you are selfish and make your own private interests your idol, God will leave you to yourself and let you promote your own interests as well as you can. But if you do not selfishly seek your own, but do seek the things that are Jesus Christ's, and the things of your own fellow-beings, then God will make your interest and happiness His own charge; and He is infinitely more able to provide for and promote it than you are."[9]

Further, the path of dying to self for Christ's sake and the path of love are the same path—one negative, the other positive. And this is the path taken by Jesus, the self-giving, humble, glorious Lord. Indeed, the path to glory for Christ and for his people is the way of the cross, the way of love, marked with self-giving for the sake of others (John 13:1–35; Phil. 2:1–11).

Notice also that our love as described in 1 Corinthians 13 reflects God's love. God is patient and kind (see both linked to God's character in Rom. 2:4; 11:22). He is not self-seeking and does not track offenses but gives and forgives. God does not delight in evil but rejoices in the

[8] John Piper, "The Greatest of These Is Love: Dying as a Means of Loving (Part 2) (1 Corinthians 13:4–7), sermon, June 25, 1995, http://www.desiringgod.org/sermons/dying-as-a-means-of-loving-part-2.

[9] Edwards, *Charity and Its Fruits*, 159.

truth. Garland notes, "Paul is describing a particular demonstration of love: God's love in Christ."[10]

First John 4 speaks similarly: God's love for us not only enables our love but also sets the pattern for our love for others (4:11). As the children of God, our lives are to reflect the character of our Father. This is a frequent biblical ethical principle (see Ex. 34:6–7 on God's character and note the similarities to godly Christian conduct depicted in 1 Cor. 13:1–7; Gal. 5:22–24). God's people are to be holy as God is holy (Lev. 11:44; 1 Pet. 1:15); be perfect as our Father is perfect (Matt. 5:48); be merciful as God is merciful (Luke 6:36); and likewise here to love as God loves (1 John 4:7, 11; cf. Eph. 5:1–2).[11]

Indeed, love necessarily stamps all true Christians' lives, even to the degree that it is the primary evidence we are genuine followers of Christ. First John 4:7–8 stresses this very point: "Beloved, let us love one another, for love is from God, and whoever loves has been born of God and knows God. Anyone who does not love does not know God, because God is love." I. Howard Marshall comments, "A person cannot come into a real relationship with a loving God without being transformed into a loving person."[12]

Such love results from God's sovereign work on the heart. Yarbrough aptly warns that to fail to love is "not merely to fail ethically; it is to fail in the whole matter of salvation. Loving other people and knowing God are components of one inseparable whole."[13] Yarbrough elaborates: "God's communicable attributes, like light and love and truth (and faithfulness), are transformative. The person who receives Christ's cleansing from sin (1:9) and seeks Christ's mediation with the Father (2:1) has a relationship with the Father established by which the Father's traits increasingly mark the believer."[14] In this sense, love will happen. It will emerge as the fruit of the Spirit (Gal. 5:22–24).

---

[10] Garland, *1 Corinthians*, 617.

[11] F. F. Bruce, *The Epistles of John* (Grand Rapids, MI: Eerdmans, 1970), 109. For more on this biblical grounding of ethics in the character of God, see Christopher J. H. Wright, *Old Testament Ethics for the People of God* (Downers Grove, IL: InterVarsity, 2004); Christopher W. Morgan, *A Theology of James: Wisdom for God's People*, Explorations in Biblical Theology (Phillipsburg, NJ: P&R, 2010), 169–85.

[12] I. Howard Marshall, *The Epistles of John*, NICNT (Grand Rapids, MI: Eerdmans, 1978), 212; for insight into the tests of love, obedience, and truth in 1 John, see John R. W. Stott, *The Letters of John*, TNTC (repr., Grand Rapids, MI: Eerdmans, 1990); Christopher D. Bass, *That You May Know: Assurance of Salvation in 1 John*, NAC Studies in Bible and Theology (Nashville: Broadman, 2008). More attention still needs to be given to 1 John's warnings as community guidelines. These "tests" are not only for individuals to gauge their salvation but are also given as guidelines for the community—to help them assess who the believers actually are and who should be in good standing in the church.

[13] Yarbrough, *1–3 John*, 235.

[14] Ibid., 237.

Yet 1 John also stresses our responsibility to love, clearly demonstrated by the commands to love in 4:7 and 4:11. So, like many other doctrines, love reflects the frequent themes of God's sovereignty and our responsibility. D. A. Carson relates these themes to love: "What is distinctive about God's love for us . . . is that it is self-originating. . . . Unlike God's love, ours is not *absolutely* self-originating; but it is self-originating in the sense that God's grace so transforms the believer that his or her responses of love emerge out of a matrix of Christian character, and are correspondingly less dependent on the loveliness of the object."[15]

Similarly, love reflects the already and not yet nature of salvation history. As believers born of God, we love—now. Love is not merely something that one day will characterize us; true believers are marked currently by love. Yet 1 John consistently calls believers to love, which shows that love is to be "sought, hallowed, nurtured, and guarded."[16] So we love now, but we need to grow in love.

Love likewise bears witness to what is often called the "indicative and imperative." We are born of God and are therefore the people of God characterized by love. Yet we are commanded to love. In a style reminiscent of the apostle Paul, John calls us to live according to who we are (1 John 4:7–8; cf. Eph. 4:1–6). Our very identity as the people of the God who is love stirs us to live in love.

So love is more expansive and integrated than we often think, as Jonathan Edwards synthesizes: "[Love] is the root and spring and, as it were, a comprehension of all virtues. It is a principle that, if implanted in the heart, is alone sufficient to produce all good practice; and every right disposition toward God and man is summed up in it and comes from it, as the fruit from the tree or stream from the fountain."[17] Edwards elaborates:

> The graces of Christianity are all connected together, and are mutually dependent on each other. . . .
>
> They so go together that where there is one, there are all. . . . Where there is faith, there are love, hope, and humility; and where there is love, there is trust; and where there is a holy trust in God, there is love for God. . . . Where there is love for God, there is a gracious love for man; and where there is a Christian love for man, there is love for God. . . .
>
> The graces of Christianity depend on one another. . . . There is also a mutual dependence between them, so that one cannot be without the

[15] Carson, *Showing the Spirit*, 65; emphasis original.
[16] Yarbrough, *1–3 John*, 235.
[17] Edwards, *Charity and Its Fruits*, 9.

> other. . . . Faith promotes love. . . . Then again, love enlarges and promotes faith. . . . So love promotes humility. . . . Humility promotes love. . . . Love tends to repentance. . . . And repentance tends to humility. . . . A true love for God tends to love for men who bear the image of God.[18]

Even more, love is the integrating center of these virtues, as Edwards shows:

> All the Christian graces are alike related to one and the same grace, namely charity, or divine love, as the sum of them all. As we have before seen, charity, or love, is the sum of all true Christian graces, however many names we may give them. And however different their modes of exercise, or the ways of their manifestation, if we do but carefully examine them, we shall find they are resolved into one. Love, or charity, is the fulfilling of them all; and they are but so many diversifications, different branches, relations, and modes of exercise of the same thing.[19]

So the indwelling Spirit communicates God's love to us, particularly displayed in Christ's coming and saving work. The Spirit gives us new life, a new nature, and communicates God's love through us back to God. The Spirit also communicates God's love through us toward others. Our love flows from, tends to, is defined by, and reflects God's own love. Just as God genuinely seeks the good of others and gives of himself for their good, as his people, we, too, genuinely seek the good of others and give ourselves for their good. And as we are a part of God's people, the community defined by love, we experience the same Spirit communicating God's love to others, through others back to God, and through others to us. So the love we share and the love we receive all flow from God's own love. This leads us to our next point.

Our Love for One Another Displays the Invisible God and His Love to the World (1 John 4:12)

At first blush, this statement seems ridiculous, even absurd. Would God really choose to reveal himself through us? After all, we are finite, fallen creatures, more capable of revealing limitations and sin than of revealing God, who is infinite in his perfections. But notice 1 John 4:12: "No one has ever seen God; if we love one another, God abides in us and his love is perfected in us."

---

[18] Ibid., 237–40.
[19] Ibid., 244.

The careful student of the Bible will likely recognize the phrase "No one has ever seen God" (4:12). It appears in another Johannine passage, John 1:18: "No one has ever seen God; the only God, who is at the Father's side, he has made him known." There John stresses that the unique and divine Son reveals the invisible God.

Here in 1 John 4:12, how is the invisible, unseen God made known? John Stott answers this question well: "Here, to our astonishment and confusion, John goes on to say that if we love each other, God lives in us and his love is made complete in us. That is, the unseen God, who once revealed himself in his Son, now also reveals himself in his people if and when they love one another. God's love is seen in their love because their love is his love imparted to them by his Spirit."[20] Put differently, our love displays God's love because our love is first his love given to us by the Spirit through union with Christ.

God's intrinsic love, which was supremely displayed in the sending of his one and only Son to the cross, is now displayed in his people. And the invisible God, who most perfectly revealed himself in his Son, now actually reveals himself through his people, particularly through their love. As we love, 1 John 4:12 instructs, there are two interrelated realities: (1) God abides in us, and (2) God's love is perfected in us. Both are related to the community of believers. Note the phrases "in us" and "among us." Yarbrough observes that here two central emphases in the letter come together: abide/remain and perfect/complete. God dwells or abides "in the midst of his people as they respond to each other with the love that he has extended to them."[21] As such, the church is the temple, the community of Jesus that manifests God's presence and character, especially his love, all through the abiding Spirit (4:13).[22]

But that is not all. Verse 12 continues: as we love one another, God's love is perfected in us/among us. John is not asserting our spiritual perfection, as he earlier rejects that idea in 1:8–10. Nor is he claiming that

[20] Stott, *Letters of John*, 166–67. See also 1 John 4:13.

[21] Yarbrough, *1–3 John*, 244–45.

[22] In Ephesians, Paul depicts the church as God's display people, the community of believers who not only showcase God's eternal purpose of cosmic unity in Christ (1:9–11; 2:11–22; 3:9–12; 4:1–16) but also reflect and communicate God himself, particularly his grace (2:7), wisdom (3:10), oneness (4:1–6), holiness (4:20–24; 5:25–27), and love (4:11–16; 5:1–2; 5:22–33). Of course, Christ is ontologically distinct from the church. He is always the head; we are always the body. And of course, the church cannot fully display God. But the church genuinely does, as God communicates his "communicable attributes" through his people. See Christopher W. Morgan, "The Church and God's Glory," in *The Community of Jesus: A Theology of the Church*, ed. Kendell H. Easley and Christopher W. Morgan (Nashville: Broadman, 2013), 213–35. For more on how God displays his purpose of unity and himself as one through the church, see Christopher W. Morgan, "Toward a Theology of the Unity of the Church," in *Why We Belong: Evangelical Unity and Denominational Diversity*, ed. Anthony L. Chute, Christopher W. Morgan, and Robert A. Peterson (Wheaton, IL: Crossway, 2013), 19–36.

there is something imperfect about God's love that somehow believers fulfill. Rather, as Yarbrough perceptively comments, "The root of the perfect participle . . . means 'to finish, complete, or bring to the desired outcome.'" He continues:

> John speaks here . . . of God's already pristine love finding its fullest possible earthly expression as people respond to the message of Christ and reach out to one another as a result. John takes a backseat to no one in Scripture in advancing a lofty view of God the Father's essential being. But in direct proportion to God's transcendence, for John, is the mandate that believers incarnate God's character, central to which is love (1 John 4:8, 16).[23]

Stott states it simply, "God's love, which originates in himself (7–8) and was manifested in his Son (9–10), is made complete in his people (12)."[24]

Synthesis

So, how does God's love shape ours? And why does God place such a premium on our loving of others?

As we have seen, the indwelling Spirit communicates God's love to us, particularly underlined in Christ's coming and saving work. The Spirit gives us new life, a new nature, and communicates God's love through us back to God. The Spirit also communicates God's love through us as we love others. As we love, the invisible God displays himself. And as we love, the invisible God's own love is extended, reproduced, expressed to the fullest, and brought to its intended outcome in and through our love. God's love is intrinsically complete when it comes to us, but its mission still remains, and thus it transforms us and shines through us not only back to God but outward to others. Every time we love, God's love is shining through us, extending his love to others, and reaching his intended goals.[25]

Therefore, John urges, "Beloved, let us love one another" (1 John 4:7), and, "Beloved, if God so loved us, we also ought to love one another" (v. 11). We are to love one another this way because God is love, and love

[23] Yarbrough, *1–3 John*, 245.

[24] Stott, *Letters of John*, 167.

[25] Collin G. Kruse, *The Letters of John*, PNTC (Grand Rapids, MI: Eerdmans, 2000), 162: "To put it in other words, the circuit of God's love is completed when we love one another." As we love, we are most fully human, as Ajith Fernando asserts: "Being made in the image of the God who is love (1 John 4:8), humans achieve their full humanity only when they live lives of love" (*Reclaiming Love*, 24). And as we love, we manifest God's presence and love. Interestingly, living out our full humanity and manifesting God's presence and love cohere in the image of God, as we become what we were always intended to be.

is from God. As we love one another, we display the invisible God and his love to the world. And as we love, we extend the love of the invisible God to the world.

Remarkably, our loves for God and others largely coincide. "God does not need our good works, but our neighbor does," Martin Luther urged.[26] So, yes, we are to love God and to love others. But we are to love and serve God largely by loving and serving our neighbors. Michael Horton ably captures Luther's point: "God descends to serve humanity through our vocations, so instead of seeing good works as our works for God, they are now to be seen as God's work for our neighbor, which God performs through us. . . . When we are overwhelmed by the superabundance of God's gracious gift, we express our gratitude in horizontal works of love and service to the neighbor."[27]

Further, God's highest commands to us—to love him fully and to love others—are united not only with each other but are interwoven with his ultimate purpose—to glorify himself.

Note that, first, God's love is the beginning, middle, and end of our salvation. Out of his love he plans to save us. Then, through Christ's saving work and uniting us to Christ, he chooses us, redeems us, adopts us, seals us, and gives us an inheritance. And through it all, the love of God is set forth on display throughout eternity, exalting God and his love (thus, the God-glorifying process of his self-giving love).

Note, second, that God's love is the beginning, middle, and end of our love for God. God's self-giving love seeks our good, bringing about our salvation. In this, God meets our needs and glorifies himself! We get our needs met, and God gets the glory. God displays his love for us in his all-sufficiency to meet our needs. And through it all, God displays himself. In turn, we worship and love him. God is at once self-giving and self-exalting!

Third, God's love is the beginning, middle, and end of our love for others. God's self-giving love seeks our good, bringing about our salvation. By giving us new life in union with Christ, God produces in us love for God and others. The Spirit brings forth fruit in us, communicating God's love to and through us. As we, as the church, love one another,

[26] Quoted in Gustav Wingren, *Luther on Vocation*, trans. Carl C. Rasmussen (Philadelphia: Muhlenberg Press, 1957; repr., Evansville, IN: Ballast, 2004), 2.

[27] Michael S. Horton, *People and Place: A Covenant Ecclesiology* (Louisville, KY: Westminster John Knox, 2008), 304. Note also Edwards, *Charity and Its Fruits*, 97: "God makes men the instruments of doing good to others. . . . Yea, He makes them like Himself, the great Fountain of all good, who is forever pouring down His blessings on mankind."

we display the invisible God to the world. As we extend God's love to others, God displays himself and thereby glorifies himself. Our needs are met, and God gets the glory. And others' needs are met, and God gets the glory. In other words, the overarching directions of Romans 11:36 apply also to God's love: "From him and through him and to him are all things. To him be glory forever."

Thus, we can simultaneously seek the glory of God and the good of others. In fact, we cannot truly seek the glory of God without also correspondingly seeking the good of others. And we cannot truly seek the good of others unless we principally seek the glory of God. But we can exalt God by loving one another, knowing that God is love, love is of God, from God, through God, and to God. Or put differently, God's love is:

1) God's own, intrinsic, Trinitarian love.
2) God's love to us, centered on Jesus' coming and saving work.
3) God's love to others, through others back to God.
4) God's love to us, through us back to God.
5) God's love to others, through others out to us.
6) God's love to us, through us out to others.
7) God's love displayed in his people (thus glorifying God).
8) God's love extended through his people.

So God is love, and love is of God, from God, through God, and to God. And God is love, and love is of God, from God, through God to others, to us, and to God. Further, God is love, and love is of God, from God, through God to us, to others—all to God.

Through it all, we not only see the importance of loving God but also can delight in the marvelous God-glorifying process of his self-giving love. And through it all, not only can we see the importance of loving others, but we can also rejoice in the God-glorifying process of our God-given self-giving love.

7

DOES THE LOVE OF GOD REQUIRE UNIVERSALISM?

DANIEL STRANGE

> Whatever may be charged against the intellectualism of the period when orthodoxy reigned supreme, it can claim credit at least for having been broad minded and well balanced in its appreciation of the infinite complexity and richness of the life of God. The music of that theology may not always please modern ears, because it seems lacking in sweetness; but it ranged over a wider scale and made better harmonies than the popular strains of today.[1]

Our finitude, fickleness, and basic "culture-boundedness" as human beings is often neatly reflected in the popular songs our culture sings to one another. Charting the history of "love lyrics" is no exception. In the face of the brash, anguished love of Miley Cyrus's "Wrecking Ball," some will laugh, and others will look back with nostalgic longing to a world fifty years earlier when Frank Sinatra could gently croon about the inseparability of "Love and Marriage" going together like "horse and carriage."

For the sake of the proclamation and spread of the gospel, Christians are called to plot a potentially perilous route that seeks *both* to confront and to connect with the culture in which God has placed them. One clear and present danger is that of the subtle allure of those zeitgeist sirens that can shipwreck a faith as it veers, at times ever so subtly, off course and is pulled into troubled currents. Even with the best intentions, what is done

[1] Geerhardus Vos, "The Scriptural Doctrine of the Love of God," in *Redemptive History and Biblical Interpretation*, ed. Richard B. Gaffin (Phillipsburg, NJ: P&R, 1980, 2001), 425–57.

in the name of cultural connection is sadly nothing other than cultural capitulation.

Whether it's understood in an overly sexualized form, a syrupy sentimental form, or some other mutation, "love" is one of those universal themes on which most people have an opinion. Put our popular understandings of love together with our popular understandings of God and what we think he/she/it/they(?) should be like, and one creates a heady "love potion" that can easily disorient. The effects here are not simply intellectual at this point: desires, hopes, and dreams can all be affected to reshape our vision of reality. What is legitimate connection and what is illegitimate compromise can be very blurry at this point. We need a firm (and sober) steer to guide us in making sure we are keeping ourselves from idols.[2]

The opening quotation of this chapter was a "revisioning" address by Geerhardus Vos,[3] a theological "steady hand" who wished to restate a biblical theology of the love of God in the face of misunderstanding and overemphases that had pulled theology worryingly out of shape: "There has developed a widespread demand that God's love, and nothing but His love, shall be made the keynote of every message Christianity has to bring to the world."[4] Vos calls us to tether our understandings of the love of God to his self-revelation in Scripture. Rather than this entailing a restrictiveness and impoverishment, our mind and imaginations will be recaptured by an amazing vision of God and his loving purposes in all their splendor, fullness, and richness. What must be noted here is that Vos didn't blog this last week. He wrote it in 1902.

In the subsequent one hundred and something years, a whole lot of "love of God" discourse has passed under the theological bridge. The cultural sirens have not gone away—indeed, their call is shriller than ever and as intoxicating as ever. Therefore, a restating of a biblical vision and resetting of the biblical compass concerning the love of God becomes necessary in every generation. Hence this volume.

In terms of the contribution of this particular chapter, we come to an assessment of a doctrinal duet where some don't hear sweet harmony but only grating dissonance. The embarrassing bickering parties are, in one corner, the love of God and, in the other, the traditional doctrine of hell. If we were once told that love and marriage could not be separated, and that

[2] 1 John 5:21.

[3] Given at the opening of the nineteenth session of Princeton Theological Seminary.

[4] Vos, "Scriptural Doctrine of the Love of God," 425.

you couldn't "have one without the other," we are now told that God's love and universalism have this same relationship. To put it another way, to affirm the doctrine of the love of God in any credible way—and still hold to a traditional doctrine of hell—is a marriage *not made* in heaven.

Of course, "love of God and universalism" combinations come in a variety of theological shapes and sizes.[5] Those accompanied by a self-confessed liberal theological method and presenting a package of doctrines totally unrecognizable to historic Christian orthodoxy are not really the focus of this chapter.[6] Then there are some more popular and "fashionable" presentations that are more overtly Christian and even orthodox, sociologically if not theologically, but that lack theological rigor (and so remain frustratingly opaque) and historical awareness (to the point of coming across as quite hubristic). These are more in our focus, although in a peripheral way.[7]

What I would like to focus on is what might be called a new "version" of "love and universalism." These are persons who still wish to call themselves evangelical and whose stated method is evangelical in the sense of wanting the entire Bible (with all the passages that speak of judgment and hell) to be the ultimate authority in determining doctrinal truth. One might call these Christian universalisms, or Christocentric universalisms.[8] One of the most prominent advocates in recent years is Robin Parry, writing under the pseudonym Gregory MacDonald in his *The Evangelical Universalist.*[9] MacDonald defends a host of orthodox doctrines save for two "unusual beliefs." First, "one's eternal destiny is not *fixed* at death and, consequently, . . . those in hell can repent and throw themselves upon the mercy of God in Christ and thus be saved."[10] Second, "*in the end* everyone will do this."[11] For MacDonald, it is these two beliefs that can resolve the long-standing and insuperable theological and philosophical problems with the traditional view of hell, whether

[5] Good introductory surveys include Richard Bauckham, "Universalism—A Historical Survey," *Them* 4/2 (1979): 48–54; Gerald McDermott, "Will All Be Saved?" *Them* 38/2 (2013): 232–43; and the essays by Ludlow, Hilborn, and Horrocks in Robin Parry and Chris Partridge, eds., *Universal Salvation: The Current Debate* (Carlisle, UK: Paternoster, 2003). For a more thorough, and generally more sympathetic, history of key universalist proponents in the history of Christian thought, see Gregory MacDonald, ed., *"All Shall Be Well": Explorations in Universal Salvation and Christian Theology from Origen to Moltmann* (Cambridge, UK: James Clarke, 2011).

[6] E.g., someone like John Hick.

[7] Here I'm thinking of something like Rob Bell's *Love Wins* (London: Collins, 2011).

[8] Although my interlocutor for this chapter will be Gregory MacDonald, I should also mention a few others who fall into this category: Thomas Talbott, *The Inescapable Love of God* (Parkland, FL: Universal, 1999); Nicholas Ansell, *The Annihilation of Hell: Universal Salvation and the Redemption of Time in the Eschatology of Jürgen Moltmann* (Eugene, OR: Cascade, 2013).

[9] Gregory MacDonald, *The Evangelical Universalist*, 2nd ed. (London: SPCK, 2008).

[10] Ibid., 6; emphasis original.

[11] Ibid.; emphasis original.

Calvinist, Arminian, Molinist, or open theist.[12] While appeals to mystery may have a place as a "last resort"[13] for the traditionalist, MacDonald's contention is that the Bible does not teach a doctrine of eternal damnation and that a universalist hermeneutic can be legitimately inferred from Scripture.[14]

Issues surrounding the love of God take a central role in this debate. MacDonald recognizes that it is often the doctrine of the love of God that drives people toward universalism. However, rather than engage in a doctrinal "pick and mix" or "top trumps" ("My wrath text beats your love text," or vice versa), he does not wish to prioritize God's love to the downplaying or exclusion of his judgment or wrath. Moreover, in terms of method, MacDonald notes that love is to be validated by the redemptive work of Christ and the entire biblical plotline. However, he believes that in the resulting hermeneutic from Genesis to Revelation, one is led to a universalist conclusion. It is worth quoting him at length here:

> God does not just *happen* to be love, nor is it true that he *chooses* to be love to certain individuals, as if he could just as easily have chosen not to love them. Rather, it is impossible for God to be God and to act in an unloving way towards anyone. If God is love, then *all* God's actions must be compatible with his love. This means that his holiness is loving, his justice is loving, and his wrath is loving. The traditional theologian often sets love up *in contrast to* justice and wrath. We are told that "God may be loving, *but he is also* just," as if the universalist has somehow forgotten about God's justice! But ironically, this objection to universalism actually exposes the weakness of more traditional accounts. The universalist has an integrated account of the divine nature in which all God's actions are manifestations of his "holy love." More traditional theology often seems less concerned about God's holy love than about God's holiness and God's love. Certain actions are seen as loving actions (saving the lost) whilst other actions are manifestations of God's holiness but most certainly not manifestations of his love (sending the lost to hell). But 1 John 4 will not allow us to conceive of any of God's actions being

[12] MacDonald describes these "problems" in *Evangelical Universalist*, 9–34.

[13] Ibid., 33.

[14] "Christian universalism yields a theology of hope, of divine love, and presents a vision of the victory of God that has significant advantages over the tradition, with its eternal hell. It also yields an inspiring ecclesiology and missiological motivation. Indeed, it accentuates the love and grace of God without diminishing his severity and wrath. It lifts the saving work of Christ to new heights without losing sight of judgement." Ibid., 8. Concerning the nature of his proposal, he writes, "I am a hopeful dogmatic universalist, a non-dogmatic dogmatic universalist, if you will. All theological systems need to be offered with a degree of humility, and one that departs significantly from the mainstream Christian tradition calls for even more. I hope to show that, in fact, universalism is not a major change to the tradition and that it actually enables us to hold key elements of the tradition together better than traditional doctrines of hell. Nevertheless, arrogance is out of place." Ibid., 4.

> incompatible with his love. Consequently, any account of hell must see hell as a manifestation of divine love and mercy even if it is a severe side of that mercy. The traditional theologian will not allow that it is possible for those in hell to find salvation; but, I ask, how is that teaching compatible with the kind of divine love revealed in the biblical story? How could God be love if he draws the line at death and says, "Beyond this point I will look for the lost sheep no more; and even if they try to return, I shall turn them away"? It seems to me that such a God would not be behaving in a loving way. In conclusion, I suggest that the problem is not that the universalist sentimentalizes God's love and forgets his wrath but, rather, that the traditional theologians underestimate God's love and unhelpfully disconnect it from his justice.[15]

It is crucial to note here that central to MacDonald's argument is that the *telos* of all divine judgment, punishment, and justice is ultimately corrective, rehabilitative, and purificatory—and never *purely* retributive, which could mean an irrevocability and irreconcilability between individuals and God.

This chapter is not about universalism per se but about the love of God and universalism. In what follows I wish to argue that the traditional coupling of the love of God and the traditional view of hell is far less conflictual and thus far more harmonious than MacDonald believes, and that there is too much at stake exegetically, hermeneutically, and theologically to file for divorce and change partners. First, I want to defend briefly a traditional hell hermeneutic that teaches a definite "separationism" between regenerate and unregenerate, and between pre-final eschatological judgment and post-eschatological judgment. Second, I want to argue that such separatism does not imperil the love of God or divine simplicity, given an understanding of divine freedom and love in Scripture, in which the objects of love can be and indeed are distinguished. *What God has separated, let no one join together.*

Before we continue, I want to end this introduction by putting up front an existential note. Ten years ago I wrote a robust Calvinistic defense of a traditional view of hell in response to another Christian universalist, Thomas Talbott.[16] Despite the different brief and audience of this current volume, my conclusions today are the same fundamentally as they were then. However, a decade on means I am ten years older and

---

[15] Ibid., 103–4; emphasis original.

[16] Daniel Strange, "A Calvinist Response to Talbott's Universalism," in Parry and Partridge, *Universal Salvation*, 145–68.

have ten more years of life experience, ten years of experiencing the death of loved ones who are not Christians. In those ten years, the cultural pressure to hope or imagine that God's love should require universalism has not lessened. Wrath, divine retribution, and eternal punishment have not suddenly come into vogue. I hope I am not in too much of a Christian bubble to know that the implausibility structure concerning the traditional doctrine of hell is pretty solid—sadly, within sectors of the church as well as outside it. And so I am happy to admit that at a personal level, it is harder than it was ten years ago not to hope, imagine, or wish that a Christian universalism might possibly be true. I would like to think that I am empathetic to Christian universalist concerns; I feel the pull of the position. The traditional doctrine of hell is totally and utterly awful. It is at this point, however, that I must be most prayerfully sensitive and on my guard to my sinful anthropocentric cultural locatedness, a locatedness that often leads with an emotional and aesthetic sensibility. As James Smith has noted:

> The new universalism is not the old universalism. Fair enough. But those of us who reject even the new universalism aren't gleeful about it. We might even *wish* it were otherwise. But we also recognize that even our wishes, hopes, and desires need discipline.[17]

The call to discipleship is to take all of my faculties and to submit them to the transcultural and theocentric locatedness of *sola Scriptura* supported by the rule of faith, that choir of faithful witnesses across *different* cultures and *different* centuries that has maintained those "better harmonies" of the love of God and the traditional doctrine of hell.[18]

A Stubborn Separationism

In such a short chapter (again, not really on universalism but on the love of God), it is impossible to do justice to the complex and increasingly voluminous exegetical, hermeneutical, philosophical, theological, historical, and pastoral debates between proponents of a Christian universalism and those of the traditional doctrine of hell. In terms of the biblical text, lexical word studies, Old Testament background, New Testament background, arguments from silence, and accusations of begging the question,

[17] J. K. Smith, "Can Hope Be Wrong? On the New Universalism," accessed July 8, 2014, http://forsclavigera.blogspot.co.uk/2011/04/can-hope-be-wrong-on-new-universalism.html; emphasis original.

[18] For a helpful exposition of the rule of faith and its relationship to *sola Scriptura*, see Carl Trueman, *The Creedal Imperative* (Wheaton, IL: Crossway, 2011).

they all come into play. These continue to be rehearsed in print and on many a discussion board.[19]

As alluded to above, what we are dealing with are two very contrasting hermeneutical paradigms that govern how one reads all the relevant biblical texts. MacDonald et al. are asking us to look over the whole of the Christian canon with fresh eyes. So, for example, in talking about Jesus' statement on hell and the nature of *gehenna*, after rehearsing the exegetical debates concerning the precise nature of *eternal* (*aiōnios*), MacDonald concludes that it cannot be clearly established whether Jesus was explicitly affirming or denying traditional Jewish beliefs about everlasting punishment, conceding that the default position would be the traditional view—"*unless we have good reason to think otherwise.*"[20] However, he believes there are compelling theological and hermeneutical reasons for doing precisely that:

> Any interpretation of Genhenna [*sic*] must be compatible with the claim that God is love and would never act in a way towards a person that was not ultimately compatible with what is best for that person. Any interpretation of Gehenna as a punishment must be compatible with the claim that divine punishment is more than retributive but has a corrective intention as well (for divine punishment of the sinner must be compatible with, and an expression of, God's love for that sinner). Any interpretation of Gehenna must be compatible with God's ultimate triumph over sin and the fulfillment of his loving purposes of redeeming all his creatures.[21]

Let us recall MacDonald's two claims: "One's eternal destiny is not *fixed* at death and, consequently, . . . those in hell can repent and throw themselves upon the mercy of God in Christ and thus be saved"; second, "*in the end* everyone will do this.[22]

Having scanned over some of the key literature once more, knowing the historic tradition, and armed with some of the basic tools of evangelical interpretation (e.g., "literal" interpretation[23] and the "analogy of faith"[24]), I do not see enough evidence to embrace these claims or this

[19] Parry (aka MacDonald, author of *The Evangelical Universalist*) seems to be on top of many of the discussions and comments on the issue at http://theologicalscribbles.blogspot.co.uk.
[20] MacDonald, *Evangelical Universalist*, 148; emphasis original.
[21] Ibid.
[22] Ibid., 6.
[23] To be distinguished from "literalistic."
[24] That is, Scripture interpreting Scripture. It may be "getting on a bit," but I still think an excellent summary of these terms is to be found in J. I. Packer, *Fundamentalism and the Word of God* (London: Inter-Varsity Fellowship, 1958), 101–7.

hermeneutic and therefore make the paradigm shift from the traditional and orthodox view of hell to that of universalism. Knowing that positive "evidence" for traditional hell positions (which MacDonald does not shirk from) need to be theologically integrated into the universalistic hermeneutic, and vice versa, I believe the far more plausible case lies in the traditional position.

On what grounds do I come to this conclusion? Put simply, there is a straightforward and stubborn "separationism" in Scripture that casts a long shadow over the entire plotline and that cannot just be scratched out with ordinary evangelical interpretative tools. This separationism has at least two overlapping aspects. The first is a fundamental separation of humanity into two types, antithetically related and described in a series of stark contrasts: seed of the women/seed of Satan; good/evil; belief/unbelief; light/darkness; sheep/goats; in Christ/in Adam. Of course, it needs to be noted that the ultimate cause of the separation will be different according to prior theological commitments.[25] However, whatever the ultimate cause, the relationship between these two groups is one described in the strongest of terms, e.g., *enmity*, *hatred*, and *hostility*. In such an inimical context, the notion that divine judgment never has a purely retributive function based on the notion of "desert"[26] does not seem to fit with the tenor of this antithesis. To put it another way, there is in Scripture a category of people repeatedly spoken of, the language of which is *not* that of corrective fatherly discipline and chastisement, even where the overarching discursive framing is parental covenantal love, however harsh that correction might need be.[27] Rather, it is finality language of losing one's soul (Mark 8:36), being denied by Christ (v. 38), and doors shutting (Matt. 25:10–11).

The second separation is between pre-parousia and post-parousia, the final judgment marking the climax and crisis between the two. From

---

[25] In a more Reformed framework, election and reprobation are based on God's foreordination; in a more Arminian framework, they are based on divine foreknowledge of free libertarian decisions.

[26] Which the traditional view holds.

[27] E.g., Deut. 29:18–21: "Make sure there is no man or woman, clan or tribe among you today whose heart turns away from the LORD our God to go and worship the gods of those nations; make sure there is no root among you that produces such bitter poison. When such a person hears the words of this oath and they invoke a blessing on themselves, thinking, 'I will be safe, even though I persist in going my own way,' they will bring disaster on the watered land as well as the dry. *The LORD will never be willing to forgive them; his wrath and zeal will burn against them. All the curses written in this book will fall on them, and the LORD will blot out their names from under heaven.* The LORD will single them out from all the tribes of Israel for disaster, according to all the curses of the covenant written in this Book of the Law." Also Matt. 12:32: "Anyone who speaks a word against the Son of Man will be forgiven, but anyone who speaks against the Holy Spirit *will not be forgiven, either in this age or in the age to come.*" Scripture quotations in this chapter are from The Holy Bible, New International Version®, NIV®. Copyright © 1973, 1978, 1984, 2011 by Biblica, Inc.™ Used by permission. All rights reserved worldwide.

a human perspective in time, these two separate arenas operate under defined and different terms and conditions—the first, which we call human history, revealing a certain fluidity, and the latter, a finality and irrevocability.

My argument is that these two forms of separation can be obviated only by a subtle demythologizing of certain texts, "literalizing" of others, and an overly speculative "going beyond what is written" when it comes to key points of argumentation. Conversely, the so-called positive universalist texts can retain a universal flavor (which admittedly we may have unduly neglected) while still embracing this stubborn separationism.[28]

Of course, because we are dealing with ways of reading texts rather than any one specific text, it is hard not to generalize here. However, I would want to highlight at least four factors that cumulatively lead to this conclusion.

First is the overwhelming and intense urgency of the need for repentance and faith now in this life to avoid facing exclusion from what is variously called the "age to come," the "kingdom," and "eternal life." Jesus' teaching and parables all have this urgent flavor, which cumulatively suggest the need for decision now while it is still possible, because there will come a time when it will not be, and the nature of this exclusion will be unimaginably terrible. The parables in Matthew 13 and 25 of the wheat and tares, good fish and bad fish, wise and foolish virgins, and sheep and goats are spoken in the starkest of terms. There is no hint that destinations can be reversed "at the end of the age" (13:40), thus the warning to act now, even if it means radical surgery (18:8). The horror of *gehenna*[29] and the urgency to avoid it does not straightforwardly suggest that its function is ultimately disciplinary and purificatory, which the universalists suggest. As Howard Marshall writes, "Luke 13:22–30 gives no hint whatever that the door will remain permanently open: it has been closed and nothing is said about re-opening it. Why is Jesus' teaching always couched in terms of final rejection with never a hint that the rejection might not be final if people will only make a post-mortem repentance?"[30]

[28] Many of these lines of criticism are taken up in Christopher W. Morgan and Robert A. Peterson, eds., *Hell Under Fire: Modern Scholarship Reinvents Eternal Punishment* (Grand Rapids, MI: Zondervan, 2004).

[29] E.g., Matt. 11:20–24; Mark 9:34–37; Luke 12:5.

[30] I. Howard Marshall, "The New Testament Does Not Teach Universal Salvation," in Parry and Partridge, *Universal Salvation*, 59. MacDonald, in *Evangelical Universalist*, 206, has responded to this critique by arguing that one can hold to a salvation-after-judgment position and still retain this sense of urgency and the "necessity of the now," in terms of stressing our need for obedience to God. However, I remain unconvinced that this accounts for the intensity of the urgency. Moreover, it uncomfortably changes the authorial meaning and intent of statements by Jesus and other NT writers.

Second is what we might call "prophecy." Not only do Jesus' parables seem to indicate that hell exists, but also that it will not be unpopulated—there will be a time when decisions made now will mean exclusion and "departing" later. Second Thessalonians 1:6–10 is perhaps the clearest indication of an irrevocability concerning this judgment:

> God is just: He will pay back trouble to those who trouble you and give relief to you who are troubled, and to us as well. This will happen when the Lord Jesus is revealed from heaven in blazing fire with his powerful angels. He will punish those who do not know God and do not obey the gospel of our Lord Jesus. They will be punished with everlasting destruction and shut out from the presence of the Lord and from the glory of his might on the day he comes to be glorified in his holy people and to be marveled at among all those who have believed. This includes you, because you believed our testimony to you.

We should also mention at this point those terrifying apocalyptic passages of Revelation 14:9–11 and 20:10–15, which traditionally have been thought to have offered some of the clearest textual evidence for separationism and a populated hell.[31]

Third is what can simply be called "history." While it is correctly pointed out that Scripture never uses the term *final* with regard to judgment, to suggest that there will opportunities for repentance and faith post-parousia and judgment seems at odds with the contours of history, where the above-named urgency is matched with a divine patience, long-suffering, and tolerance that, while totally gracious, will cease at judgment day. There is nowness about history, again linked to urgency. The universalist has to decouple a fixed judgment day from this divine forbearance.

[31] Knowing, maybe, the "evidence" of these two passages against universalism, MacDonald and others spend a great deal of time on them. MacDonald has a detailed and sophisticated chapter on the structure and exegesis of Revelation, which yields universalist conclusions. His basic argument is that there are two universalistic postscripts in 15:2–4 and 21:12–21, which demonstrate that the future is not fixed for those judged in 14:9–11 and 20:10–15. In other words, the "kings of the nations" in chap. 15 are identical to those condemned in chap. 14, and the New Jerusalem in chap. 21, with its open gates that are never closed, means those judged in chap. 20 can enter, having been purified. See MacDonald, *Evangelical Universalist*, 106–32. MacDonald's main interlocutor here is Greg Beale in *The Book of Revelation*, NIGTC (Grand Rapids, MI: Eerdmans, 1999), who comments on why universalist readings are illegitimate (see 797–98, 1097–98). There is not space to comment on the details, but I would like to make two points. First, we are back to wider hermeneutical considerations. Commenting on Beale, MacDonald writes, "He takes the fixed point as the damnation texts and re-reads Revelation 21 to fit in with them. Universalists will take their interpretation of Revelation 21 as the starting point and attempt a re-interpretation of the damnation texts. . . . Prior to considering the results of such attempts one cannot say that either is *obviously* the correct approach. I would, though, remind the reader of the hermeneutical principle governing this book, in which the dice is loaded in favor of the universalist should an impasse be reached" (117). Second, one central question, picked up by Beale, revolves around the "fixity" of the Lamb's book of life in 21:27b and whether names can be added or deleted. In an appendix on this, MacDonald begins by admitting that "given Revelation 21:27, it is clear that a universalist interpretation of Revelation will only work if a non-Calvinist interpretation can be given to the Book of Life" (192).

However, not only is there no explicit evidence for such a decoupling, but it also appears to skew the natural shape and flow of history. What is naturally portrayed as historical climax and end is now in actuality a penultimate and false end and therefore something of an anticlimax. The doctrine of "final judgment" has been so named because it traditionally has been seen to be final and irrevocable. It is the future event that casts a shadow over present reality, the resurrection of Christ being evidence of its inevitability (Acts 17:30). Evangelicalism has traditionally affirmed a realized or inaugurated eschatology, the now and the not yet. Some stress more continuity between the present age and the age to come, while some stress more discontinuity. However, there is an understanding of biblical limits or brakes on what one can affirm regarding both continuity and discontinuity. In the universalist structure, there is a lack of discontinuity and separation between now and not yet that does not sit comfortably with the data of Scripture.

This takes us neatly to my final point here, which is the issue of agency. The overwhelming stress in Scripture is on the need to hear the gospel from a human messenger in this life.[32] While some texts have been cited to suggest postmortem evangelism,[33] these are both sparse and highly speculative in terms of their exegesis.[34] For Scripture to be virtually silent on what is a central theme in the universalist argument is, to my ears, quite deafening, particularly when we consider the loud themes we have discerned above concerning urgency, prophecy, and history. As Bavinck puts it, in his own refutation of postmortem evangelism: "If it is not in scripture, theology is not free to advocate it."[35]

My argument so far has been simply that in Scripture there is a clear separationism that cannot be overcome without great eisegetical effort. Where does this leave us? For the universalist, it leaves the evangelical who holds to the traditional view of hell and judgment with insurmountable theological problems pertaining to God's love, a doctrine so precious and primary that the "problem" has to lie with the separationist exegesis; hence the revisionism. So the question becomes, can one hold to separationism *and* the biblical doctrine of the love of God? It is to this we now turn.

---

[32] For a detailed defense of this see Daniel Strange, *The Possibility of Salvation among the Unevangelized* (Carlisle, UK: Paternoster, 2000).
[33] Most noticeably 1 Pet. 3:18.
[34] On the notoriously tricky 1 Peter passages, I have found most helpful Karen Jobes, *1 Peter*, BECNT (Grand Rapids, MI: Baker, 2005).
[35] Herman Bavinck, *Holy Spirit, Church, and New Creation*, in *Reformed Dogmatics*, vol. 4, ed. John Bolt, trans. John Vriend (Grand Rapids, MI: Baker, 2008), 4:631.

A Many-Splendored Love

> A dull uniformity has taken place of the wealth of form and color that used to delight the eye, not merely of the theologian, but of the simple Christian also, because both recognized in it a reflection of the infinite fullness of life in God. Thus the watchword, God is love, has not only silenced all other voices from the realm of truth, it has likewise rendered many incapable of appreciating broad distinctions in a matter where even the most delicate shadings are of importance.[36]

In our first section I have argued that Scripture presents us with a separationism, the clarity of which has meant that traditional evangelical theology has been compelled to stitch this pattern of teaching, however aesthetically distasteful and garish, into its distinctive confessional garments. However, for universalists like MacDonald, the clash with other biblical patterns, most noticeably the love of God, is unbearable, hence the questioning and subsequent reinterpretation of the separationism.

If we cannot deny this separationism, then we have to affirm it while at the same time affirming the biblical doctrine of the love of God, a doctrine no authentic evangelical denies. Given the nature of God's truth and our evangelical doctrine of Scripture, we have to be able to do this in such a way that affirms the unity of God and his revelation and that is faithful in expounding both separationism and divine love.[37]

What I wish to defend in this final section is a doctrine of the love of God that affirms separationism. Rather than focusing on issues concerning human freedom and God's love,[38] a more legitimate target concerns the nature of God's freedom and God's love. Here I wish to make a number of interrelated statements concerning the love of God and its compatibility with the separationism we have affirmed above. What I wish to argue, in the words of Bettis, is this:

---

[36] Vos, "Scriptural Doctrine of the Love of God," 3.

[37] At this point in our argument, we come to another intraevangelical separation or fork in the road. Historically within evangelicalism there have been different ways of theologically reconciling God's love with eternal separationism. These tradition-specific theological formulations show many of the evangelical family resemblances (due to the common biblical "gene"), but definitely have their own distinctive identities. Without wanting to caricature them, for those who are operating out of a more Arminian or Molinist (or even Open Theist) theological framework, *the* center of theological activity concerns the relationship between God's love and the nature of human freedom. In the Arminian configuration, God loves all humanity without exception and desires for all to be saved without exception, but humans have the freedom not to choose God's offer in Christ. After death, such a choice is fixed, hence separationism and the urgency to respond now. For those who affirm such libertarian freedom and the other presuppositions associated with this evangelical tradition (e.g., providential foreordination, a universal salvific will, an unlimited atonement, a resistibility of saving grace), we part company at this point. These brothers and sisters can fend for themselves from here on out.

[38] Which, if we mean "libertarian freedom," is a concept I reject.

> The real question must be raised not about the universalist's premise that God's love is good and sovereign, but about his conclusion that the best way to describe the sovereignty and goodness of God's love is universalism. . . . The theologian's task is the description of the goodness of God's love. Universalism *appears* to provide the fullest description of God's love for men. At issue is whether or not it is *actually* the best description.[39]

The Language of Love

What kind of statement are we making when we say that God is love? The Bible is replete with personal names, descriptions, and actions of God.[40] God's love, of course, is one of these descriptions. It is divinely revealed love, true love, real love. However, given the fundamental metaphysical building block of the Creator/creature distinction, all religious language, including statements about the love of God, are analogous and anthropomorphic—what Calvin evocatively called God's "lisping."[41] Such accommodation is testimony to our creaturely ectypal dependence upon and distinction from a totally independent Creator whose knowledge is archetypal. Indeed, just to make sure we get the direction right, maybe referring to religious language as "anthropomorphic" is misleading: "It is important to keep in mind that, according to the Scriptures, God created humanity in *his* image (contra Feuerbach). The human capacities to know, will and love are themselves theomorphic: 'God's unconditional concern for justice is not an anthropomorphism. Rather man's concern for justice is a theomorphism.'"[42] All this is to say that there is a qualitative difference between human love and God's love.

Why labor this point? Because it recognizes a certain epistemic humility and limitedness we must always have when we speak of God and his love. I agree with MacDonald that there can be an appeal to mystery that is no more than an unbecoming theological cop-out (remember that I *am* a systematic theologian). And yet I, and I hope MacDonald too, still want to recognize that we comprehend God's infinite and perfect love

---

[39] See Joseph Dabney Bettis, "A Critique of the Doctrine of Universal Salvation," *Religious Studies* 6 (Dec. 1970): 329–44; emphasis original.

[40] One thinks of Barth's words here: "The doubtful thing is not whether God is a person, but whether we are." Karl Barth, *Church Dogmatics*: *Study Edition* 1.1 (London: T&T Clark, 2010), 136.

[41] John Calvin, *Institutes of the Christian Religion*, ed. John T. McNeill, trans. Ford Lewis Battles, 2 vols. (Philadelphia: Westminster, 1960), 1.13.1.

[42] Kevin Vanhoozer, *Remythologizing Theology: Divine Action, Passion, and Authorship* (Cambridge, UK: University Press), 64, quoting Abraham Heschel, *The Prophets* (New York: HarperCollins, 2001), 349. The emphasis in the main text is in the original. Paul Helm articulates these same ideas by using the terms "themotion" and "refraction" in "The Impossibility of Divine Passibility," in *The Power and Weakness of God: Impassibility and Orthodoxy*, ed. Nigel M. de S. Cameron (Edinburgh: Rutherford, 1990), 119–40.

only as finite, created beings. We must be careful not to put our theological method into reverse gear (also known as idolatry) by starting to make human love the norm and judge of what God's love must be like for him to be truly loving. Although we can never avoid systematizing God's revelation, we must be careful with speculations that not only go beyond what is written, but actually steamroll over what is written.

The Shadings of Love

When we come to what is written about God's love in Scripture, we see, to quote another classic from Ol' Blue Eyes himself, that love is a "many-splendored thing."[43] As many have pointed out, it is crucial to distinguish, because the Bible distinguishes, the delicate shadings of God's love.[44] First and foremost there is the perfect, self-sufficient, fully complete love between the persons of the Trinity: Father, Son, and Spirit. God is love because God is Trinity; God is Trinity because God is love, the antithesis of narcissism, and the definition of utter self-giving. As the late Robert Reymond put it: "God loves himself with holy love and with all his heart, soul, mind, and strength, . . . he himself is at the center of his affections, and . . . the impulse that drives him and the thing he pursues in everything he does is his own glory."[45] Turning to the objects of love outside of God,[46] there is, second, a universal benevolence in God's providence and common grace that is bestowed on all creation and includes the very act of creation itself.[47] Third is God's love for the human race and the world (John 3:16). Last is the particular, special, saving, covenantal lovingkindness (*hesed*) bestowed on God's elect (those chosen before the foundation

[43] Vos's address is as good as any in offering a detailed biblical theology of love.

[44] For those who make these distinctions see Vos, "Scriptural Doctrine of the Love of God"; J. I. Packer, "The Love of God: Universal and Particular," in J. I. Packer, *Collected Shorter Writings: Celebrating the Saving Work of God*, vol. 1 (Carlisle, UK: Paternoster, 1998), 145–60; D. A. Carson, *The Difficult Doctrine of the Love of God* (Leicester, UK: Inter-Varsity, 2000); Geoffrey Grogan, "A Biblical Theology of the Love of God," in Kevin J. Vanhoozer, ed., *Nothing Greater, Nothing Better: Theological Essays on the Love of God* (Grand Rapids, MI: Eerdmans, 2001), 47–66. For more philosophical defenses of this kind of particularism, see Oliver Crisp, "Is Universalism a Problem for Particularists?" *SJT* 63/1 (2010): 1–23; Paul Helm, "Can God Love the World?" in *Nothing Greater, Nothing Better*, 168–85.

[45] Robert Reymond, *A New Systematic Theology of the Christian Faith* (Nashville: Thomas Nelson, 1998), 343.

[46] Which are not necessary acts but free in the sense that God does not have to create or redeem to be God or to be love, etc.

[47] Bettis, in "A Critique of the Doctrine of Universal Salvation," writes, "The common assumption of all these positions [universalist] is that the essence or integrity of man is his own possession. Their problem is to define that essence in order to show how God's love is related to it. If men do have their integrity in themselves, then God's love must be discussed as relating God in some way to the object or recipient of that love. But the integrity of men, what makes them really human, is neither their being, their activity, nor their participation in humanity. What defines them is their relationship to God. Apart from the relation to God through his love, they are literally nothing. There is no humanity prior to God's love. Contrary to the humanistic premise, traditional Christianity has insisted that men have no existence whatsoever on their own and apart from God's love. Men are not pre-existing objects for God to love. They are the *results* of his creative, sustaining and redeeming love" (337); emphasis original.

of the world and written in the Lamb's book of life[48]), those for whom Christ died[49] and who the Spirit irresistibly calls. The recipients of this *hesed* love are not every individual who has ever lived but rather those God has chosen for his own good and sovereign purposes. MacDonald is quite right when he affirms the doctrine of divine simplicity. God is never self-conflicted; his attributes are never compartmentalized. Whoever God is, he is so completely, maximally, and simultaneously.[50] But in this one simple act of God's love, creatures experience this love in different ways. One simple, eternal, and free act of God's love does not mean there is, in time and space, a blanket, uniform effect upon all creatures. Psalm 136 demonstrates this very well:

> Give thanks to the LORD, for he is good.
> His love endures forever. . . .
> who spread out the earth upon the waters,
> His love endures forever. . . .
> to him who struck down the firstborn of Egypt
> His love endures forever. . . .
> but swept Pharaoh and his army into the Red Sea;
> His love endures forever.
> to him who led his people through the wilderness;
> His love endures forever. . . .
> to him who struck down great kings,
> His love endures forever.
> and killed mighty kings—
> His love endures forever. . . .
> He remembered us in our low estate
> His love endures forever.
> and freed us from our enemies.
> His love endures forever.
> He gives food to every creature.
> His love endures forever. (Ps. 136:1, 6, 10, 15–18, 23–25)

God's *hesed* for his people means that he strikes down mighty kings and kills kings of splendor, those who have been sustained by his common

[48] Eph. 1:4; Rev. 13:8.

[49] The doctrine of particular redemption. See David Gibson and Jonathan Gibson, eds., *From Heaven He Came and Sought Her: Definite Atonement in Historical, Biblical, Theological, and Pastoral Perspective* (Wheaton, IL: Crossway, 2013).

[50] "His eternal love for His people is more real, more powerful, and more enduring than any earthly emotion that ever bore the label 'love.' Unlike human love, God's love is unfailing, unwavering, and eternally constant. That fact alone ought to convince us that God's affections are not like human passions." Philip R. Johnson, "God without Mood Swings," in *Bound Only Once: The Failure of Open Theism*, ed. Douglas Wilson (Moscow, ID: Canon Press, 2001), 109–21.

grace. God's love means God's wrath against those who offend his holiness. God's simple love is not inconsistent with an eternity in hell for those who reject him, but perfectly consistent.[51]

There is biblical universalism that we must not only accept but also celebrate. God's love is breathtaking in its scope, gratuity, and efficacy. It is a boundary-crossing love that saves from among every nation and every type of background a multitude that no one can number.[52] It is a full-orbed "widescreen and surround sound" cosmic love that will save the world as an organism and bring renewal and restoration, as Colossians 1:20 suggests.[53] As Kuyper notes:

> He so loves his world that He has given Himself to it, in the person of His Son, and thus he has brought our race, His whole Cosmos, into a renewed contact with eternal life. To be sure, many branches and leaves fall off the tree of the human race, yet the tree itself shall be saved; on its new root in Christ, it shall once more blossom gloriously. For regeneration does not save a few isolated individuals, finally to be joined together mechanically as an aggregate heap. Regeneration saves the organism, itself, of our race.[54]

But, as Kuyper states—and this is the crucial point—this cosmic love that will save the race and save the world does not mean that all individuals will be saved ("the many branches and leaves"), or even need to be saved, for God to be love.[55] As I have shown in the first part of this chapter, the

[51] As Lane puts it, "There may be situations, such as with God's wrath against the impenitent in the final judgement, where wrath expresses love without expressing love for its object." Tony Lane, "The Wrath of God as an Aspect of the Love of God," in Vanhoozer, *Nothing Greater*, 167.

[52] Rev. 7:9.

[53] It is worth mentioning here a strand of thinking in the traditionalist tradition called "reconciliationism" or the divine conquest view. Advocates include Henri Blocher, Stephen Williams, and, most recently, Shawn Bawulski, "Reconciliationism, A Better View of Hell: Reconciliationism and Eternal Punishment," *JETS* 56/1 (2013): 123–38; Shawn Bawulski, "Reconciliationism Part 2: a Divine Conquest View of Hell" (unpublished paper provided by author). While affirming the reality of a retributive hell and a fixed eternal separationism (not annihilation), this view holds that hell is included in God's total and victorious triumph over evil (Colossians 1). Therefore, while the reprobate are not and never will be saved, they do not continue to sin but rather acquiesce with remorse and shame to their just judgment and punishment (this arguably making better sense of Phil. 2:9–11). Bawulski writes, "How does God show love to the unrepentant? In my view, God shows them love in various items of grace and mercy realized in their final fate: continued existence where God metaphysically sustains their being, the grace shown in taking away their ability to further sin and damage themselves, the grace to put them in a place where they, in judgment, are in awe of the truth and of God's goodness, the grace of the dignity to eternally display truth about God, the grace of continuing to bear worth rather than be discarded, etc. It is mercy for God to make the truth unavoidable, to make his character and power undeniable. In showing them the sort of grace and mercy described above, God is not mitigating their punishment; they receive, to the full extent, exactly the degree of punishment that justice requires." Bawulski, "Reconciliationism Part 2," 3.

[54] Abraham Kuyper, *Lectures on Calvinism* (Grand Rapids, MI: Eerdmans, 1931), 59.

[55] Helm deals with the logic of mercy understood as "undeserved love" in "The Logic of Limited Atonement," *Scottish Bulletin of Evangelical Theology* 3/2 (1985): 47–54. He writes, "What is essential to such love is that it could, consistently with all else that God is, be withheld by him. If God cannot but exercise mercy as he cannot

Bible tells us that this is not the case and that there will be a perfectly just retributive punishment for those not in Christ: eternal separation from God.

Conclusion

Gregory MacDonald believes it is deeply troubling to believe in a "God who could save everyone but chooses instead to send some to suffer eternal torment in hell to demonstrate the glory of his justice (a glory that could have been demonstrated without sending anyone to hell)."[56] While I do not find it deeply troubling, I admit that my understanding as a creature is pushed near its limits if I choose to speculate why God might not be more glorified and more loving by ultimately saving everyone.[57]

But at this point, surely such speculation is illegitimate, even idolatrous, given the rehearsal of this very situation in Scripture: "What if he did this to make the riches of his glory known to the objects of his mercy, whom he prepared in advance for glory . . . ?" (Rom. 9:23).[58] Rebuking visions of the potter and the clay should and do float into my consciousness at this point.[59] I must never forget or turn aside the creatureliness of my knowledge.

---

but exercise justice, then its character as mercy vanishes. If God has to exercise mercy as he has to exercise justice, then such 'mercy' would not be mercy. For the character of mercy is such that each person who receives it is bound to say, 'I have no right to what I have received. It would have been perfectly consistent with God's justice had I not received it.' And so in this respect the logical character of mercy is vastly different from that of justice. A justice that could be unilaterally waived would not be justice, and mercy which could not be unilaterally waived would not be mercy" (50).

[56] MacDonald, *Evangelical Universalist*, 22.

[57] While I think we need to be cautious here, we might be able to speak about God's continuing love for those in hell. Once again see Bettis, "A Critique of the Doctrine of Universal Salvation": "God is God for St Thomas not because he is good to men, but because his love so completely transcends human well-being that it can include all variety and possibilities. The universalist argues that God's love is better and greater if it results in the salvation of all men. But St Thomas insists that the goodness and greatness of God's love is reflected in the unfathomable variety of created being. The reality of hell and the possibility of permanent reprobation were aspects of God's love without which it would have been less great and less good" (341). See also John M. Frame, *The Doctrine of God: A Theology of Lordship* (Phillipsburg, NJ: P&R, 2002), who notes that the displaying of his glory and mitigating punishments might be benevolence even in hell. However, he concludes here, "God is good to all his creatures in different ways and at different times, depending on their natures and their roles in God's plan for history. His goodness does not obligate him to give the same blessings to all, or to give the same blessings to any creature throughout his existence. If the lost in hell are now receiving no blessings at all, they cannot complain that God was never good to them. During this life they were surrounded by God's goodness just like all other creatures" (413).

[58] Commentating on these verses in Romans, Schreiner concludes, "When the vessels of mercy perceive the fearsome wrath of God upon the disobedient and reflect on the fact that they deserve the same, then they appreciate in a deeper way the riches of God's glory and the grace lavished upon them. The mercy of God is set forth in clarity against the backdrop of his wrath. . . . Thereby God displays the full range of his attributes: both his powerful wrath and the sunshine of his mercy. The mercy of God would not be impressed on the consciousness of human beings apart from the exercise of God's wrath, just as one delights more richly in the warmth, beauty, and tenderness of spring after one has experienced the cold blast of winter. . . . God's ultimate purpose is to display his glory to all people. His glory is exhibited through both wrath and mercy, but especially through mercy." Thomas R. Schreiner, *Romans*, BECNT (Grand Rapids, MI: Baker, 2008), 523.

[59] Rom. 9:21.

Returning to where we started, what I do know, or better hear with great clarity and less straining, is this: a harmonious duet that is a constant refrain within God's revealed Word. On the one hand, the affirmation of the amazing God of love and love of God with all its shadings and inflections, which include Jesus' wonderful offer that whoever comes to him will never be driven away (John 6:37); on the other hand, the terrible reality and finality of hell, eternal punishment, and separationism. It is not simply that this combination best coheres with the biblical revelation (which it does), but it is that this combination provides Christians with categories of "love" and "the lost," which, when put together, give us that missionary motivation and urgency to "love the lost." We do this with greatest effect when we follow our Lord's revealed will to proclaim this good news of Jesus *now*, with its call for repentance and faith *now*, before it is too late.

Just as he did in 1902, Geerhardus Vos will give us our benediction as we go out:

> May God grant that, whatever the outcome of the present crisis, we may firmly hold to this and that the year's work upon which we are entering may help us all to become more efficient and abounding in the execution of this solemn charge of our Lord.[60]

[60] Vos, "Scriptural Doctrine of the Love of God," 457.

8

HOW DOES GOD'S LOVE IN CHRIST RELATE TO ISLAM?

DANIEL J. EBERT IV

A year after 9/11, Paul Marshall wrote an article titled "Failing to understand the Islamic world is failing to understand the twenty-first century."[1] Is this an overstatement? It remains to be seen. One thing is clear: Christians have a new opportunity to bear faithful and compassionate witness to Muslim neighbors. To do this, Christians must develop a more careful theology, not least because Muslim scholars are doing their own theological work. For example, in 2007 a significant group of Muslim leaders published an open letter in the *New York Times*, "A Common Word between Us and You." In this document Muslim theologians challenged Christians to find common ground with them in the public square on the basis of "loving God and neighbor." Christian responses ranged from incredulity to enthusiasm.[2] Surely an appropriate response to Islam ought to be intellectually virtuous, theologically careful, and relationally Christlike. This is our Christian responsibility.[3]

In an attempt to illustrate such an approach, we will address the question of the love of God in Christ in relationship to Islam. This is no easy task. We will try to answer, at least in an exploratory way, the following three questions:

[1] In Paul A. Marshall et al., *Islam at the Crossroads: Understanding Its Beliefs, History, and Conflicts* (Grand Rapids, MI: Baker, 2002), 15.

[2] See www.acommonword.com for the document as well as responses. See also Miroslav Volf et al., *A Common Word: Muslims and Christians on Loving God and Neighbor* (Grand Rapids, MI: Eerdmans, 2010).

[3] For a thoughtful response, see Daniel Migliore, "The Love Commandments: An Opening for Christian-Muslim Dialogue?," *Theology Today* 65 (2008): 312–30.

- How do we approach a theological topic such as God's love when engaging a religious community such as Islam, with beliefs so different from our own? Here we will focus on what it means to be intellectually virtuous.
- What are the basic similarities and differences between the Christian understanding of God and his love and the Islamic conception? Here we must strive to be theologically rigorous.
- How should we respond to the challenge of sharing the love of God in Christ with adherents of Islam? Here we will reflect on what it means to be Christlike in our engagement with Muslims.

Virtuous Engagement with Muslims concerning God's Love

Doctrine is often ironed out in the midst of controversy. One of the challenges for Christians is to engage in theological discussion and debate with our brothers and sisters in a way that is virtuous. The constant danger is to win the debate but deny the truth by our conduct. If this is true for theology within our own community, how much greater is the peril of failing to exhibit the fruit of the Spirit when we engage those of other religious traditions. This danger is further magnified when the topic is the love of God. How do we engage a person whose faith overlaps with ours and yet at the same time denies so many doctrines essential to the gospel? If we fail the test here, we may come away feeling self-satisfied and triumphant, yet we will have betrayed the Lord by our failure to be virtuous.[4]

Sustained and gracious engagement with those of another religious tradition can be a special problem for Western Christians, who in their individualism tend to be in a hurry, culturally unaware, and unkind. My wife and I recently visited northern India and "enjoyed" a very different driving experience. In the United States, the typical American drives fast, is only faintly aware that others are on the road, and when occasionally interfered with will impatiently lay on the horn. In northern India, everyone shares the road. It is a grand community experience, including all creatures great and small (monkeys, cows, and an occasional elephant). We learned the three keys to driving in India: slow down, know the exact dimensions of your vehicle and those of others around you, and "horn please" (in a gentle way that lets others know of your presence). What does this have to do with engaging another religion about the love of God? Let me explain.[5]

[4] Unfortunately it is not hard to find examples of such unloving behavior, even from church pulpits. For helpful attempts to engage Islam on the Internet, see www.answering-islam.org, and from a Catholic perspective, but with useful material, see "Muslims Ask, Christians Answer" at aam.s1205.t3isp.de/?L=1.

[5] Credit for these insights from the Indian road go to Brian Dunn, chaplain of Woodstock School in Mussoorie, Uttarakhand, India.

If we are going to think through God's love in relationship to Islam, then we cannot rush in headlong. We must slow down and do three things. First, we must take the time to treat Islam in its best forms, not its worst. God expects us to exhibit the virtues of fair-mindedness and empathy. Besides, this is the best way to get at the essential differences. It does not accomplish anything useful to hold up an ideal Christianity against a poor representation of Islam, all the while ignoring the best thoughts Muslims have about God's love.

Second, we must slow down long enough to realize that there are interested Muslims listening to our theological conversations. When teaching world religions, I like to use an empty chair at the front of the class to remind students that an adherent of the religion we are studying is in attendance. We must write, speak, and act as though sincere and thoughtful Muslims were reading, listening, and watching. This is only right, and consistent with submission to the lordship of Jesus. It illustrates humility on our part, and also helps us to be honest. I write this essay fully aware that some of my Muslim friends will read it. We ask the Lord to help us to be humble, honest, and clear in our work.

Third, we need to slow down long enough to let Muslim scholars tell us how they understand God's love. Rather than imposing on Islam our ideas, we must let careful Muslim thinkers tell us how they interpret the Qur'an and their religion. This exhibits both fair-mindedness and the intellectual virtue of curiosity. While we long for our Muslim friends to come to faith in Christ and enjoy the wonderful blessings of the gospel, this does not mean we have nothing to learn in return—if only we would slow down to listen. Like on an Indian road, slowing down in this way increases the likelihood of a safe and successful journey.

The second lesson relates to knowing the size of your vehicle and that of others around you—there are some very tight places along the Indian road. It is important that we know as accurately as possible not only the dimensions of our own faith but also what Muslims believe if we are to engage them for Christ. Because Islam and Christianity differ on several essential points, disagreements are inevitable. However, as on the Indian road, unnecessary accidents can be avoided if we attend to each other's faith with care.

Some Christians do not understand the love of God; this does not mean that there is not a deep doctrine of divine love in the gospel. In the same way, although many Muslims do not know the teachings of the Qur'an on Allah's love, there are Muslims who find expressions of divine love in their religion. There is no room for sloppy thinking or analysis here. The virtues of carefulness, tenacity, and honesty are required. From the Christian perspective, as we shall see, Muslim teachers deeply qualify God's love. Yet we must seek to understand Islamic views of divine love as accurately and fairly as possible. This requires being sensitive to historical perspectives on God's love in Islamic thought as well as to the range of contemporary views.[6]

The final lesson from the Indian road that helps us engage Muslims with God's love is "horn please." One will see this appeal colorfully emblazoned on the backs of trucks and other vehicles all over India. On the Indian road there is a constant cacophony of horn blowing. But no one seems to be upset. It is simply a way, on crowded streets shared by all, to make one's presence known.

As we engage Muslims with God's love in Christ, we want to slow down and empathetically understand what Muslims believe; but we must also, in obedience to the Lord, and for their sake, bear faithful and Christlike witness to the gospel. We must make our presence known. Horn please! The Qur'an and Islam, as well as the Bible and Christianity, both teach about God's love. We must have the courage to clarify how the respective teachings are similar and how they are different. Then we must bear witness to this difference. I wonder, however, if we have been blowing our horns more in the Western style, with impatience and perhaps some irritation. In part, this essay is a call to live in the love of God toward all people, especially toward Muslims, and a confession that we have not always done so.

Theological Engagement with Muslims regarding God's Love

While good theologians confess, as my first theology teacher taught, that God is what he is through and through, Islam and Christianity put the emphasis on different attributes. For Islam it is the *Takbīr*—the confession *Allāhu akbar,* "God is greater" (or "God is the greatest"). For Christianity it is the confession "God is love" (1 John 4:8).[7]

These affirmations reflect a more basic difference. Fundamental confessions about the essence of God are at the heart of each faith. For Islam it is the confession of *tawhīd,* God's oneness: "There is no God but God"

[6] We should be careful to avoid "essentialism"—that is, imposing on all Muslims a preconceived stereotypical list of criteria. For a broad and useful introduction to Islam, see Roger Allen and Shawkat Toorawa, *Islam: A Short Guide to the Faith* (Grand Rapids, MI: Eerdmans, 2011).

[7] Scripture quotations in this chapter are from The Holy Bible, New International Version®, NIV®. Copyright © 1973, 1978, 1984, 2011 by Biblica, Inc.™ Used by permission. All rights reserved worldwide.

(*lā ilāha illa 'Llāh*). For the Christian it is the confession of the Trinity: "There is only one God, both immanent and transcendent, who eternally exists in three personal distinctions—Father, Son, and Holy Spirit." How we understand God's essential nature (whether monistic or triune) relates directly to how we conceive of God's love. One cannot discuss one without the other. So in this essay we will first consider the identity of the God who loves before turning to the question of the nature of God's love itself.

The God Who Loves

We come to the disputed question of whether the God of Islam and the God of Christianity are the same God. As Timothy George put it in his book title, *Is the Father of Jesus the God of Muhammad?*,[8] Theologian Miroslav Volf has given serious attention to this question, including an important edited work, *Do We Worship the Same God?*[9] Despite the titles, the question is deep and complex (as both authors recognize). To frame it in a way that requires a yes or no response is inadequate and misleading. Timothy George points us in the right direction:

> Is the Father of Jesus the God of Muhammad? The answer to this question is surely both yes and no. Yes, in the sense that the Father of Jesus is the only God there is. He is the sovereign Creator and Judge of Muhammad, Confucius, Buddha—indeed of every person who has ever lived, except Jesus, the one through whom God made the world and will one day judge it (Acts 17:31; Col 1:16). . . . It is also true that Christians and Muslims can together affirm many important truths about this great God—his oneness, eternity, power, majesty. As the Qur'an puts it, God is "the Living, the Everlasting, the All-High, the All-Glorious" (2:256).
>
> But the answer is also no, for Muslim theology rejects the fatherhood of God, the deity of Jesus, and the personhood of the Holy Spirit—each of which is an essential component of the Christian understanding of God.[10]

There is much wisdom here. It does not advance our witness to sincere Muslims to tell them they worship a false God, or that they are not seeking to direct their thoughts and worship to God.

It is helpful to distinguish here between intended referent and

[8] Timothy George, *Is the Father of Jesus the God of Muhammad? Understanding the Differences between Christianity and Islam* (Grand Rapids, MI: Zondervan, 2002).
[9] Miroslav Volf, *Allah: A Christian Response* (New York: HarperOne, 2011); Miroslav Volf, ed., *Do We Worship the Same God?: Jews, Christians, and Muslims in Dialogue* (Grand Rapids, MI: Eerdmans, 2012).
[10] George, *Is the Father of Jesus*, 69. See also Kenneth Cragg, "Islamic Theology: Limits and Bridges," in *The Gospel and Islam: A 1978 Compendium*, ed. Don McCurry (Monrovia, CA: MARC, 1979), 198.

meaning. Muhammad clearly intended to refer to the God of creation, the one true and living God. However, the way that Muslims understand this one God with regard to his mode of existence, his nature, his relationship to the creation, and his revelation differs significantly. The intended referent is the same; the meaning is not. This divergence also results in serious differences in the way God's love is understood.

What is the intended referent for god in Islam and Christianity? Monotheism operates on the assumption that there is only one true God, the sovereign creator of all. Alternatives include polytheism, pantheism, panentheism, atheism, and various forms of idolatry. But there cannot be two Gods who are both sovereign creator of all. Clearly Christ and the apostolic church, when speaking of God, intended to refer to the God of creation, the God of the Old Testament and of antecedent Judaism. As Paul says, "We know that . . . 'There is no God but one'" (1 Cor. 8:4).[11] Likewise, the Qur'an and the early Muslim community clearly intended to refer to this one God, the God of the Jews and Christians of Muhammad's day. To make it explicit the Qur'an says, "There is no god except one God" (Q 5:73).[12]

This understanding about God is the theological foundation for Islam: everything starts here. The Qur'an and Islam emerged in contest with a polytheistic culture. So affirming monotheism, and consequently God's unity (*tawhīd*), is the religion's most fundamental tenet. The aim of the Islamic movement was to put an end to polytheism and idolatry in the Arabian Peninsula. With regard to other monotheists, the Qur'an instructs, "Do not argue with the People of the Scripture except in a way that is best . . . and say, 'We believe in that which has been revealed to us and revealed to you. And our God and your God is one'" (Q 29:46; cf. 5:73).[13]

The recognition that both Christians and Muslims intend to refer to the one God is significant and has functional value. It provides a sort of lowest common denominator, a shared theological premise: there is one God who is the creator of heaven and earth, and it is the believer's intention to worship him alone.[14] Miroslav Volf's thesis is that this recognition

[11] Paul goes on to include both the Father and the Son in this one divine identity (1 Cor. 8:6).

[12] References in the Qur'an can be searched online conveniently by typing the reference for the URL, illustrated here for Qur'an 4:171, after the following pattern: www.quran.com/4/171. Simply change the chapter and/or verse number after the slash. Various translations can also be selected. Quotes in this essay are from the Sahih International translation.

[13] Many other Qur'anic references purport that the God of Islam and the God of Christianity are the same, including 5:46–48, 59; 2:136, 285; 22:39–40; 42:13, 15.

[14] However, even Christian and Islamic accounts of this "theological minimum" will reflect the contours of their respective thicker theologies. Cf. Amy Plantinga Pauw, "The Same God?," in Volf, *Do We Worship*, 47.

of a common referent also allows for mutual respect and better fosters civic coexistence in the public square.[15] This recognition also provides a possible starting point from which Christians and Muslims can bear witness to one another. Paul arguably did this when he said to the philosophically minded Athenians about the inscription to the unknown God, "You are ignorant of the very thing you worship—and this is what I am going to proclaim to you" (Acts 17:23).

While the intended referent is the same, Christians and Muslims both believe the others are largely mistaken about God's nature. For Christians the move from a thin theological agreement about monotheism to the richer theological understanding of the triune God's saving self-revelation in Christ and the Spirit has significant implications for how one understands God's love. Here we move from intended referent to meaning.

What is the meaning of God in the Muslim view? Jewish, Christian, and Muslim monotheists, while referring to the one God who is the creator of all, tell rather distinct stories about the nature of this God and his relation to humanity. Their diverging narratives result in irreducible theological differences. Virtue requires us to face these differences honestly and respectfully when we engage our Muslim neighbors and friends.

The Qur'an identifies Islam as true religion (Q 3:19, "Religion in the sight of Allah is Islam"). The most elementary components of Islam appear in a single verse (called an *ayah*) that begins, "The Messenger has believed in what was revealed to him from his Lord, and [so have] the believers. All of them have believed in Allah" (Q 2:285).

This earliest Islamic creed is also found in the Hadiths, which are collections of the sayings and practices of Muhammad.[16] One such narrative, or *sunna*, about the prophet has Muhammad answering the questions of a visitor, who turns out to be the angel Gabriel. The angel first asks, "What is Islam?" The Prophet answers, "To bear witness that there is no god, but God." He is asked further, "What is faith?" The prophet says, "That one should believe in God!" The angel asks a third question, "What is virtue?" Muhammad answers, "That you should worship God."[17]

Believing in or calling on any deity other than God is termed *shirk*

[15] Volf, *Allah*, esp. chaps. 10–11.

[16] The Qur'an states that Muhammad is "an excellent example" for all Muslims (Q 33:21). But the Qur'an says little about Muhammad's life. So his followers collected his *sunna*, customs or practices, and preserved them in the Hadiths, nine canonical collections of various reputation. Shi'ites have their own Hadith traditions, which uniquely focus on the descendants of Muhammad through the line of Ali. Muslims accept the Hadiths as a second source for Islamic doctrine and practice.

[17] Cyril Glassé, *The New Encyclopedia of Islam*, 3rd ed. (Lanham: Rowman & Littlefield, 2008), 119.

(partnership), which is an unforgivable sin (Q 4:116): "Indeed, Allah does not forgive association with Him, but He forgives what is less than that for whom He wills. And he who associates others with Allah has certainly gone far astray." According to Qur'an 25:68–70, anyone who worships God with another god will be punished on judgment day with a double penalty, "except for those who repent, believe and do righteous work. For them Allah will replace their evil deeds with good. And ever is Allah Forgiving and Merciful" (Q 25:70). Clearly Islam situated itself to oppose anything but monotheism. The Christian conception of God as triune, whether correctly understood or not, was viewed as a threat to this strict conception of God as monistic.

It is from this starting point that Islam continues to deny explicitly and vehemently the Christian understanding of God as triune. A few Muslim thinkers have attempted to mitigate or even find creative ways of affirming a Trinity, but such voices are clearly outliers. Such attempts to collapse the Christian and Islamic views into a common theological construction, however well-intentioned, ultimately fail. Such moves succeed only in denying both Islamic and Christian confessions.

The most fundamental confession of the Muslim creed is an affirmation of divine oneness (*tawhīd*), which by implication denies any personal distinctions within the Godhead, and as a result the possibility of the incarnation. The problem for Christian theology is clear: if these doctrines are denied, then the unique revelation of God's love in Christ is also denied.

Traditional Islamic theology begins with the affirmation of divine oneness found in the Qur'an and interprets it in philosophical terms that necessarily eliminate the possibility of the Trinity. The Qur'an tells the Christians of Muhammad's day to stop all talk of "threeness" in relation to God, as well as from confessing the incarnation. Two texts from the Qur'an are sufficient to make the point.

After the opening chapter, the remaining 113 chapters of the Qur'an (called *suras*) are organized for the most part from longest to shortest. The antepenultimate (Q 112) is titled *Surat al-'Iklās*, or "The Chapter of Purity." It consists of the following four lines:

> Say, "He is Allah, [who is] One,
> Allah, the Eternal Refuge.
> He neither begets nor is born,
> Nor is there to Him any equivalent."

A longer passage, taken from *Surat an-Nisā'* ("The Woman"), amplifies both points:

> O People of the Scripture, do not commit excess in your religion or say about Allah except the truth. The Messiah, Jesus, the son of Mary, was but a messenger of Allah and His word which He directed to Mary and a soul [created at a command] from Him. So believe in Allah and His messengers. And do not say, "Three"; desist—it is better for you. Indeed, Allah is but one God. Exalted is He above having a son. (Q 4:171)

As one Islamic writer says, we have a "theological impasse here, a fundamental incompatibility between the respective conceptual forms taken by belief in the same God."[18] Christians can respond that we do not believe in three gods; we affirm God's oneness. We can argue that we believe not in a carnal begetting of the Son by the Father and a cohort but that God has an inner relational life. In this regard, we do not believe that the one divine essence was begotten, or that this essence begot another essence. We confess rather that the three persons, Father, Son, and Spirit, exist together as the relational life of the one essence, and that within this divine life, the Father is not begotten, though he does beget the Son. However, the response of the Qur'an, and that of orthodox Islamic theology, is insistent: "And do not say, 'Three'; desist—it is better for you." A theological impasse indeed!

When the Christian understanding of God as triune and the Islamic response are brought into close proximity, great care is required in order not to misunderstand the other unnecessarily. Much like on the Indian road! Here we need to look closely at three questions: (1) What does the Qur'an actually say about the Trinity? (2) How does Islamic theology build on the Trinity? And (3) Is there a valid way to bridge theologically this divide between Islam and Christianity—without jeopardizing the uniqueness of God's love in Christ?

Shah-Kazemi, an Ismaili Muslim, acknowledges, "Although the idea of 'threeness' is censured in a general way in the Qur'an, the only specific 'trinity' mentioned in the Qur'an is not the Trinity affirmed in Christian dogma."[19] There are just two instances in which the Qur'an gives specific configurations of the Trinity. The first seems to identify God, Jesus, and Mary as three gods:

[18] Reza Shah-Kazemi, "Do Muslims and Christians Believe in the Same God?," in Volf, *Do We Worship*, 81.
[19] Quoted in ibid., 87.

> [Beware the day] when Allah will say, "O Jesus, Son of Mary, did you say to the people, 'Take me and my mother as deities besides Allah?'" He will say, "Exalted are You! It was not for me to say that to which I have no right." (Q 5:116)

The Qur'an is not explicitly rejecting the orthodox understanding of the Trinity. It rejects rather a triad of gods: God, Jesus, and Mary. Jesus himself is portrayed as rejecting such a conception of the Trinity.

The second Qur'anic reference gives what Christians would agree is another heretical understanding of the Trinity:

> They have certainly disbelieved who say, "Allah is the third of three." And there is no god except one God. And if they do not desist from what they are saying, there will surely afflict the disbelievers among them a painful punishment. (Q 5:73)

The Qur'an rightly rejects this distortion of the Trinity. It is not at all clear that the Qur'an addresses the concept of one God in whom three persons subsist in the Christian Trinitarian sense. Nowhere—in its opposition to the beliefs of the day, for example—does the Qur'an reference the Spirit as a person of the Trinity. One can find among Muslim theologians astonishingly perceptive accounts of the Christian doctrine of the three divine persons in one God. Some even acknowledge that Christianity is a genuine form of monotheism.[20]

This does not mean that the Qur'an and Islam allow for the orthodox understanding of the Trinity. The objection is twofold. First, the idea of "threeness" is censured in a general way in the Qur'an (Q 4:171). Second, it is assumed that the very definition of oneness (*tawhīd*) rationally rules out any understanding of personal distinctions within God himself. Qur'an 112, as we saw, expresses an affirmation of God's oneness in the most emphatic language. Such Qur'anic material, along with the Hadiths and classic Islamic theology, tends to portray a rather strict philosophic conception of God as a bare monistic being.

The transcendence of God, wrapped up in this conception of *tawhīd*, means that God is utterly different from everything that has been cre-

[20] See, e.g., the philosophically sophisticated, early ninth-century work of Abu Isa Muhammad ibn Harun Al-Warraq, *Anti-Christian Polemic in Early Islam: Abu Isa Al-Warraq's "Against the Trinity,"* ed. and trans. David Thomas (Cambridge, UK: Cambridge University Press, 1992). For a detailed discussion, see Nader al-Bizri, "God's Essence and Attributes," in *The Cambridge Companion to Classical Islamic Theology*, ed. Tim Winter (Cambridge, UK: Cambridge University Press, 2008), esp. 129–31. Cf. Shah-Kazemi, "Do Muslims and Christians Believe," esp. "The Trinity: Muslim Critique," 87–103.

ated. Muslims feel thoroughly horrified by every attempt to associate with God anything from the created order (human beings included). To place anything beside God or to assimilate anyone with God is considered *shirk*, an unpardonable sin. This feeling of horror is entirely in harmony with the Qur'an, which condemns any such attempt repeatedly and vehemently. Because of the problems of polytheism and idolatry in Arabia at the time of the rise of Islam, along with misunderstandings of the Christian doctrine of the Trinity, this is certainly understandable. But it creates one of the greatest difficulties in leading Muslims to Christ and the life-giving message of the gospel. Is there a theological way to bridge this divide?

Is there a God behind the God of Christianity and Islam? In his influential work, religious pluralist John Hick starts with a theologically minimal conception of divinity and then calls on others to see the various great religious traditions as different ways of conceiving and experiencing this one ultimate reality.[21] However, to accept his premise Christians must give up any theological claim that stands in the way of this theologically minimal God behind the Trinity. The cost is too high. The same problem attends theological strategies used in attempts to bridge the divide between the Muslim and Christian views of God. We will consider one of these briefly. It illustrates how such attempts tend to collapse the Christian view into an Islamic view, and as a result do injustice to the Christian conception of God's love in Christ.

In an impressively argued article, Reza Shah-Kazemi defines the intended referent of the monotheistic faiths (Judaism, Christianity, and Islam) as the "transcendent Absolute, ultimate Reality, the unique source of Being."[22] He then argues that when this Reality is conceived in human thought, fundamental differences between Islam and Christianity surface. His solution is to appeal to a higher plane of discourse, beyond the conceptual limits of theology. He argues that the differences can be resolved "on the higher plane of metaphysics and the deeper plane of mysticism—planes that are not constrained, doctrinally as regards metaphysics or experientially as regards mysticism, by the limitations of theology."[23]

---

[21] John Hick, *Problems of Religious Pluralism* (New York: St. Martin's, 1985), 102.

[22] Shah-Kazemi, "Do Muslims and Christians Believe," 78.

[23] Ibid. There is a parallel move among certain Hindu philosophers to distinguish between *Nirguna Brahman* (God as he is in himself, without attributes) and *Saguna Brahman* (God as he is revealed in his various manifestations). Cf. Timothy C. Tennent, *Building Christianity on Indian Foundations: The Legacy of Brahmabāndhav Upādhyāy* (Delhi: ISPCK, 2000).

Shah-Kazemi writes, "The very nature of theological debate renders it all but inevitable that fundamental disagreements about the nature of God will prevail."[24] However, he argues:

> [If] we look beyond the theological definition of *Allāh*, and to its supratheological or metaphysical referent—that ultimate Essence (*al-Dhāt*) which is absolutely ineffable and thus unnamable, and if, likewise we look beyond the theological definition of the Trinitarian conception of God, and focus instead on its supratheological or metaphysical referent . . . then we shall be in a position to affirm that, despite the different names by which the ultimate Reality is denoted in the two traditions, the Reality thus alluded to is indeed one and the same.[25]

The mysticism of Shah-Kazemi, despite his admirable attempts to be sensitive to the Christian position, is problematic. For Christians there can be no higher plane of metaphysics or mysticism that trumps God's definitive self-revelation in Christ and the gospel. There is no spiritual essence that escapes the theological form, rendering it the "relatively accidental features of conceptual belief."[26] Such a move denies God's self-revelation as embedded in the New Testament and undercuts the love of Christ that flows from God's own triune life.

Shah-Kazemi turns the Trinity into a second-order manifestation of the Supreme Reality (which he argues transcends number).[27] This denies the Trinity and effectively removes genuine relationality from within God's own life. As a result, it transforms the Christian conception of God into a virtual mirror image of the Muslim conception.

This move, as all moves that find a God behind the triune God, results in two fatal blows to Christianity. First, it leaves the gospel without any grounding in God as he is in himself. We understand that God is triune because of the way the Father has acted in his Son and Spirit. As we reflect on this revelatory, creative, and saving work of God from the vantage point of the New Testament, we begin to glimpse how God exists in inter-Trinitarian relation. This is why theologians say we know the ontological (or immanent) Trinity (God as he exists in his own being) via the functional Trinity (God as he reveals himself by his work in the

[24] Shah-Kazemi, "Do Muslims and Christians Believe," 79.
[25] Ibid.
[26] Ibid.
[27] Ibid., 116. He appeals to both Christian and Islamic mystics for support: "Both Eckhart and Ibn al-'Arabi situate plurality within the divine nature on a plane that is below that of the Essence, a plane that pertains to the relationship of Essence and the domain of manifestation."

world).[28] The gospel and our understanding of God as triune cannot be severed.

Second, Shah-Kazemi's view eliminates the ultimate grounding of love in the eternal relational life of God as Father, Son, and Spirit. For the Christian there can be no God behind the triune one! All such attempts both redefine the orthodox Christian view of God and have significant implications for how the love of God is understood. The point is straightforward: to argue for a philosophical or mystical abstraction of a God behind the triune God is to eliminate the triune relationality that grounds divine love in God's own nature and life. This may be acceptable to Islam, but it is a denial of Christianity and the gospel and therefore no safe bridge between the two faiths.[29]

The critical difference is whether God is the triune one of the gospel. Attempts to advocate for a God behind the God of Islam and Christianity—that is, a God of the first order, who is the explanation of a second-order Trinitarian God—necessarily distort the gospel. Such efforts tend to exchange the triune God of Scripture with the very God that the advocate started with. As a result, this both denies the Trinity and also rejects the saving gift of God's love in Christ.

What is the meaning of God in the Christian view? Is the one true and living God a bare monistic being, as implied by traditional Islam, or is the God of the universe, the creator and judge of all, actually one divine nature that subsists as a unique plurality of persons? This is not a question that can be resolved by human reason and philosophy but one that depends ultimately on supernatural revelation. Only God himself can reveal to us his own nature; only he can disclose to us how he exists. So theology proper leads us to ask questions about revelation. Is the picture presented in the Qur'an an adequate picture of God, or is the distinctly triune God presented in the Bible the way God actually exists?

While Islam begins with the Qur'anic affirmation of divine oneness and interprets it in philosophical terms that eliminate the reality of the Trinity, the gospel leads Christians in another direction. The church begins with the confession that God is one, but interprets it in light of the

[28] This has been most forcefully stated and argued by Karl Rahner, who put it this way: "The economic Trinity is the immanent Trinity, and the immanent Trinity is the economic Trinity." This is known as "Rahner's Rule." It is a bit of an overstatement, since there are some truths about God as he is in himself that are not manifest by his work in the world. Karl Rahner, *The Trinity*, trans. Joseph Donceel (New York: Crossword-Herder, 1927), 22. Cf. Randal Rauser, "Rahner's Rule: An Emperor without Clothes?," in *IJST* 7.1 (2005): 81–94.

[29] Contra Shah-Kazemi, "Do Muslims and Christians Believe," 134, who argues: "The Trinity is essential to Christian belief, but it is possible to conceptually abstract this aspect of belief, and still retain an adequate conception of the essence of God, the Essence of that divinity believed in and worshiped by Muslims."

biblical narrative that culminates in the life of Jesus and the ministry of the Spirit. This revealed storyline leads us to understand God's identity as triune. It is out of this narrative and divine identity that the love of God in Christ flows.

Recent discussions of the social model of the Trinity stress the relational life of God, from which his love emanates, and help us to articulate for our Muslim friends the connection between God's communal nature and his love. J. Scott Horrell offers this careful statement: "[The Trinity] as the one divine Being eternally exists as three distinct centers of consciousness [i.e., 'persons'], wholly equal in nature, genuinely personal in relationships, and each mutually indwelling the other."[30] This definition systematizes God's historical and biblically embedded self-disclosure.[31] It contains several critical elements. First, there is a strong affirmation of monotheism. There is only one set of attributes that make up the divine nature.[32] There is only one divine being. Here we agree with the confessions of Judaism ("Hear, O Israel: The LORD our God, the LORD is one!" Deut. 6:4) and Islam ("There is no god but God!").

Second, from the gospel we learn that within this one divine nature there are three relational distinctions: Father, Son, and Spirit. God subsists (lives or exists) as three internal relationalities. These internal distinctions are traditionally called "persons." But this special theological use of the term *person* should not be confused with the human idea of three *people* (in the sense of beings with distinct and individual natures), for there is only one divine nature.[33] There is mystery here because God is *sui generis*, a one-of-a-kind being.

Finally, with respect to relational distinctions, each of the three persons is distinct, preserving his own unique identity. The Father is not the Son; the Son is not the Spirit. Again, with regard to the divine nature, they are one and the same; with regard to their persons, they are "individual centers of consciousness" in mutual relationship. Furthermore, the unique identity of each person is mutually constituted; that is, the Father

---

[30] J. Scott Horrell, "Towards a Biblical Model of the Social Trinity: Avoiding Equivocation of Nature and Order," *JETS* 47 (Sept. 2004): 399, 420.

[31] Our thinking about the Trinity as a theological construct, and our application of insights gained from such conceptual work, must never be abstracted from the storyline of the NT, with its focus on the atonement and God's mission in the world by Christ and the Spirit. Cf. Colin Gunton, *The Promise of Trinitarian Theology*, 2nd ed. (New York: T&T Clark, 2003) *xx–xxi*.

[32] Horrell, "Towards a Biblical Model," 403, helpfully defines the Christian understanding of "nature" in this context as the "generic essence, universal property, attributes of Godness manifest equally in the Father, Son, and Holy Spirit."

[33] Horrell, ibid., defines *person* "in the divine and ideal sense as a center of self-consciousness existing in relationship to others."

is not the Father without the Son, and the Son is not the Son without the Spirit.[34] If you sense that we are in over our heads, you are right—we are! We are speaking of the very way in which God exists, the glorious three-in-one. Human words are inadequate to convey fully God's own life. *Mostly, we should be silent and worship!*

We do not claim that we can know God exhaustively, but simply that the God who is incomprehensible and utterly beyond our imagination and intelligence has nonetheless truly made himself known to us as he is in his inner life—he is one who exists as a triune relational being. Because God is the infinite and ultimately incomprehensible Creator of all that exists, theological constructs, even the most viable ones, necessarily fall short of full and perfect explanation of God.[35] This is as it should be in light of creaturely finitude. However, it is the witness of Christians that God's self-revelation in Christ and by the Spirit is true and faithful. This divine revelation is necessary and sufficient for salvation, a life pleasing to God, and participation in God's work in the world. This "good news" reveals God to be the triune God of love. Any abstraction from this revelation to another God behind the Trinity leaves a message that is not the Christian message and that negates the Christian understanding of divine love.

The Love of God

Intended referent. Both the Muslim and the Christian talk about God's love; as with the divine identity, the understandings overlap, but there are also critical differences. These varied conceptions derive from the distinct scriptures of Christianity and Islam, with their dissimilar narratives about God's nature and saving work. Again, comparing and contrasting the Christian faith with Islam requires virtuous thinking, rigorous theological analysis, and Christlike engagement.

The meaning of the Muslim view of God's love compared with the Christian view. We should not assume that we understand how each Muslim thinks or feels about God. "As in other religions, Muslims run

[34] According to Horrell, ibid., this basic definition of *person* should be filled out with four aspects by which each divine person is constituted: (1) generic nature of deity; that is, the attributes that distinguish God from creature; (2) full self-consciousness (actual reality of self, with distinct mental properties and internal relations); (3) unique relatedness, distinguishing each member of Godhead from the others in "I-you" relationships; (4) *perichoresis*, the mutual indwelling of each in the other without confusion of self-consciousness.

[35] When it comes to our knowledge of God, it is helpful to distinguish between *apprehension* and *comprehension*. We can know truth about God (sufficient for our needs as his creatures), but we cannot know God exhaustively. "While there may be hiddenness, incomprehensibility, and even (in apophatic theology) *darkness*, there are no masks—as the incarnation and the cross powerfully demonstrate. God is honest, true, and genuine in communicating himself" (ibid., 400). On the mysterious nature of the Trinity, see Oliver D. Crisp, "Problems with Perichoresis," *TynBul* 56/1 (2005): 120.

the gamut, from extremely devout to lapsed, from extremist to ultra-liberal, from converted to merely cultural, and of course everything in between."[36] There are family resemblances among the varied Islamic traditions and a numerically dominant approach (Sunni traditionalism); but there are also many other streams and great personal variety among individual Muslims. There are also a variety of theological and experiential approaches to relationship with God. In broad feature, some of this variety includes the unique Shia perspective on God's continued revelatory work through imams; the fascinating sense of a personal experience of God by Sufi mystics, like Rumi; the progressive and even postmodern thinking about God by various contemporary Muslims; and, at the other end of the spectrum, the animistic thinking of less-educated Muslims. In what follows we will simply compare and contrast a representation of careful Islamic thinking on God's love with the Christian view.[37] The value of this approach is that it helps to identify foundational differences. We begin with two Qur'anic features of God's love that differ from the New Testament picture.

First, where explicit words for *love* are concerned, there is relatively little emphasis in the Qur'an on God's love for people.[38] This is not to say that God's love is not present in the Qur'an. We need to avoid the linguistic fallacy of thinking that the meaning of God's love is strictly limited to the occurrence of the primary word for love (*hub*). For a full study, one needs to study the semantic range of related words.[39] Expressions such as "God is merciful" or "compassionate" occur often in the Qur'an (e.g., see the opening of every *sura*, except the ninth). Nevertheless, compared to the New Testament, the explicit use of the word *love* in the Qur'an is rare as a way of expressing God's affection for people. The expression "God is love" (*Allahu muhibba*), for example, is absent from the Qur'an. Muslims point out that *al-Wudūd* is one of the ninety-nine names for God and can be translated loosely as "the Loving One" (Q 11:90; 85:14).[40] Nonetheless, the low frequency of the use of the term *love*, as well as other terms for

[36] Allen and Toorawa, *Islam*, 4.

[37] For an influential study from the Islamic perspective, see Ghazi bin Muhammad, *Love in the Holy Qur'an*, trans. of 6th Arabic ed. (Chicago: Kazi, 2010).

[38] On the use of *love* in the Qur'an, see Farid Mahally, "A Study of the Word 'Love' in the Qur'an: *Hubb Allah fi al-Qur'an*," www.answering-islam.org/Quran/Themes/love.htm.

[39] Cf. Volf, *Allah*, 155–56. The range of Arabic words related to love in the Qur'an is nicely summarized in Ghazi, *Love in the Holy Qur'an*, chap. 21, and also 404–5.

[40] It is variously translated as "affectionate," "most loving," "full of lovingkindness," and "full of love." See www.quran.com/11/90 and www.quran.com/85/14. The word *al-wudūd* should not be confused with *al-muhibb*, the standard Arabic word for "loving." God's lovingkindness is associated in these texts with his being "merciful" and "forgiving," respectively. Except in the mystical tradition, as we shall see, Muslim exegetes prefer to point to God's mercy, not his love, as an essential divine attribute.

love, while not the whole picture, is suggestive and reflects the different orientation of Islam toward questions of God and his love.[41] The significance of this different orientation has to be fleshed out by the distinct Islamic narrative about God's nature and relationship to his creation.

Second, when God's love for people is made explicit in the Qur'an, there is often an emphasis on its limited or conditional nature. The word *love,* along with its cognates, is used some sixty-nine times in the Qur'an.[42] More than half of these occurrences refer to human love for things, people, or God (2:165; 3:31; 5:54). When the love of God comes up in popular discussion, the tendency is for Muslims to think first of human love for God rather than God's love for humans.[43]

In regard to God's love for people, there are about twenty references that identify those God does *not* love. Examples include those who exceed God's limits (2:190; 5:87; 7:55), the ungrateful and wicked (2:276), disbelievers (3:32), and the wasteful (6:141; 7:31). This list stresses the conditional nature of God's love.[44]

References that speak of God's love in a positive sense also stress love's conditional nature. God loves those who do good (2:195; 3:76), trust him (2:222; 3:146, 159), keep themselves pure (2:222), are firm and steadfast (3:146), judge in equity (5:42), and fight for God's sake (61:4).[45] This conditional emphasis is problematic for Christian theology. The Bible occasionally speaks of a conditional aspect to God's love. But Christian theology understands the condition as relating primarily to the sin of creatures, not a reservation on God's part. As Volf argues, "The critical test of whether we have understood God's love correctly is whether we affirm that God loves the ungodly—those who are unlike God and even those opposed to God."[46]

How do Islamic theologians respond to this Christian concern? Two contrasting approaches are illustrative and lead back to the underlying question of God's nature. The first approach places an emphasis on God's transcendence and the corollary that love is properly a human activity

[41] Even if one includes the vast Hadith material, the pattern is similar. Mahally, in "Study of the Word 'Love,'" helpfully summarizes the evidence from four of the most reputable collections: Bukhari lists ninety-five uses of "love" and thirty-six of "loved." Muslim lists twenty-two usages of "love" and four for "loved." Abu Dawud lists only ten for "love," one for "loved." Malik's Muwatta lists "love" twelve times and "loved" four times. Most of these have to do with human love or love of things; only a limited number refer to God's love.

[42] Mahally, "Study of the Word 'Love,'" notes by contrast that the Bible contains 409 uses of love, with 223 in the NT alone.

[43] A popular *aya* reads, "But those who believe are stronger in their love for Allah" (Q 2:165).

[44] For a more complete list see Volf, *Allah,* 172–73.

[45] Reza Shah-Kazemi identifies eight categories of people whom God loves; cited in Volf, *Allah,* 172.

[46] Ibid., 172–73.

quite incompatible with God's nature.[47] Hofmann writes, "The idea that God might 'love' what He created is not self evident. On the contrary, one might argue that love establishes a longing and dependency between the lover and the loved one that is irreconcilable with God."[48] Hofmann cites a reference in the Qur'an that speaks of Allah as being "free of need" (Q 64:6). In the context of this *sura*, certain ones had rejected God's messengers. But God does not need them. In other words, God is self-sufficient. In contrast to this transcendence, Hofmann treats love as a human, needy, and imperfect affection. He then concludes, "God cannot possibly love his creation that human way! Therefore it is safer and more accurate not to speak of 'love' when addressing His clemency, compassion, benevolence, goodness, or mercy."[49]

This, of course, is a caricature of the Christian understanding of God's love. It reverses the analogy. In Christian theology, human love is a frail reflection of the perfect pattern of divine love; God's love is not patterned after human love, with its tendency to be selfish and codependent. Besides, the qualities of compassion and mercy are subject to the same line of reasoning.

With regard to the Qur'anic verses that describe God as "loving" people, Hofmann writes, "In all these cases Allah 'loves' must be understood as Allah 'approves,' 'is content with,' or 'views positively' those who act as described. 'Love' here does not refer to emotional involvement."[50] In those few places where the Qur'an does speak of God's love, the tendency is to downplay the language. Hofmann acknowledges that God is said to love those who attain to faith and do good works (Q 19:96); God will love you if you love him (Q 3:31); and God can create a people that he loves and that will love him (Q 5:54). But, Hofmann argues, to think of such divine love as comparable in any way to human love "must be ruled out as incompatible with the very nature of God as sublime and totally self-sufficient."[51] Ghazi bin Muhammad points out that Muslim scholars stress either that God's love is ineffable and only its effects can be discussed, or that love, which by definition is an inclination toward another, is not applicable to God.[52] So, God's love is not only stressed as conditional, it is also limited by defini-

[47] Cf. Murad Wilfried Hofman, "Differences between the Muslim and Christian Concept of Divine Love," a paper delivered at the 14th General Conference of the Royal Aal al-Bayt Institute for Islamic Thought, Amman, Jordan, 2007, aalalbayt.org/en/respapers.html#rd14. Ghazi, *Love in the Holy Qur'an*, 414–22, provides a helpful list of quotations from various Islamic scholars on the subject.

[48] Hofmann, "Differences," 7.

[49] Ibid., 9.

[50] Ibid.

[51] Ibid. Ghazi provides a helpful list of quotations from various Islamic scholars on the subject (414–22).

[52] Ghazi, *Love in the Holy Qur'an*, 414.

tion—it rules out the kind of intimate and yet appropriate divine love that the gospel presents.

This line of approach appears to work from a Greek philosophic conception of God and divine love rather than a biblical one. At the end of the day, it starts not with an understanding of God based on his own self-revelation but with a preconceived notion of how God must exist and love. The best Christian theologians are careful to affirm God's perfection, but they also insist that there is a proper analogy between divine love and true human love. This human ability to love after the divine analogy begins with our creation in the *imago Dei*; it will finally come to perfection through our redemption and transformation by the Spirit into the likeness of Christ.

The alternative Islamic approach to God's love is more positive and stems from the spiritual masters of Islam. Here we find some of the most moving and expressive understandings of divine love in Islamic thought. The development of mysticism within classical Islam climaxed with Abu Hamid al-Ghazali (d. 1111). Samuel Zwemer, the famed missionary to Muslims, described Al-Ghazali in his 1920 book title as "A Moslem Seeker after God: Showing Islam at Its Best."[53] Al-Ghazali describes God's mercy to be "perfect inasmuch as it wants to fulfill the need of those in need and does meet them; and inclusive inasmuch as it embraces both deserving and undeserving, encompassing this world and the next, and includes bare necessities and needs, and special gifts over and above them. So He is truly and utterly merciful."[54]

In contemporary discussions, Shah Kazemi represents this more mystical stream of Islam. He works with the fuller range of vocabulary related to the semantic domain of love, especially words for God's mercy. Along with the great spiritual teachers of Islam, Kazemi builds his view of God's encompassing love on two important points. First, God's mercy is the overarching way that he relates to his creation (Q 7:156); second, this mercy is an essential attribute of God (Q 6:12).[55] According to his version of Islam, God's nature is characterized by "loving mercy."

[53] Samuel M. Zwemer, *A Moslem Seeker after God: Showing Islam at Its Best in the Life and Teaching of al-Ghazali, Mystic and Theologian of the Eleventh Century* (New York: Revell, 1920). Al-Ghazali makes a case for assimilating mysticism into normative Islam through his magnum opus, *Revivification of the Religious Sciences*. This is one of the greatest works of Muslim spirituality. Al-Ghazali wanted to invigorate the traditional religious disciplines of Islam (exegesis of the Qur'an, study of philosophic theology, and the Hadiths, along with the work of the jurists) by instilling them with spiritual experience.

[54] As cited in Volf, *Allah*, 159. Whether we agree or not with the thesis of Volf's book, we ought to appreciate his desire to address Islam in its best light. He writes, "For me here the 'paradigmatic' Muslim is the great and immensely influential thinker Abu Hamid al-Ghazali (1,056–1,111), and not, for instance, Sayyid Qutb (1,906–66), the most popular representative of radical Islam." Ibid., 11.

[55] Ibid., 174.

While this is a more positive emphasis on God's love, two problems remain for Christian theology: its manifestation toward creatures leans toward mercy rather than love itself (or at least a more qualified understanding of love), and the tendency is to explain God's love in terms of his self-love.

God's love for his creatures, even when stressed in this version, tends to be abridged to mercy rather than the fullness of love itself. There remains, even for the great spiritual giant Al-Ghazali, a concern about the suitability of love as a divine attribute. He argues that love is the disposition to something pleasant, something that suits and pleases. This, he claims, can apply only to an imperfect being inclining toward something it lacks and is, therefore, impossible for God.[56] So, when divine love turns towards the creature, it of necessity must be limited.

More importantly, when this more positive form of love in Islam is stressed, it becomes what from the Christian perspective appears to be an enclosed form of self-love. Miroslav Volf summarizes this conclusion of Islamic theology in the form taught by Ahmad ibn Taymiyya.[57] Ibn Taymiyya argued that since God loves his creatures (Q 85:14), it cannot be from any self-deficiency. So, when he loves people, it cannot be because he needs them, but neither can it be that God loves them without a reason. His love is not groundless. Ibn Taymiyya concludes, then, that God loves because he first loves his own self. God loves apart from the contingent creation, and this love is an essential aspect of God's eternal being. This is an amazing insight and begins to approximate the Christian understanding. We can surely appreciate aspects of this Islamic version of God's love. But, at the same time, it raises two critical problems. First, how can a monistic being truly love his own self, without love becoming something other than love? And second, on this view, God can show mercy toward his creatures, but he can actually love only himself. This helps to explain why God's love for creatures in the Islamic conception is described better as mercy than as love.[58]

We can draw three important conclusions with regard to God's love in Christ as compared to the Islamic view. First, while Muslims can say that love is an essential characteristic of God's nature and can affirm that God is loving in the sense of being merciful to people, they usually stop

[56] See Ghazi, *Love in the Holy Qur'an*, 414–15.

[57] Volf, *Allah*, 166–67. Ahmad ibn Taymiyya (1263–1328) was a formative thinker for modern Salafists, an extremely conservative Islamic movement. He influenced Muhammad ibn Abd al-Wahhab (1703–1793), the founder of Wahhabism, with its center of influence in modern Saudi Arabia.

[58] See Volf's careful discussion of this in *Allah*, 168–69.

short of saying that God is love. Second, "Christians say that God's eternal love includes love of the other, the divine other within the godhead and, derivatively, a creaturely other. When Muslims speak of God's eternal love, they affirm God's self-love and see in it the foundation of divine love of creatures."[59] However, when turned toward creatures, this love is better termed "mercy," as we have seen. Finally, for Christians God unequivocally loves the ungodly, not only with his merciful care but also with a saving love in Christ.[60] As the apostle Paul writes, "God demonstrates his own love for us in this: While we were still sinners, Christ died for us."[61] No one captures the essence of these three conclusions about God's love in more dense expression, and with their practical application, than John the Beloved:

> Dear friends, let us love one another, for love comes from God. Everyone who loves has been born of God and knows God. Whoever does not love does not know God, because God is love. This is how God showed his love among us: He sent his one and only Son into the world that we might live through him. This is love: not that we loved God, but that he loved us and sent his Son as an atoning sacrifice for our sins. Dear friends, since God so loved us, we also ought to love one another.[62]

Toward a Christlike Engagement with Muslims regarding God's Love

To return to the analogy of the Indian road, we have tried to slow down to listen carefully to Muslim scholars' speaking about their understanding of God's love. We have tried to compare the size of our two vehicles, comparing and contrasting our distinctive ways of talking about God and his love. As Christians and Muslims we both intend to refer to the one and only God, and we both speak about this God's love. But how we understand God's nature and the nature of his love are different, and the consequences are significant. What then, after the Indian road analogy, is the appropriate way to "blow our horn"? How do we bear faithful witness to the love of God in Christ to our Muslim friends?

The experience and witness of followers of Jesus is that God has revealed himself to be Father, Son, and Spirit. He is one God, as Islam

---

[59] Ibid., 181–82.

[60] Ibid., 182. Volf points out an important implication for human love: "Christians affirm unequivocally that God commands people to love even their enemies. As God loves the 'ungodly,' we should love our enemies. Though Muslims insist that we should be kind to all, including those who do us harm, most reject the idea that the love of neighbor includes the love of enemy."

[61] Rom. 5:8.

[62] 1 John 4:7–11.

confesses, but he exists in the mystery of his own divine life as three unique persons. This understanding of God is not merely the result of Christian reason or philosophy but rather a necessary conclusion derived from God's self-revelation in redemptive history. For Christian theology, *this* is the theological foundation—everything else starts here.[63] This is the God who exists, the one who has spoken in his Word and by his Spirit, who has both created the world and reconciled us to himself. God, as he is in himself—in his own divine life as Father, Son, and Spirit—is indeed a great mystery. Yet it is one that perfectly meets our needs; through this mystery we come to know the true depths of God's love in Christ.

In thinking about the relationship between the Muslim conception of God and his love and the Christian understanding, we have seen that there are both similarities and differences. As we have seen, it can be argued that Muslims from an historical perspective are referring to the same God as Christians do. When Muhammad came on the scene, he identified the God he wanted to call the tribes of Arabia to worship as the God of the people of the Book, the God of the Jews and Christians. He was speaking of the same God and calling on the Arab tribes to worship that God alone (not idols, nor the tribal gods).

In part the theology is the same: God is one, and he is Creator and judge—omniscient, omnipotent, and omnipresent. But the monistic interior life of Allah is a different conception than the communal and relational life of the triune one; a God who is imagined as radically transcendent is theologically different from the God who in the person of the Son became incarnate. These are huge theological differences, with significant implications for how we understand divine love.[64]

There is not only an historical and theological perspective on the question of God's identity; there is also a relational question: are Muslims in the same relationship with God as Christians? Again there can be a partial yes here, but there must also be a significant no. We must be cautious here. There are some questions we should best leave with God himself. As Muslims say, "God knows best" (Q 6:57–58). But what does the New Testament reveal about how God relates to those outside of Christ? As followers of Jesus, we confess that salvation is in him alone. But God does relate to the non-Christians, wooing them to himself by his Spirit,

[63] On God's love in the work of Father, Son, and Spirit with relevance for Islam, see John Gilchrist, *The Love of God in the Qur'an and the Bible*, published by Jesus to the Muslims, 1989, www.answering-islam.org/Gilchrist/love.html.

[64] See Cragg, "Islamic Theology," for some helpful suggestions for engaging Muslims about these differences.

convicting them of sin, righteousness, and judgment. He does cause his common grace to fall on the just and the unjust—because he is the God of the whole creation.

Yet Muslims do not personally acknowledge God as Father, nor have they entered by faith into the new covenant that Jesus instituted by his sacrifice, nor are they indwelt by that Holy Spirit given to those who confess Jesus as Lord, the Spirit who regenerates and sanctifies. In these respects they are not related to God. They recognize him as sovereign and judge, but not as Savior. And this is where we can, and must, bring our Muslim friends the good news, the glad tidings of how they can fully enter into a saving relationship with God and experience his perfect love. This leads us to a fourth and final perspective about the relationship of Muslims to God.

This is the missional question. Does God love Muslims? Here the answer is a resounding yes. The Father manifests his infinite love for all people in the redemptive work of Christ, in the ministry of the Spirit, and then in the mission of the church.[65] But we must ask ourselves; do we love our Muslim neighbors and friends? The answer ought to be an unqualified, self-sacrificing yes. Samuel Zwemer was an exemplary missionary of the last century who sought to reflect faithfully God's love for Muslims. He wrote, "After forty years experience, I am convinced that the nearest way to the Muslim heart is the way of the love of God, the way of the cross."[66]

In this light, the question as to whether the Father of Jesus is the God of the Muslim takes on a powerful missional dimension. God's love calls us to reflect his missional heart by giving our lives, as he gave his in Christ, in self-sacrificing love for our Muslim friends, that they, too, might be reconciled to God and enjoy the riches of his love.[67] This means that we must enter into the lives and experiences of Muslims everywhere—we should do this, even as the Son of God came and dwelt among us in our human condition.

We also need to enter into the theological world of Islam. We must seek to understand accurately, sympathetically, and intimately the thought

[65] David Bosch put it this way: "Mission has its origin in the heart of God. God is the fountain of sending love. This is the deepest source of mission. It is impossible to penetrate deeper still; there is mission because God loves people." David J. Bosch, *Transforming Mission: Paradigm Shifts in Theology of Mission* (Maryknoll, NY: Orbis, 2011), 384.

[66] Samuel Zwemer, *The Cross and the Crescent* (Grand Rapids, MI: Zondervan, 1941), 246.

[67] For a collection of fascinating biographical essays by men and women who have given their lives to the study of Islam, see Christian W. Troll and C. T. R. Hewer, *Christian Lives Given to the Study of Islam* (New York: Fordham University Press, 2012).

world of Islam, especially on the doctrine of God. In this way we can "blow our horn" more skillfully and so bear witness to the distinctive blessings of the gospel. From a more informed vantage point, we can see both the strengths and weaknesses of the Muslim understanding of God and begin to show in a loving, respectful way the beauty and wonder of God's love in Christ.

By understanding the Islamic story, with its aspirations and problems, we can situate ourselves inside their hearts and minds in a way that enables us to point to what alone can satisfy. Then we can reveal how their best spiritual aspirations (e.g., to submit to God and love him), as well as their limitations (e.g., the human proneness to wander into sin, the human inability to reach a God who is so transcendent), are answered marvelously in the love of God in Christ.[68]

[68] This strategy is argued and illustrated by Curtis Chang in *Engaging Unbelief: A Captivating Strategy from Augustine and Aquinas* (Downers Grove, IL: InterVarsity, 2000).

9

HOW DOES GOD'S LOVE SHAPE THE CHRISTIAN WALK?

C. D. "JIMMY" AGAN III

"Walking" is frequently used in Scripture as a metaphor for the holy life to which God has called his people. To cite only a few examples, the Old Testament calls us to walk in God's law (Ex. 16:4), walk in his ways (Deut. 10:12; Ps. 81:13), and walk humbly with God (Mic. 6:8). Similarly, the New Testament urges us to walk "in newness of life" (Rom. 6:4), "in a manner worthy of the Lord" (Col. 1:10), and even "in the same way in which [Jesus] walked" (1 John 2:6). The image of walking captures well what theologians mean by "progressive sanctification," a process by which, over time (and with the help of the Holy Spirit), God's people make progress in the kind of holy living he desires.[1]

What, though, does this holy walk have to do with the love of God? This chapter hopes to help readers answer that question by surveying biblical texts in which (1) the vocabulary of "love" is used to describe God's love for his people and/or their love for God,[2] and (2) some aspect of holy living is touched on. While space does not allow for the inclusion of every such text—let alone texts in which the concept of the love of God is conveyed without "love" vocabulary—our survey addresses a wide range of texts from a variety of biblical books, highlighting a number of topics. These are organized around four headings:

[1] See WCF 13, Westminster Larger Catechism Q. 75, and Westminster Shorter Catechism Q. 35. Note also the definition provided by Anthony A. Hoekema, *Saved by Grace* (Grand Rapids, MI: Eerdmans, 1989), 208.

[2] Texts included in our survey feature terms rendered in the ESV by some form of the English words "love" or "beloved." Most frequently represented are the Hebrew words *chesed* ("steadfast love") and *ahab* ("to love"), and the many Greek words built on the *-agap-* and *-phil-* roots (both translated "love").

- Our Point of Departure: The Love of God and the Beginning of the Christian Walk
- Our Path: The Love of God and the Shape of the Christian Walk
- Our Source of Power: The Love of God and Progress in the Christian Walk
- Our Destination: The Love of God and the Goal of the Christian Walk

A brief conclusion draws out important implications for walking more faithfully in the kind of holiness that is informed by the love of God.

Our Point of Departure: The Love of God and the Beginning of the Christian Walk

Every walk begins somewhere. If we want to know where the Christian walk begins and how that beginning relates to the love of God, we can find no clearer summary than 1 John 4:19: "We love because he first loved us."[3] Here we briefly consider the significance of John's statement, along with parallel themes from Paul, the Psalms, and Deuteronomy.

The Love of God as the Beginning of a Life of Love

The logic of 1 John 4:19 is unmistakably clear: to live a life of love, one must first be loved by God. And since all of Christian duty can be summed up in terms of love for God and neighbor, we may conclude that God's love for us is the starting point for any progress we make in living a life that pleases him. This is true for at least two reasons: first, since God is love (that is, God's loving actions reveal his essential character), it is only in knowing him and his love revealed in the gift of his Son that we know what love is (vv. 8–18); second, it is impossible for us to love unless God has given us a second birth, lavishing on us the love that makes us his children (3:1–3; 4:7). Thus, while there are many ways to describe the Christian life accurately, its fundamental rhythm is one of response to the love of God, supremely revealed in the work of his Son (3:16; 4:10). According to John, deeper appreciation for this rhythm sustains our progress in the Christian life.

The Love of God as the Beginning of a Transformed Life

We find similar logic in Pauline passages that contrast life apart from God's love with the new life we have because of the grace of Christ. In Titus 3, for instance, Paul reminds us that Christians were once enslaved

[3] The text-critical and grammatical issues impacting the interpretation of this verse are discussed briefly in Stephen S. Smalley, *1, 2, 3, John*, WBC 51, rev. ed. (Nashville: Thomas Nelson, 2007), 223, 249–50. For a similar point stated more cryptically, see 1 Cor. 8:3.

to sinful passions, living lives characterized by hatred (v. 3). But now that the "goodness and loving kindness[4] of God our Savior" have appeared (v. 4), we are cleansed and renewed by the Holy Spirit (v. 5). In Ephesians 2 we learn that though we "once walked" in the ways of sin, the Devil, and the flesh (vv. 1–3), we are now able to do the "good works" for which we were created (v. 10). This new walk is possible because of the "great love with which [God] loved us" when he lavished his grace on us in Christ (vv. 4–7). The thought is expressed more succinctly when Paul addresses the Roman church as those "loved by God and called to be saints" (Rom. 1:7).[5] God's love transforms us, setting us on a new path of holiness—a starting point that beckons us to further progress on the path.[6]

The Love of God as the Beginning of a Life of Covenant Faithfulness

To find this two-beat rhythm of holiness as a response to God's love in the Old Testament, we might look to Psalm 136:1: "Give thanks to the Lord, for he is good, for his steadfast love endures forever."[7] Repeating the final phrase twenty-five times, the psalm invites us to look at all of biblical history, and even at our daily lives, for evidence of God's faithful love;[8] once we have seen it, the appropriate response is a posture of worship, thanksgiving, and praise. Similarly, in Psalm 26:2–3 David invites the Lord to "test my heart and my mind. For your steadfast love is before my eyes, and I walk in your faithfulness." This is no self-righteous boasting on David's part; rather, it is an indication that the "ideal covenant participant" will pursue holiness on the basis of the steadfast love and faithfulness of God.[9]

The Love of God as the Beginning of a Life of Obedience

The book of Deuteronomy links more explicitly this love-and-response rhythm to the origins of Israel's relationship with God. Moses' words in 10:12–16 particularly highlight the pattern:

---

[4] *Philanthropia*; lit., "love for human beings/humanity."

[5] Paul's use of "saints" in this context points to both definitive sanctification (believers' new status as God's holy people) and progressive sanctification (our calling to grow in holiness); so C. E. B. Cranfield, *A Critical and Exegetical Commentary on the Epistle to the Romans*, ICC, 2 vols. (Edinburgh: T&T Clark, 1975), 1:70. Cf. 2 Thess. 2:13.

[6] Ultimately, of course, this starting point can be traced to God's electing love. See Ps. 78:67–68; Mal. 1:2–3; Rom. 9:13–16, 25; 11:28–29; Eph. 1:3–6; 1 Thess. 1:4.

[7] See also 1 Chron. 16:34, 41; 2 Chron. 5:13; 7:3, 6; 20:21; Ezra 3:11; Pss. 100:4–5; 106:1; 107:1; 118:1, 29; Jer. 33:11.

[8] Note Gen. 32:10, where Jacob refers to "all the deeds of steadfast love" that God has shown him, inviting the reader to see God's love at work throughout the biblical narrative, even where the language of love is not employed.

[9] C. John Collins, note on Psalm 26, in *ESV Study Bible*, ed. Wayne Grudem (Wheaton, IL: Crossway, 2008), 969.

> Now, Israel, what does the LORD your God require of you, but to fear the LORD your God, to walk in all his ways, to love him . . . and to keep the commandments and statutes of the LORD . . . ? [Though he could have chosen any nation,] the LORD set his heart in love on your fathers and chose . . . you above all peoples. . . . Circumcise therefore the foreskin of your heart, and be no longer stubborn.[10]

God's love initiates, and his people respond with loving obedience—a truth intended to renew even hardened hearts. Both the Old and New Testaments point, then, to the same conclusion: progress on the path of holiness begins (and sometimes begins anew) with the faithful love of God for his people.

Our Path: The Love of God and the Shape of the Christian Walk

As we have seen, the Christian walk begins at the place where God's love intersects our lives, calling forth a response of holy dedication to him and his purposes. But what shape should this response take? In other words, if we desire to walk the path of holiness, where are we required—or forbidden—to put our feet? In what follows, we will consider how the love of God determines the shape of the holy walk to which God's people are called.

A Holy Walk Expresses Desire to Abide in the Love of God

To understand the relationship between the love of God and the shape of a holy life, we may begin with Jesus' words in John 15:9–10: "As the Father has loved me, so have I loved you. Abide in my love. If you keep my commandments, you will abide in my love, just as I have kept my Father's commandments and abide in his love." When a person experiences divine love—as Jesus has experienced the Father's love, and as believers have experienced Jesus' love—the result is a desire to experience continually ("abide in") such love. According to Jesus, the road map for abiding in divine love is to be found in the commandments he and his Father have given. Rather than being a burdensome system of rule keeping, the holy life marked out for us by biblical commands is rooted in the love of God, simultaneously *expressing* our love for God (1 John 5:3, "This is the love of God, that we keep his commandments") and *enabling* us to enjoy his love for us.[11]

[10] Cf. Deut. 4:37–40; 7:6–13.

[11] Indeed, the OT envisions the giving of the law as an expression of God's love; see Deut. 33:3 and Ps. 147:11, 19–20.

A Holy Walk Prioritizes Love for God

If divine commands show us how to abide in a relationship of love with God, it comes as no surprise that the "great and first commandment" (Matt. 22:38) involves love for God: "Hear, O Israel: The LORD our God, the LORD is one. You shall love the LORD your God with all your heart and with all your soul and with all your might" (Deut. 6:4–5; cf. Matt. 22:36–38; Mark 12:28–30; Luke 10:25–27). When we have been loved by the one true God, the only fitting response is wholehearted, exclusive commitment to him. Such commitment takes the form of loving obedience to God's commands (Deut. 6:1–3, 6–9; cf. Josh. 22:5), which in turn leads to blessing ("that it may go well with you," Deut. 6:3, 18). Every requirement made of us in Scripture is thus an outworking of our love for God and a means of enjoying his love for us. So essential is this mark of holiness that many Scripture texts identify believers simply as those who love God (Pss. 122:6; 145:20; Rom. 8:28; 1 Cor. 2:9; James 1:12; 2:5; 1 Pet. 1:8), his name (Pss. 5:11; 69:36; 119:132; Isa. 56:6), or the Lord Jesus (1 Cor. 16:22; Eph. 6:24).

A Holy Walk Marries Love for God and Love for Neighbor

When asked to name one great commandment, Jesus also names a second: "You shall love your neighbor as yourself" (Lev. 19:18; Matt. 22:39; Mark 12:31; Luke 10:27; cf. 1 John 4:21). Scripture relates love of neighbor to love of God in the following ways:

- *Love for neighbor mirrors the character of the God we love.* Following Israel's sin with the golden calf, God reveals himself to Moses as "the LORD, the LORD, a God merciful and gracious, slow to anger, and abounding in steadfast love and faithfulness" (Ex. 34:6). Leviticus 19:18 is therefore a call to reflect God's character as we relate to our neighbors: "You shall not take vengeance or bear a grudge . . . , but you shall love your neighbor as yourself. I am the LORD."[12]

- *Concern for our neighbor's welfare is a sign that we love what God loves.* God delights in "steadfast love, justice, and righteousness in the earth" (Jer. 9:23–24). His people are therefore called to "hate evil, and love good, and establish justice in the gate" (Amos 5:15),[13] caring for the vulnerable as God himself does (Deut. 10:18–19). As the Davidic king was called to embody steadfast love, faithfulness, justice, and righteousness (Isa. 16:5; cf.

[12] Note the similar logic of Matt. 5:44–45; Luke 6:35.

[13] Cf. Ps. 97:10; Isa. 61:8; Lam. 3:33–36; Hos. 4:1–2; Mic. 3:1–2; 6:8; Zech. 8:16–19; Rom. 12:9.

Ps. 45:6–7; Heb. 1:8–9), how much more are those who serve the kingdom inaugurated by Jesus, David's greater son![14]

- *Love for neighbor finds its motive and its standard in God's love for us.* Leviticus 19:34 commands Israel to love the stranger in her midst "as yourself, for you were strangers in the land of Egypt: I am the Lord your God." Appealing to a demonstration of redeeming love even more decisive than the exodus, Jesus says, "A new commandment I give to you, that you love one another: just as I have loved you, you also are to love one another" (John 13:34; cf. 15:12–13).[15] When we love as we have been loved, we learn to set aside our own freedoms in order to build up weaker brothers and sisters (Rom. 14:1–21; 1 Cor. 8:1–11:1).

As should be clear, God's love for us also prohibits mistreatment of our neighbors. First John 3:16–18 makes the point concisely: because Jesus has loved us by laying down his life for us, we may not close our hearts to a brother in need, nor may we love merely in "word or talk." God's love sets us apart for him, and his path of holiness will never carry us toward loveless deeds.

A Holy Walk Forbids Love for Idols

Also out of bounds for those who know the love of God is idolatry in any of its forms. If there is only one God who has promised his steadfast love to our fathers—and fulfilled that promise through the work of his Son—then there is only one who deserves our love in return. Jesus presupposes this truth when he warns against the idol of wealth: "No one can serve two masters, for either he will hate the one and love the other, or he will be devoted to the one and despise the other. You cannot serve God and money" (Matt. 6:24; cf. Luke 16:13). In addition to love of money (1 Tim. 3:3; 6:10; 2 Tim. 3:2; Heb. 13:5), the New Testament identifies a host of rival masters who vie for our love; we list them here from most generic/abstract to most specific/concrete:

- the world (2 Tim. 4:10; 1 John 2:15)
- falsehood (Rev. 22:15; cf. 2 Thess. 2:10)
- one's own life/self (John 12:25; 2 Tim. 3:2; Rev. 12:11)[16]

[14] The Scripture texts cited here, and their contexts, indicate that holy concern for our neighbor's good has corporate as well as individual dimensions.

[15] By "one another," Jesus refers specifically to fellow believers; however, since life within the redeemed community is intended as a microcosm of God's purpose in creation as a whole, calls to love the "household of faith" are closely connected to our duty to "do good to everyone" (Gal. 6:10).

[16] Prov. 19:8—"Whoever gets sense loves his own soul"—makes it clear that it is appropriate to love oneself by walking in paths of wisdom God has promised to bless; an idolatrous love of self arises when we seek blessedness apart from God. For a summary of the debate concerning the propriety of self-love from Augustine

- "what is exalted among men" (Luke 16:15)
- pleasure (2 Tim. 3:4)
- family members (Matt. 10:37–38)
- public recognition of status/praise (Matt. 23:6–7; Luke 11:43; 20:46; John 12:43)
- ill-gotten gain (2 Pet. 2:15).

Whatever rival love threatens to divide our hearts, holiness demands that we resist it with all our might; otherwise, says Jesus, we are hating and despising God. Expressed in Old Testament terms, when we trust in human resources or in gods of human invention, we are denying that God's "steadfast love" is worthy of our trust (Pss. 33:16–18; 52:7–8; 115:1–11; 147:10–11).[17]

A Holy Walk Requires Passionate Delight in God

The heart that is growing is holiness will understand the relational reality behind the preceding point: when we set our affections on an idol, we are saying that God is just as likely to disappoint and abandon us as any other faithless lover.[18] In truth, our God is the only one who has made himself "one flesh" with us, cherishing us as his own body (Eph. 5:29–32). Only his love pursues us when we go astray.[19] Three implications follow regarding the content of holy living:

- *A holy life will be characterized by burning passion for God's infinite perfections.* We will never be able to resist sin if we see its fruits as gifts from a rival more desirable than God. Meditating on and praising God's perfections (Ex. 15:11; Pss. 16:5–11; 84:2, 10), rehearsing his faithfulness (Pss. 35:9–10; 71:19; 136), fixing our eyes on Jesus (Heb. 12:2)—these are ways to increase our soul's thirst for the one whose "steadfast love is better than life" (Ps. 63:1–4).

- *A holy life will be characterized by delight in obeying God's will.* "Oh how I love your law! It is my meditation all the day!" (Ps. 119:97). True holiness

to modern times, see Stephen G. Post, *Christian Love and Self-Denial: An Historical and Normative Study of Jonathan Edwards, Samuel Hopkins, and American Theological Ethics* (Lanham, MD: University Press of America, 1987).

[17] As this conclusion suggests, there is a close link between love for God and faith/trust in God; however, it is a mistake to follow Anders Nygren, *Agape and Eros*, trans. Philip S. Watson (London: SPCK, 1957), who argues that faith replaces love for God in the NT.

[18] See esp. Jer. 2:2–5; Ezek. 16:8–43.

[19] The intensity of sin, and of God's faithful love, is often expressed in strong language: God speaks as though he has abandoned or deserted his people, only to remember his everlasting love (Isa. 54:7–10; Jer. 11:14–17; 12:7; 16:5; 31:1–3; Lam. 3:26–33; Hos. 9:15; 14:4), tenderly wooing them back to himself (Hos. 2:14–23). Even in exile Israel remains "precious" to God (Isa. 43:4), his "darling child" (Jer. 31:20).

is never a matter of halfhearted or begrudging fulfillment of God's commands. The heart that burns with passion for God will not only obey him but delight to do so.

- *A holy life will be characterized by repentance and confession.* Even those who delight in God and his law will not obey perfectly. Therefore, holiness requires that we be ready to repent of and confess sin. Prayers connected with Israel's return from exile demonstrate the principle: Israel is drawn to repentance by God's "steadfast love" (Ezra 9:9; Neh. 9:32; Dan. 9:3); in turn, God's readiness to forgive elicits renewed commitment to "lov[ing] him and keep[ing] his commandments" (Dan. 9:4; cf. Ezra 10:3; Neh. 10:29).

The love of God provides key signposts that shape the path of holiness. Since we desire to abide in the love he has shown us, we must obey his commandments, beginning with wholehearted love for him and radical love for our neighbors. Since such obedience entails resisting all competing loves, it requires us to cultivate passion for God.[20] But as we consider passion for God and abiding in his love, it is clear that we are dealing not simply with the question of *where* God's holy people should walk, but *why* we should want to walk there and *how* we will find the strength to do so. Our next section examines these questions in further detail.

Our Source of Power: The Love of God and Progress in the Christian Walk

Thus far we have seen biblical evidence for two major conclusions: first, the love of God initiates the Christian walk of holiness, as God's love for us produces in us holy love for him; second, the love of God defines the path of holiness, as we abide in his love by obeying his commandments. Here our focus shifts to a new question: once we are put on this path, and its shape is marked out for us, how does the love of God motivate, empower, and sustain our progress in holiness? By way of response, we now consider nine scriptural themes that link the love of God to the believer's power for pursuing sanctification.

The Love of God Gives Power for Progress in Holiness

Several psalms depict God's love for his people as the transforming power that motivates and enables our ongoing commitment to holiness. Psalm

[20] So Peter Kreeft, *Knowing the Truth of God's Love: The One Thing We Can't Live Without*, Knowing the Truth (Ann Arbor, MI: Servant, 1988), 152: "[God] doesn't want merely the fruits and effect of love but our love itself, our hearts. He wants *us*. The lover . . . wants the beloved herself."

106 teaches this lesson through contrast: the heart that praises God for his "steadfast love" will also consider it a joy to "observe justice" and "do righteousness at all times" (vv. 1–3); but those who forget the "abundance of [his] steadfast love," especially as demonstrated in the exodus from Egypt, commit "iniquity" and "wickedness" (vv. 6–7).[21] According to Psalm 5:4–8, the "abundance of [God's] steadfast love" leads us to worship him,[22] increasing both our hatred of sin ("You are not a God who delights in wickedness") and desire for faithful living ("Lead me, O Lord, in your righteousness"). Proper—that is, covenantal, and not merely cognitive—remembrance of divine love severs the root of rebellion and sin by strengthening our devotion to God. If we delight to declare the steadfast love and faithfulness of the God in whom there is no unrighteousness (Ps. 92:2, 15), we will naturally long to be found among the righteous rather than the wicked (vv. 6–14).

We see a similar pattern in Psalm 107. Following an exhortation to "give thanks to the Lord, for he is good, for his steadfast love endures forever" (v. 1), the psalm recounts various ways in which God has redeemed the people of Judah from the afflictions associated with the Babylonian exile. This narrative, punctuated by a fourfold admonition to "thank the Lord for his steadfast love" (vv. 8, 15, 21, 31), builds to a concluding exhortation: "The upright see it [i.e., God's redemption] and are glad, and all wickedness shuts its mouth. Whoever is wise, let him attend to these things; let them consider the steadfast love of the Lord" (vv. 42–43). When the story of God's redeeming love is rehearsed, three effects follow: the joy of the upright is increased, the power of wickedness is diminished, and the wise—people who "genuinely seek to be skillful in godly living"[23]—are spurred on in their pursuit of godliness.

The Love of Christ Gives Power for Progress in Holiness

Given what we have learned from the Psalms, it should come as no surprise that Paul's epistles depict the love of God the Son as the motivating power for holy living.[24] We may think, for instance, of Galatians 2:20: "It is no longer I who live, but Christ who lives in me. And the life I now live in the flesh I live by faith in the Son of God, who loved me and gave himself for me."[25] When we cherish Christ's self-sacrificing love for us, our faith is

---

[21] Cf. Isa. 63:7–10.

[22] See Pss. 100:4–5 (calling Israel to worship) and 117 (calling all nations to worship).

[23] Collins, note on Ps. 107:43, in *ESV Study Bible*, 1081.

[24] The one scriptural reference to the "love of the Spirit" (Rom. 15:30) likely has in view not the love of God the Holy Spirit for his people, but believers' Spirit-prompted love for one another.

[25] Though the context of the verse focuses on justification, Paul's use of the present tense "live/lives" points to one's ongoing manner of life as well; cf. 2:14, 19; 5:25.

strengthened—and along with it, our power to love (Gal. 5:6, "faith working through love") and thus fulfill the whole of God's law (vv. 13–14). We find similar language and concepts at 2 Corinthians 5:14–15, where Paul presents his apostolic demeanor as a paradigm for the life of all Christians: "The love of Christ controls us, because we have concluded this: that one has died for all, . . . that those who live might no longer live for themselves but for him who for their sake died and was raised." Our lives will serve Christ's purposes and not our own, as the gospel narrative of his dying-and-rising love for us[26] exercises control over our thoughts and actions. This is why Paul, wanting the Ephesian church to come to complete spiritual maturity, prays that they, along with "all the saints," might come to a fuller knowledge of the "love of Christ that surpasses knowledge" (Eph. 3:18–19). When we know the love of Christ, grasping experientially its significance for who we are and who we are meant to be, we find strength to live for him.

The Love of God Gives Power for Holiness in Everyday Relationships

With this foundation in place, the New Testament often appeals to the love of Christ, or the love of God shown in Christ, as the basis for very specific expressions of holiness. Titus 2:8–3:11, for example, indicates that because the "grace of God" (2:11)—also described as the "goodness and loving kindness of God our Savior" (3:4)—has "appeared" in Christ, God's people are to devote themselves to good works of every kind. But the text moves beyond this general truth into the concrete realities of our everyday relationships: we are to be respectful of authority, gentle, and courteous (3:1–2); we must "speak evil of no one," avoid quarreling, and eschew conduct that divides the church (3:2, 9–11). Lest we should miss the point, it is underscored throughout the New Testament:

- Jesus calls his followers to love one another as he has loved us and laid down his life for us (John 13:34; 15:12–13).

- John tells us that we "ought to lay down our lives for the brothers," especially in such mundane matters as sharing our material possessions, because Jesus, embodying the very definition of love, "laid down his life for us" (1 John 3:16–17).

- According to Paul, relationships among God's people should be characterized by kindness, gentleness, mutual forbearance, forgiveness, and self-

[26] When Paul speaks of the "love of Christ" elsewhere, the genitive clearly is subjective: Rom. 8:35; Eph. 3:19.

> sacrificial love—all because we enjoy the love of God the Father through the work of God the Son (Eph. 4:32–5:2, 25–33; Col 3:12–14), who "loved us and gave himself up for us" (Eph. 5:2, 25).

In none of these texts are we told of the love of God/Christ simply as a reminder of our duty; rather, in each case, the story of God's saving love in Christ is recounted because it has power to strengthen us for costly, practical holiness in the warp and woof of daily life.

The Love of God Expressed in Forgiveness Fuels a Radical Response of Love

Implied in much of what has been said to this point is a key biblical truth—namely, that the joy resulting from forgiveness of sin is a powerful motive for holy living. In Psalm 51, for instance, after appealing to God for forgiveness "according to your steadfast love" (v. 1), David prays, "Restore to me the joy of your salvation, and uphold me with a willing spirit.[27] Then I will teach transgressors your ways, and sinners will return to you" (vv. 12–13). Forgiveness leads to renewed joy, which prompts such zeal for God's holy ways that we would seek to help others who have turned from them.[28] We may compare Exodus 34:6–7, where—just after Israel's sin with the golden calf—God reveals himself to Moses as a "God merciful and gracious, slow to anger, and abounding in steadfast love and faithfulness, keeping steadfast love for thousands, forgiving iniquity and transgression and sin." Though he will not clear the guilty (i.e., those who do not seek refuge in his mercy) and will punish sin "to the third and fourth generation" (v. 7), God's self-revelation emphasizes his disposition to forgive.[29] That this forgiveness should motivate repentance and renewed faithfulness is made clear by the covenant renewal in verses 10–28, which includes a reissuing of the Ten Commandments.[30] Jonah's allusion to Exodus 34:6–7 (Jonah 4:1–2) shows that he knew, but resented, this truth: God's love, revealed in his readiness to forgive sin, powerfully draws sinners to return to the way of faithfulness.[31]

---

[27] I.e., "May your s/Spirit sustain me so that my spirit is able to continue in its restored condition." See Marvin E. Tate, *Psalms 51–100*, WBC 20 (Dallas: Word, 1990), 25.

[28] Cf. Ps. 25:6–10.

[29] So D. A. Baer and R. P. Gordon, "*chesed*," *NIDOTTE*, ed. Willem A. VanGemeren (Grand Rapids, MI: Zondervan, 1997), 2:214: "Wrath is a true word, a right word, sometimes an inevitable word. . . . But God would not have it be his last word. That honor is reserved for his unfailing love."

[30] Cf. Neh. 9:17–18; Joel 2:12–13.

[31] For further celebrations of God's forgiving love, see Pss. 103:1–13; 130:7–8; Isa. 38:17; Mic. 7:18–20. Note that in Ps. 103:17–18, those who experience such love are said to fear God, keep his covenant, and obey his commandments.

This truth becomes most explicit in Luke 7:36–50, where Jesus commends a woman who has just anointed his feet not only with perfume, but with her tears. Contrasting the extravagant act of this "sinner" (vv. 37, 39) with the lack of hospitality shown by his host, Simon the Pharisee, Jesus declares, "Therefore I tell you, her sins, which are many, are forgiven—for she loved much. But he who is forgiven little, loves little" (v. 47). The accompanying parable of the moneylender (vv. 41–43) demonstrates that the woman's great love for Jesus is a consequence, not the cause, of her forgiveness. Once again we see a key principle for progress in the Christian life: forgiveness fuels our love for God and for Jesus, leading us to radical acts of repentance and devotion.[32]

The Love of God Expressed in Discipline Keeps Us on the Path of Holiness

Like forgiveness, discipline is an expression of God's love that is essential to sustaining a holy life: "My son, do not regard lightly the discipline of the Lord. . . . For the Lord disciplines the one he loves, and chastises every son whom he receives" (Heb. 12:5–6, citing Prov. 3:11–12 LXX). This loving discipline takes two forms. In some cases, God trains us in righteousness by allowing us to endure trials that test our faith (Heb. 12:4, 10–11). Knowing that he uses even such difficulties for our good strengthens us to "strive for . . . holiness" (vv. 12–14). In other cases, discipline is a response to sin on our part, as Jesus reminds the lukewarm church at Laodicea: "Those whom I love, I reprove and discipline, so be zealous and repent" (Rev. 3:19). Similar are Jeremiah's words to Israel after her sin has led to the destruction of Jerusalem: "The steadfast love of the Lord never ceases. . . . Though he cause grief, he will have compassion according to the abundance of his steadfast love" (Lam. 3:22, 32).[33] As divine love can motivate us to pursue the path of holiness, it can also train us to remain on—or call us to return to—that path.

The Love of God Sustains Holiness in Times of Persecution

As our discussion of discipline reminds us, we live in a world where trials and pressures hinder our progress on the path of holiness; as Paul says to Timothy, "all who desire to live a godly life in Christ Jesus will be persecuted" (2 Tim. 3:12). Thankfully, Scripture frequently reminds us that the love of God is our hope and strength in times of persecution. Psalm 119:87–88 expresses the pattern concisely: "They have almost made an

[32] A similar combination of themes is found in Jesus' restoration of Peter (John 21:15–19).

[33] Cf. Ps. 119:75–76; Zeph. 3:16–17.

end of me on earth, but I have not forsaken your precepts. In your steadfast love give me life [or, 'revive me'], that I may keep the testimonies of your mouth." Similar in theme, but more desperate in tone, is the following plea: "Answer me quickly, O LORD! My spirit fails! . . . Let me hear in the morning of your steadfast love, for in you I trust. Make me know the way I should go, for to you I lift up my soul. . . . Teach me to do your will, for you are my God!" (Ps. 143:7–8, 10). When wicked men pressure us to abandon God's ways, we trust his love to renew our strength, enabling us to bear the fruit of holiness even in the withering heat of persecution.[34]

As we might expect, this pattern continues in the New Testament. For instance, knowing that the believers at Thessalonica have endured much affliction (1 Thess. 1:6), Paul encourages them in their "work of faith and labor of love and steadfastness of hope" by reminding them that they are "loved by God" and chosen by him (vv. 3–4). In the midst of a second wave of persecution, the apostle develops the thought further: though many in our world refuse to "love the truth" and instead take "pleasure in unrighteousness" (2 Thess. 2:10, 12), the Thessalonians are "beloved by the Lord," chosen by God for salvation "through sanctification by the Spirit and belief in the truth" (v. 13); this status as God's beloved, chosen, sanctified people strengthens the church to "stand firm" (v. 15). Thus Paul concludes this section with a prayer: "May our Lord Jesus Christ himself, and God our Father, who loved us and gave us eternal comfort and good hope through grace, comfort your hearts and establish them in every good work and word" (2:16–17; cf. 3:5). The world is hostile to truth, to faith, and to holiness. But God has loved us, and this truth strengthens us to persevere in Spirit-empowered holiness. Even a church that has "but little power" finds new strength when it learns that Christ will one day say, in the hearing of its persecutors, "I have loved you" (Rev. 3:8–9; cf. 1:5).

The Love of God Multiplies Holiness in Times of Persecution

In some psalms, this pattern becomes more complex, as God's loving deliverance from persecution is not only anticipated but also remembered. In Psalm 31, for example, even as many plot to take David's life (v. 13), he recalls past experiences of God's steadfast love; these leave him not only hating idolatry (vv. 6–8) and pride (vv. 18, 23), but also encouraging others to devote themselves to God: "Love the LORD, all you his saints! The LORD preserves the faithful" (v. 23). Likewise, in Psalm 40, David speaks

[34] For hope in God's steadfast love linked (sometimes implicitly) with commitment to obey him, see also Pss. 6:4, 8; 17:3–7; 31:16–18; 36:10–12; 44:17–21, 26; 86:5, 11, 13, 15; 119:124, 149–151, 159.

in the "great congregation" of the "steadfast love and . . . faithfulness" God has shown him in the past (vv. 9–10).[35] As part of his testimony, David declares, "I delight to do your will, O my God; your law is within my heart" (v. 8). As the psalm closes, David expresses both confidence that God's steadfast love will deliver him from present affliction (vv. 11–15) and hope that many others will seek the Lord and "love [his] salvation" (v. 16).[36] When God saves us in his steadfast love, our commitment to holy obedience is not only strengthened but multiplied, as our testimony to his love enables others to "be strong" and "take courage" (Ps. 31:24).

The Love of God Promised to a Holy People Motivates a Life of Loving Obedience

Among the many means by which Scripture motivates holiness is the promise that God blesses his people. Expressions of this promise sometimes make explicit reference to the love of God, according to one of the four patterns summarized here:

- *Love as a descriptor of the blessing.* In some Scripture texts, God promises his love to those who are holy and righteous. Thus Solomon praises God as one who "keep[s] covenant and show[s] steadfast love to your servants who walk before you with all their heart" (2 Chron. 6:14), and Hosea calls Israel to "sow for yourselves righteousness; reap steadfast love" (Hos. 10:12).

- *Love as a descriptor of the blessed.* Here, God promises blessing on those who love him. In Psalm 145:20 ("The Lord preserves all who love him, but all the wicked he will destroy"), love for God represents a broader commitment to holiness. At Psalm 91:14 ("Because he [the Israelite facing distress] holds fast to me in love, I will deliver him"), clinging to God in love refers to knowing God and calling on him for deliverance/salvation.

- *Love as a descriptor of the blessing and the blessed.* The two previous patterns are combined in the second commandment, where God reveals himself as one who "show[s] steadfast love to thousands of those who love me and keep my commandments" (Ex. 20:6; Deut. 5:10; cf. Deut. 7:9). Nehemiah 1:5 cites the same formula almost verbatim in the context of a prayer of repentance.

- *Love as a condition for blessing.* A final pattern, characteristic of the book of Deuteronomy, emphasizes more strongly that love for God is a condi-

[35] For other expressions of joy in response to God's saving love, see Pss. 48:4–9; 66:18–20; 98:1–6; 106:44–46; 118:1–5. Of special grammatical interest is Ps. 116:1, where the Hebrew supplies no object for the verb "love"; literally, the verse reads, "I love the Lord, because he has heard my voice and my pleas for mercy."
[36] Note that Psalm 70 is a near-verbatim repetition of Ps. 40:13–17.

> tion for receiving his promised blessings. Deuteronomy 30:16 is representative: "If you obey the commandments of the Lord your God . . . by loving the Lord your God, by walking in his ways, and by keeping his commandments . . . , then you shall live and multiply, and the Lord your God will bless you in the land."[37]

In none of these instances does Scripture intend to motivate holiness through a theology of merit, as though our love for God could obligate him to love us.[38] Phrases such as "those who love me" and "the righteous" describe not the cause of God's favor but the character of those whose commitment to God is sincere.[39] In addition, Deuteronomy 30:6 demonstrates that our capacity for loving God, and thus for receiving his promised blessings, is itself a gift of God's grace: "The Lord your God will circumcise your heart and the heart of your offspring, so that you will love the Lord your God with all your heart and with all your soul, that you may live."[40] Yet the biblical framework of grace is not intended to diminish the urgent necessity of holy living; if God showers his blessings, including his steadfast love, on the righteous, it would be insane to live as though we were at home among the wicked. There is a "holiness without which no one will see the Lord" (Heb. 12:14), and the patterns cited here provide powerful incentive to pursue it.

The Love of God Expressed in Providence Fuels a Life of Reverent Obedience

A final source of strength for walking the path of holiness is wonder at the love of God expressed in his providential care for the world he has made. According to Psalm 33:5, our God "loves righteousness and justice; the earth is full of the steadfast love of the Lord." When we marvel at our Father's love in creation, gratitude moves us to love what he loves—and thus to be "righteous" and "upright" ourselves (Ps. 33:1). Psalm 119:64 echoes the thought: "The earth, O Lord, is full of your steadfast love; teach me your statutes!" In Psalm 147 the signs of God's "steadfast love" that should lead us to "fear him" (v. 11) and uphold his "statutes and rules" (v. 19) in-

[37] For the same pattern, see Deut. 7:12–13; 11:13–14, 22–23; 19:8–9; 30:19–20.

[38] Note that the promises cited above (a) occur in the context of repentance/need for forgiveness (2 Chron. 6:24–27, 36; Neh. 1:5; Hos. 10:12), (b) follow Israel's gracious redemption from slavery in Egypt (Ex. 20:6; Deut. 5:10), or (c) are made to those who are weak and needy (Psalm 91; 145).

[39] Contra J. G. McConville, *Deuteronomy*, ApOTC 5 (Downers Grove, IL: InterVarsity, 2002), 127: "Those who enjoy God's 'faithful love' do so because of their own righteousness."

[40] Cf. Deut. 7:7–9: it is not because of Israel's greatness that God has "set his love" on them, but simply because "the Lord loves [them] and is keeping the oath" he made with their forefathers; it is in this light that Israel is called to know that God "keeps covenant and steadfast love with those who love him."

clude not only his mercy to the humble and brokenhearted, but also his rule over the stars and the weather, and his gifts of food to beasts, birds, and his people.[41] If we wish to persevere in all that holiness demands, we must tune our hearts to discern the love of our heavenly Father in simple things such as daily bread, lilies, and sparrows (Matt. 6:26–30; 10:29–31).

Our Destination: The Love of God and the Goal of the Christian Walk

Sometimes we walk for the sheer pleasure of it, with no particular destination in mind. But the Christian walk, which follows the path of holiness on which God has set us, and along which he strengthens us, is aimed at a particular end point. We focus here on three New Testament texts that motivate our present pursuit of holiness by giving us glimpses of this destination—a glorious, unending future in which we will experience the fullness of the love of God.

Believers Are Empowered by God's Love in Christ Jesus

In the latter half of Romans 8, in order to sustain us in the "sufferings of this present time," Paul points us to the "glory that is to be revealed to us" (Rom. 8:18)—a glory that includes resurrected bodies (vv. 11, 30) fit for life in a renewed creation (v. 21) as rightful heirs of "all things" (v. 32; cf. v. 17). Yet the climactic promise of the chapter concerns not these blessings but the love that has permanently secured them: no matter what afflictions face us, nothing in this world or the next will ever be able to "separate us from the love of God in Christ Jesus our Lord" (vv. 35–39).

The context suggests that the love that makes us "more than conquerors" (v. 37) also strengthens us for our ongoing battle against sin: as our loving Father adopts us as his "sons" (v. 15) and conforms us to the "image of his Son" (v. 29), he also gives us power through his Spirit to put to death our sinful deeds (v. 13). Put simply, while the most glorious expressions of the "love of God in Christ Jesus" will be revealed only in the future, this love gives us the power and courage to pursue holiness in the present.

Believers Pursue Radical Purity as God's Beloved Children

First John 3:1–3 similarly links the love of God, the promise of future glory, and the believer's pursuit of holiness in the present. God has lav-

[41] Cf. Job 37:13; Pss. 36:5–9; 127:2; 145:8–9, 14–16. For the gift of life itself as an expression of God's steadfast love, see Job 10:11–12.

ished his love on us, so that we not only are called but actually *are* his children (3:1). Yet we will reach full maturity only when Jesus returns and, seeing him "as he is," we are made "like him" (v. 2). Until then, strengthened by this hope, we commit ourselves to Christlike living, purifying ourselves "as he is pure" (v. 3).[42] We should note at this point that while both John and Paul appeal to the love of God and our future experience of its fullness, neither does so in the interest of a shallow, pie-in-the-sky piety. Instead, both apostles have in mind a radical obedience: Paul speaks of a continual putting to death[43] of sinful deeds, and John sets forth a standard of Christlike purity that leaves no room for compromise (note v. 5, "in him there is no sin"). It is precisely because the pursuit of holiness demands so much that we need the hope of God's love to strengthen us.

Believers Are Promised the Privilege of Entering into God's Love for God

In John 14 and 15, obedience is again connected to the ultimate blessedness of God's people. Here, however, the promise is not simply that believers will experience the fullness of God's love for us, but that we will participate in the love shared between God the Father and God the Son. Three themes point to this conclusion:

- First, Jesus teaches that he obeys his Father's commands "so that the world may know that I love the Father" (14:31; cf. 15:10). Thus when we obey Jesus out of love for him (14:15, 21, 23–24; 15:14), we are mirroring his own love for his heavenly Father.

- Second, Jesus makes the astounding promise that "if anyone loves me, he will keep my word, and my Father will love him, and we will come to him and make our home with him" (14:23; cf. 14:21; 15:10; 16:26–27). While believers begin to enjoy this promise in the present (see 14:17), it also points to a future reality—an eternity in our "Father's house" (14:2–3). Our desire to obey is sharpened by the hope that we can be, both now and for ever, "at home" in the loving presence of the Father and the Son.

- Third, Jesus desires for his followers to be united to him and to his Father, being loved by the Father just as Jesus has been loved by the Father from eternity past (John 17:20–26). Jesus therefore promises that obedience leads to abiding not just in his love for us, but in the Father's love for him:

[42] Cf. Ps. 11:7: "The LORD is righteous; he loves righteous deeds: the upright shall behold his face."
[43] Note the present imperative *thanatoute* in Rom. 8:13.

> "As the Father has loved me, so have I loved you. Abide in my love. If you keep my commandments, you will abide in my love" (15:9–10).

To be sure, there is mystery here beyond our power to comprehend. And yet the logic is simple: desire to one day love the Father as the Son does,[44] and to experience the Father's love as the Son does,[45] is a compelling motive for pursuing holy obedience in the present. And how could it be otherwise? For to be drawn into the eternal reality of God's love for God is infinite kindness multiplied by infinite joy.

Conclusion: Walking in Holiness, Walking in the Love of God

The testimony of Scripture is clear: if we want to walk in the way of holiness, the love of God is indispensable to our progress. God's love for his people is the foundation for all holy living and our love for him its most essential mark. In turn, to remain on the path of holy obedience, we need the power of God's love in the present and the hope of its fullness in the future. For Christians who want their growth in holiness to be informed by these biblical truths, five implications follow:

1) To Walk in Holiness, We Must Avoid Basic Mistakes

Scripture holds together truths that God's people are prone to separate. Holiness is motivated by the grace of God's love for us *and* requires the work of loving him by obeying his commands; God's love is freely offered in forgiveness *and* is a blessing promised on condition of obedience; loving him is a matter of the heart *and* the will.[46] Though the relationship between the love of God and growth in holiness has a fundamental rhythm ("We love because he first loved us" (1 John 4:19), it is a mistake to allow one aspect of biblical truth to drown out others. Likewise, it is a mistake to conceive of love for God in a way that divorces passion for him from obedience to him.

2) To Walk in Holiness, We Must Combat Grave Dangers

The steadfast love of God should thrill us as "better than life" (Ps. 63:3). But as the case of Jonah reminds us, it is possible for God's love to be-

[44] Though only John 14:31 says explicitly that Jesus loves his Father, the concept is present on nearly every page of the Gospels. See C. D. "Jimmy" Agan III, *The Imitation of Christ in the Gospel of Luke: Growing in Christlike Love for God and Neighbor* (Phillipsburg, NJ: P&R, 2014), esp. chap. 5.

[45] See Matt. 3:17; 12:18 (citing Isa. 42:1); 17:5; Mark 1:11; 9:7; 12:6; Luke 3:22; 20:13; John 3:35; 5:20; 10:17; 17:23–24, 26; Col. 1:13; 2 Pet. 1:17. These texts are to be understood in light of various OT references to God's love for David and David's seed; see 2 Sam. 12:24; 22:51; 1 Chron. 17:13; 2 Chron. 1:8; 6:42; Neh. 13:26; Pss. 18:50; 21:7; 61:7; 89:24, 28, 33, 49; Isa. 55:3.

[46] In classical terms, love for God requires both *complacentia* (satisfaction) and *benevolentia* (good will); see David Clyde Jones, *Biblical Christian Ethics* (Grand Rapids, MI: Baker, 1994), 44–48.

come nothing more than a sterile fact that we recite and resent (Jonah 4:2). Jesus similarly warns that in the last days, as "lawlessness" increases, "the love of many will grow cold" (Matt. 24:12).[47] In a hostile world, surrounded with temptations to idolatry and given to hardness of heart, we can sustain a holy life only through passionate love for God and appreciation of his love for us.

3) To Walk in Holiness, We Must Cultivate Joyful Dependence

To combat danger, we must cultivate passion—but how? Jesus teaches that where many sins are forgiven, much love results (Luke 7:40–47); to state the principle more broadly, divine love is best appreciated by those who need it most. Passionate love for God will therefore flourish best when we joyfully embrace our utter dependence on his love—whether as sinners in need of forgiveness or as creatures in need of daily bread. Let us then "keep [our]selves in the love of God" (Jude 21), employing every means possible to discover in all of Scripture, and in all of life, the ever-enduring, earth-filling, steadfast love of the Lord!

4) To Walk in Holiness, We Must Recapture a Biblical Vision

Rather than softening the demands of holiness, emphasis on the love of God intensifies them: to properly honor God's love for us, we must love him, and him alone, with all that we are (Deut. 6:5), and we must be ready to serve sacrificially not only neighbors but even enemies (Rom. 5:8). Nor, if we truly love what God loves, can we be satisfied with a privatized piety, for we are called to delight, as he does, in "practic[ing] steadfast love, justice, and righteousness" in all the earth (Jer. 9:24). Simply put, God's vision for the world, and for the role of his holy people in it, is too spectacular to be achieved in response to anything less than his love.

5) To Walk in Holiness, We Must Be Recaptured by a Powerful Story

Thankfully, the love of God not only defines the demands of holiness but provides us with strength to pursue it. Therefore God's vision for the world, and for his people, also includes frequent retelling of the story of his powerful love. It is powerful enough to awaken the dead: "God . . . because of the great love with which he loved us, even when we were dead

---

[47] In view is love for Christ and the gospel; G. K. Beale, *The Book of Revelation: A Commentary on the Greek Text*, NIGTC (Grand Rapids, MI: Eerdmans, 1999), 230–31. Cf. Rev. 2:4 with Hos. 6:4.

in our trespasses, made us alive together with Christ" (Eph. 2:4–5); powerful enough to save the world: "God so loved the world, that he gave his only Son" (John 3:16); powerful enough, even, to change the way we live: "I live by faith in the Son of God, who loved me and gave himself for me" (Gal. 2:20).[48]

[48] Can sanctification really be accomplished by storytelling? Only if (a) the story is heard in faith and (b) the story itself is a powerful speech-act by which God accomplishes the transformation of lives; see Kevin J. Vanhoozer, "God's Mighty Speech-Acts: The Doctrine of Scripture Today," in *A Pathway into the Holy Scripture*, ed. P. E. Satterthwaite and D. F. Wright (Grand Rapids, MI: Eerdmans, 1994).

10

HOW DOES GOD'S LOVE INSPIRE SOCIAL JUSTICE?

MARIAM J. KAMELL

What does it mean that God is just? This question was posed to me two times in one month by two vastly different people. One was a student from El Salvador, seeking answers regarding how to understand God and the world he found himself in. The other was a professor from Germany who already had an answer and was simply curious about what mine would be. To the student, raised in a world of liberation theology and yet living in Canada, the justice of a God who simply overturns the order of things was coming into question, and yet some overturning did seem needed. To the professor, justice was an academic or judicial issue—in a court of law, neither the wealthy nor the poor should have the advantage. Justice is meted out with impartiality. For the one for whom injustice had been part of his entire life, the question of God's justice was of deep personal concern. For the scholar it was an intense issue, but one that could be discussed dispassionately.[1]

What does it mean that God is just, and how does this relate to the situation of the world's poorest and most vulnerable? And what does it mean for those who claim to be his people? The phenomenon of a social-justice gospel is sweeping evangelical Christianity, with conferences, books, courses, and culture shapers all providing answers to what Christian social justice is and what each person's responsibility in it is. Social

[1] To the objection that I may be too easily charged with coming from a position of privilege, I find Wolterstorff's challenge encouraging: "My response is that to think about justice from the standpoint of university professor, who is neither himself systematically wronged nor empathetically identified with those who are, is not to think about justice from *no* standpoint; it is to think about justice from *that* standpoint," in Nicholas Wolterstorff, *Journey toward Justice* (Grand Rapids, MI: Baker Academic, 2013), 19.

justice provides a common interest across diverse groups of Christianity, but competing definitions of justice create conflicting goals. For some, justice is distributive, or redistributive, making sure everyone has the same—or appropriate—amount (at least to start). For others, justice is fair results, granting to each person what they've earned for the work they've done.[2] For some, justice is equal access to resources and opportunities, regardless of any other considerations, while others think that questions of morality are on par with questions of opportunity—but who determines what is moral remains contested.[3] Likewise, debate rages whether justice must be enacted at the social/structural level or at the individual and spiritual level.[4] *Social justice* is a slippery term, and often the starting point is people's background and experience.

And yet the Bible has an immense amount to say about justice, about justice as the outflow of God's love for his broken creation, and that God's people *must* work for justice here on earth because we have experienced his grace. We might consider the story told in the Bible as the story of God's working for justice in the world he loves, particularly for the oppressed. The world God initially created was one in which justice would protect and shape the culture, where relationships would be *right* and people and all of creation could flourish. This would be partly because of the structure God put into his creation, a well-ordered place itself the temple of God.[5] Even more than that, however, the daily walk with God in the garden, the close relationship with God created by and nurtured within a daily walk with God, created the space within which rightness could flourish, where the guardians would be shaped to be the image bearers of their very God and so treat each other and his creation the way he would want.[6] In Israel, Christopher Wright argues, "Justice was no abstract concept or philosophical definition. Justice was essentially theo-

[2] See the discussion in Kim Hawtrey, "Economic Justice: A Twin Axiom Framework," *RTR* 50 (1991): 98–105; also in Ondrej Hron, *The Mirage Shall Become a Pool: A New Testament Theology of Social Justice and Charity* (Eugene, OR: Pickwick, 2012), 17–23.

[3] See here Kim Hawtrey, "Evangelicals and Economics," *Association of Christian Economists Journal* 2 (1986): 47–60, such as where she calls "freedom" a secondary yet highly contentious category in ethics (54).

[4] See, e.g., the discussion in Gustavo Gutiérrez, *A Theology of Liberation*, 15th anniversary ed. (Maryknoll, NY: Orbis, 1988), 39–46.

[5] Cf. Iain Provan, *Seriously Dangerous Religion* (Waco, TX: Baylor University Press, 2014), 32–46. He writes that in Gen. 1:1–2:4, "the cosmos is presented *as* God's temple" (33). See also John Walton, *Ancient Near Eastern Thought and the Old Testament: Introducing the Conceptual World of the Hebrew Bible* (Grand Rapids, MI: Baker Academic, 2006), 87–112.

[6] Provan, *Seriously Dangerous*, 38–39: As with creation as temple, so also the garden "is not a specific *location* in the world. It is, rather, a *state of being* in the world, in which God exists in harmony with his creatures and in which his creatures exist in harmony with each other." This temple/garden reality grants a "biblical perspective, then, the work of human beings in God's world is religious work. We are to look after sacred space—the dwelling place of God—on behalf of the one who created it" (37).

logical. It was rooted in the character of the LORD, their God. . . . Justice on earth flows from justice in heaven."[7] Any definition of justice must be rooted in the character and work of God and the subsequent shaping of God's people as his image bearers to be people who reflect his character and love for the marginalized in his world.

This raises the question of whether there is such a thing as justice outside a relationship with the God who created this world to function in a specific way and who has subsequently been working through his people to right what has gone sideways since the fall. To answer this, we will first address two embedded questions. First, we must look at how God chooses to reveal himself (in relationship and story) and what the method of revelation makes known. Second, we must examine the significance of humans created in the *imago Dei*, and what this tells us about God's design for justice in creation.

God's Self-Revelation

Guillermo Mendez, writing "Justification and Social Justice," warns against ideological approaches to the biblical text. He cautions, "We must go back to the Bible to learn who God is, what his demands are, and the basis from which he judges the human injustices of each and all social systems" before we hope to define justice and injustice.[8] The ideal places to begin building a definition of justice would be texts of God's self-revelation, preeminent of which is Deuteronomy 10:12–11:1. This text provides a programmatic statement of Israel's relationship with their God:

> So now, O Israel, what does the LORD your God require of you? Only to fear the LORD your God, to walk in all his ways, to love him, to serve the LORD your God with all your heart and with all your soul, and to keep the commandments of the LORD your God and his decrees that I am commanding you today, for your own well-being. Although heaven and the heaven of heavens belong to the LORD your God, the earth with all that is in it, yet the LORD set his heart in love on your ancestors alone and chose you, their descendants after them, out of all the peoples, as it is today. Circumcise, then, the foreskin of your heart, and do not be stubborn any longer. *For the LORD your God is God of gods and Lord of lords, the great God, mighty and awesome, who is not partial and takes no bribe, who executes justice for the orphan and the widow, and who*

[7] Christopher J. H. Wright, *Old Testament Ethics for the People of God* (Downers Grove, IL: IVP Academic, 2004), 254.

[8] Guillermo Mendez, "Justification and Social Justice," in *Right with God: Justification in the Bible and the World*, ed. D. A. Carson (Eugene, OR: Wipf & Stock, 2002), 190.

> *loves the strangers, providing them food and clothing. You shall also love the stranger, for you were strangers in the land of Egypt.* You shall fear the LORD your God; him alone you shall worship; to him you shall hold fast, and by his name you shall swear. He is your praise; he is your God, who has done for you these great and awesome things that your own eyes have seen. Your ancestors went down to Egypt seventy persons; and now the LORD your God has made you as numerous as the stars in heaven. You shall love the LORD your God, therefore, and keep his charge, his decrees, his ordinances, and his commandments always.[9]

This text shows how central justice, aid, and protection are to the very character of God. This is not a tangential work; it is inherent to his very character to protect the helpless. Consistently throughout Deuteronomy, commands are put in place to protect and provide for the most helpless, guaranteed by the stock characters of widow, orphan, slave, and foreigner (e.g., Deut. 1:16; 5:14; 14:29; 16:11–14; 24:14–22;[10] 26:12–13; 27:19; etc.). But in this text, God does far more than simply command. Instead, inherent to God's self-revelation is that it is in his very nature to protect those whose place in society is precarious.[11] He moves from the height of the heavenly realms to the lowliest of our places. Although "mighty and awesome," his rectitude is irreproachable. He *does not* take bribes, but he is the one who provides justice for those with no representative in the world and the bodily needs of those who are placeless.

This is such a repeated refrain that later authors highlight it, such as in Psalm 68:5: "Father of orphans and protector of widows is God in his holy habitation." Or again in 146:9: "The LORD watches over the strangers; he upholds the orphan and the widow, but the way of the wicked he brings to ruin." Christopher Wright observes, "The frequent expression 'the *mis-*

[9] Biblical quotations in this chapter are from *The New Revised Standard Version*. Copyright © 1989 by the Division of Christian Education of the National Council of the Churches of Christ in the U.S.A. Published by Thomas Nelson, Inc. Used by permission of the National Council of the Churches of Christ in the U.S.A.

[10] Embedded in this last text is the command in v. 16, "Parents shall not be put to death for their children, nor shall children be put to death for their parents; only for their own crimes may persons be put to death," which should caution us to remember our *individual* responsibility to act in accordance with God's care for these marginalized groups. This command is framed by commands that deal with the protection of the poor, the widow, orphan, slave, and alien in context of pay and social order, and the setting of v. 16 does not allow us to say that those commands are irrelevant to any one of us.

[11] It is worth noting here at the outset that these references to "the poor" in society referred first and primarily to the community of Israel. God's society was to be worked out with justice and equity, with particular care for those who were marginalized in its smooth operation. In the NT this can be seen in particular focus in James 2:14–16, where it is a "brother or sister" without his or her basic needs. God's people come under indictment for creating a society that itself functions to protect its own—and with such failure cannot therefore represent God's ideal to the world. The addition of the category of alien/foreigner opens this society to care for those from outside, as "Israel itself originated as a nation of runaway slaves," and thus her sympathies should always be with the oppressed person, whether of her own people or no. See Richard Bauckham, *God and the Crisis of Freedom* (Louisville, KY: Westminster John Knox, 2002), 13.

pat of the orphan and widow' means their rightful case against those who would exploit them. . . . *Mispat* is what needs to be done in a given situation if people and circumstances are to be restored to conformity with *sedeq/sedaqâ*. . . . Justice as an appeal for a response means *taking upon oneself the cause of those who are weak in their own defense*."[12] Justice, righteousness, *rightness* in relationships are concrete nouns, not abstract concepts, terms that must be *done*.[13] Moreover, they are highly relational terms, *covenantal* terms of God's relation with Israel and therefore Israel's relation with her world. Gossai notes that "*sdq* is not simply an objective norm which is present in society, and which must be kept, but rather it is a concept which derives its meaning from the relationship in which it finds itself. So we are able to say that right judging, right governing, right worshipping and gracious activity are all covenantal and righteous, despite their diversity."[14] To be righteous and act justly is to act in accordance with the very character of God, something we know only because he has covenanted with his people and revealed himself to them/us.

The flow of text in Deuteronomy 10 indicates a certain logical movement from the height of God's greatness to his extreme sensitivity toward the helpless of his creation. The text consistently reiterates God's power and control, then descends toward his choice and protection of those at the opposite extreme. The first iteration contrasts God's place as ruler of heaven and earth with his choice of Israel, implying that his choice of them "out of all the peoples" (Ex. 19:5) is nothing short of a surprise they did not earn. His people are his people solely by his choice, his mercy. Deuteronomy, in retelling Israel's story, repeatedly reminds them that God did not choose them because of their strength or power or any other feature; his choice of them rested solely on his loving faithfulness to Abraham.[15] God's choice of Israel, out of all the nations of the earth, already reveals that God is not bound up in power, politics, or wealth but in relationship.

The second iteration intensifies the contrast. Not simply God of the created world (heavens/earth), he is now proclaimed "God of gods and

[12] Wright, *Old Testament Ethics*, 257.

[13] John Goldingay, "Justice and Salvation for Israel and Canaan," in *Reading the Hebrew Bible for a New Millennium: Form, Concept, and Theological Perspective*, ed. Deborah Ellens et al. (Harrisburg, PA: Trinity, 2000), 169–87.

[14] Hemchand Gossai, *Justice, Righteousness and the Social Critique of the Eighth-Century Prophets*, American University Studies 141 (New York: Peter Lang, 1993), 55–56.

[15] Cf. Deut. 6:20–21; 7:6–8, particularly 7:7: "It was not because you were more numerous than any other people that the LORD set his heart on you and chose you—for you were the fewest of all peoples"; 9:4–5, particularly v. 5: "It is not because of your righteousness or the uprightness of your heart that you are going in to occupy their land; but because of the wickedness of these nations the LORD your God is dispossessing them before you, in order to fulfill the promise that the LORD made on oath to your ancestors, to Abraham, to Isaac, and to Jacob."

Lord of lords, the great God, mighty and awesome" (Deut. 10:17). He reigns over every power that could be, and words fail to contain his splendor. But the illustration of his magnificence does not come in mighty displays of that power but in shocking acts of caring for the least and lowest. He first reveals his grandeur in his absolute justice, for he "is not partial and takes no bribe" (v. 17). What this looks like, however, is not simply strict justice—or perhaps, better, blind justice—but rather a justice attentive to the physical realities of the people involved. He is the God "who executes justice for the orphan and the widow, and who loves the strangers, providing them food and clothing" (v. 18). As Christopher Wright describes it, "The Lord is especially attentive to the needs of the marginalized (see Deut. 10:18–19). . . . The poor as a particular group in society receive God's special attention because they are the ones who are on the 'wronged' side of a situation of chronic injustice—a situation God abhors and wishes to have redressed."[16] While Latin American liberation scholar Pedrito Maynard-Reid goes beyond the text when he argues, "There is no hope for any rich persons as long as they are members of that class; there is only judgment and damnation,"[17] we find consistently throughout Scripture a pattern wherein God refuses to be co-opted to the agenda of the wealthy and powerful, and this speaks to his impartiality.[18]

Kloppenborg notes that, at least in the time of the New Testament, the courts were "instruments of social control . . . one way in which superior social status was displayed and maintained."[19] And Longenecker notes, "Those with power did everything to acquire more power, often in blatantly calculating and oppressive measures that compounded life's difficulties for those less secure than themselves."[20] While those two scholars speak to life under the Roman Empire, one does not have to go far afield in Israel's history to see Jezebel expressing this worldly sentiment when she asks Ahab, "Do you now govern Israel? Get up, eat some food, and be cheerful; I will give you the vineyard of Naboth the Jezreelite" (1 Kings 21:7), and proceeds to manipulate Naboth's murder. While the king of Israel was supposed to reflect God in how he provided justice (e.g., Prov.

[16] Wright, *Old Testament Ethics*, 268.

[17] Pedrito U. Maynard-Reid, *Poverty and Wealth in James* (Eugene, OR: Wipf & Stock, 2004), 82. Cf. Gutiérrez, *Theology*, 120: "The future of history belongs to the poor and exploited."

[18] Wright, *Old Testament Ethics*, 269.

[19] John S. Kloppenborg, "Egalitarianism in the Myth and Rhetoric of Pauline Churches," in *Reimagining Christian Origins: A Colloquium Honoring Burton L. Mack*, ed. Elizabeth A. Caselli and Hal Taussig (Philadelphia: Trinity, 1996), 255–56.

[20] Bruce W. Longenecker, *Remember the Poor: Paul, Poverty, and the Greco-Roman World* (Grand Rapids, MI: Eerdmans, 2010), 27.

8:15; 16:10; 29:4, 14), Ahab is said to have "sold [himself] to do what was evil in the sight of the LORD" (1 Kings 21:20, 25), a reality summarized in the sordid story of injustice against Naboth.[21] In contrast, Solomon begins his reign by asking for "an understanding mind to govern your people, able to discern between good and evil" in order to be able to govern God's people according to God's justice (3:9). It is only by submitting to God and following faithfully that one can possibly judge fellow humans with the Lord's impartiality.[22]

True Worship Responds to the Love of God

Another text of God's self-revelation that must be considered is Exodus 33–34, in which Moses pleads for God to show his face. God replies, "I will make all my goodness pass before you, and will proclaim before you the name, 'The LORD'; and I will be gracious to whom I will be gracious, and will show mercy on whom I will show mercy" (33:19). In 34:6–8, when God passes by, what Moses learns is not so much what God looks like, as though some physical representation would tell him something about God. Rather, Moses learns of God's character:

> The LORD passed before him, and proclaimed, "The LORD, the LORD, a God merciful and gracious, slow to anger, and abounding in steadfast love and faithfulness, keeping steadfast love for the thousandth generation, forgiving iniquity and transgression and sin, yet by no means clearing the guilty, but visiting the iniquity of the parents upon the children and the children's children, to the third and the fourth generation." And Moses quickly bowed his head toward the earth, and worshiped.

Meeting God, Moses becomes overwhelmed with his mercy and faithfulness, and he worships. When we encounter the love of God as revealed in his very character, adoration and doxology should be our response. Walter Brueggemann warns:

> Prophecy cannot be separated very long from doxology, or it will either wither or become ideology. . . . In a world where jingles replace doxology, God is not free and the people know no justice or compassion.

[21] Ahab, of course, violated all the prohibitions in Deuteronomy 17 for the character of a king, particularly in taking a foreign wife and acquiring possessions for his own enjoyment, and he fulfilled the prophecy of Samuel in 1 Samuel 8 regarding the problem of Israel rejecting God "from being king over them" (v. 7). See also the ignoble story of David with Bathsheba, in which David attempts to use his power as king to gain immunity for his sin, manipulating the death of his friend. God judges him for this abuse of his position.

[22] The outcome of this scene comes in 3:28: "All Israel heard of the judgment that the king had rendered; and they stood in awe of the king, because they perceived that *the wisdom of God was in him, to execute justice*."

> Doxology is the ultimate challenge to the language of managed reality, and it alone is the universe of discourse in which energy is possible. . . . Only where there is doxology is there any emergence of compassion. . . . The Sinai theme speaks of God's freedom for the neighbor.[23]

As Longenecker observes, "There is . . . a fairly consistent 'prophetic' voice denouncing the way in which the elite can all too easily work the socio-economic machinery to acquire resources for themselves."[24] This prophetic tradition remains energized and truly prophetic because it remains sourced in God's character and laws for his people, that their society might shine a light to the nations in its justice and mercy to all.[25]

And so it makes sense that in close proximity to God's revelation of his own character in Exodus 34 are extensive laws about loving our neighbor, grounded in iterations of God's compassionate character. For instance, Exodus 22 includes several reminders: "You shall not wrong or oppress a resident alien, for you were aliens in the land of Egypt. You shall not abuse any widow or orphan. If you do abuse them, when they cry out to me, I will surely heed their cry. . . . And if your neighbor cries out to me, I will listen, for I am compassionate" (vv. 21–23, 27). God's character is compassionate and merciful but just and profoundly concerned about accountability for sin.

Christopher Wright observes, "The question . . . 'Do you believe in God?' means very little (as does any answer given to such a question), unless one specifies what the last word refers to in objective reality."[26] A Christian, biblical theology of social justice *must* be based in the character of God, or we will wander into idolatry, worshiping a god in our image who approves what we approve and condemns what we condemn.[27] And so we can end up with a free-market "Jesus" that cares not for the cost to those who cannot compete, or a "spirit" that "inspires" us with words of "'Peace, peace' when there is no peace" (Jer. 6:14), or a "god" who condemns only sexual sins but does not care about the plight of refugees trapped at our borders. God demands our worship, and as we worship

---

[23] Walter Brueggemann, *Prophetic Imagination*, 2nd ed. (Minneapolis: Fortress, 2001), 17–18.

[24] Longenecker, *Remember the Poor*, 29.

[25] Cf. the goal in Rev. 7:9, where the multitude is drawn "from every nation, from all tribes and peoples and languages."

[26] Wright, *Old Testament Ethics*, 24.

[27] Gary Haugen, *Good News about Injustice: A Witness of Courage in a Hurting World* (Downers Grove, IL: InterVarsity, 1999), 15, notes that Israel's prophets presented a "God whose core hatred of injustice was rivaled only by his hatred of idolatry." What this phrase masks is that idolatry consistently leads to injustice, and God's hatred is due in part to the fact that as his people fall into idolatry, they change their actions toward the impoverished.

him, our character is shaped by that relationship and his laws into the image of his own. This is of crucial importance:

> Biblically, idolatry is not confined to some spiritual or religious sphere of life, unconnected to the realities of the social, economic and political order. Rather, the identity and character of the god or gods you worship will profoundly affect the kind of society you advocate (or tolerate). "There is no wrong-doing without worship of false gods and there is no worship of false gods without wrong-doing" is the stark crystallization of this point by Ulrich Duchrow.[28]

As our worship goes astray, as we re-create God into a more congenial image who approves of our lifestyles, we become idolaters. And as we walk unconsciously into idolatry, we shape our societies to match our own priorities rather than allowing God to shape us to his society. Here it should be highlighted that *individual* idolatry and greed, personal sin in giving way to consumerism and selfishness, leads to *societal* sins, on a macroscale of what is essentially corporate slavery and environmental disregard in the two-thirds world. While no single individual may be responsible, as we excuse our personal sins we conform to the fallen world, worshiping at its idols, drawn by and imitating its selfishness, greed, or even legalism, believing that our way is the only right way to live and care for others.[29] As we worship anything but God, we become dehumanized, unable to fully care for and love our neighbor, instead looking first to our own interests and concerns.

God recognizes it is not intuitive to humans to live in his world order, and so he reminds the Israelites why *they* should also engage in this work. One would expect that since the Israelites had experienced marginalization, they would develop sensitivity toward those outside the community boundaries. Instead, they are the very ones in need of reminder, and so in Deuteronomy 10 the announcement of God's grand power over the universe and his justice for the weak is immediately followed by the reminder of their own history: *you shall also* care for the foreigners in your midst. "Israel's worship was to be marked by a deepened commitment to ethical response at the horizontal level. . . . It was to have humanitarian

[28] Wright, *Old Testament Ethics*, 276n26.

[29] Isa. 42:14–25; 44:9–20 clearly presents the image that those who worship idols (at that time physical objects that could not see nor hear) become like them, able neither to see nor understand (44:18). Thus, the text teaches that we become like that which we worship, and as we stray into worshiping things other than the true God, the image of God in us becomes further twisted rather than redeemed (see below).

implications."[30] Worship of Israel's God was intimately tied to how they lived their lives, particularly as it concerned justice and mercy, because they had experienced God's mercy.

When Israel fell short in loving the weakest members of her society, she came under condemnation for failing to act like her God. Their worship, Isaiah 58 teaches, should shape them in God's image: "Is not this the fast that I choose: to loose the bonds of injustice, to undo the thongs of the yoke, to let the oppressed go free, and to break every yoke? Is it not to share your bread with the hungry, and bring the homeless poor into your house; when you see the naked, to cover them, and not to hide yourself from your own kin?" (vv. 6–7). The great condemnations throughout Isaiah were heaviest against the leaders of Israel, who chose to act like the leaders of the nations instead of humbly caring for the people entrusted to them. In contrast, what Isaiah 58 teaches us is that when Israel *acted* like her God in love and protection of the oppressed, *then* she worshiped. Without a concrete change in character, Israel's worship failed to please God.

God is compassionate, and God hears. Indeed, that is the very pivotal starting point of the entire exodus narrative and ought never be forgotten by God's people: "I have heard their cry" (see Ex. 3:7) as they labored in oppression, and he acted to rescue them. However, the problem is that we too often become comfortable and then forget, or rather choose to forget, the work of God on our behalf. The great covenant text of Deuteronomy 6 warns of this very concern. Following the great *Shema*, the text in verse 10 cautions the Israelites against the pride of comfort:

> When the LORD your God has brought you into the land that he swore to your ancestors, to Abraham, to Isaac, and to Jacob, to give you—a land with fine, large cities that you did not build, houses filled with all sorts of goods that you did not fill, hewn cisterns that you did not hew, vineyards and olive groves that you did not plant—and when you have eaten your fill, *take care that you do not forget the LORD*, who brought you out of the land of Egypt, out of the house of slavery. The LORD your God you shall fear; him you shall serve, and by his name alone you shall swear. Do not follow other gods, any of the gods of the peoples who are all around you, because the LORD your God, who is present with you, is a jealous God. The anger of the LORD your God would be kindled against you and he would destroy you from the face of the earth. (vv. 10–15)

[30] Wright, *Old Testament Ethics*, 45.

It is worth noticing the concern of this passage. Human tendency is that when we become comfortable, when the immediate pressures of survival, of oppression, of daily need lift, we move to worship other gods, gods of comfort, luxury, self-indulgence, gods that satisfy our desire to justify our lifestyle and tell us we're special and deserve the good we have and that those who are not in our situation clearly don't deserve to be. In contrast, faced with the story of their God, Israel is stuck remembering that they *did not build* their cities; they *did not plant* their vineyards; in fact, *they had been slaves and God had rescued them*. From such a position they were therefore always to remain in humble gratitude, protecting those the machine of culture would oppress, always remembering that what they have is gift and given.

The prophet Malachi warns in 3:5: "I will draw near to you for judgment; I will be swift to bear witness against the sorcerers, against the adulterers, against those who swear falsely, against those who oppress the hired workers in their wages, the widow and the orphan, against those who thrust aside the alien, and do not fear me, says the LORD of hosts." The list of commands in this prophetic warning are all recognizable to those familiar with the holiness code of Leviticus, but it is worth noting that God appears to find equally offensive to adulterers and sorcerers those who fail to pay hired workers fairly, or oppress the orphan, or cast aside the foreigner in need of help.[31] All of these can be summarized in the command "Do not fear me." In a day when some sins are elevated and others dismissed (and often ranked differently by different groups), it is worth seeing the lists that God puts together in his Word, which show up all throughout Scripture, and meditating on what they tell us about what *God* sees as worthy of warning. John Walton cautions, "The laws were given as examples of the implications of the holiness of God."[32] Love of our defenseless neighbor is intimately linked to love and obedience to God, an outpouring of his love into his temple/creation.

We need to repeat the story—as Israel was instructed to do—about God's character and mighty works on our behalf, particularly the story of the cross, lest we, like Israel, become comfortable and forget this calling, acting instead to protect our own interests primarily. And this im-

[31] John N. Oswalt, *The Book of Isaiah Chapters 1–39* (Grand Rapids, MI: Eerdmans, 1986), 180, observes that in contrast to other deities, "The remarkable thing about the OT conception of holiness is a function of the OT understanding of God's character. What was distinct about this deity was not so much his origin, his essence, or his numinous power. Rather, it was his attitude toward ethical behavior. . . . [No other nation] saw [its] laws as being an essential expression of what made God to be God."

[32] John H. Walton, *Covenant: God's Purpose, God's Plan* (Grand Rapids, MI: Zondervan, 1994), 171.

pinges on our very worship. As the prophets rejected the worship of a people who oppressed the poor and trampled the rights of the helpless, so James also condemns those who would claim to be worshiping God and yet curry favor with the wealthy. James has a simple definition: "Religion that is pure and undefiled before God, the Father, is this: to care for orphans and widows in their distress, and to keep oneself unstained by the world" (1:27). Dual commands reflect so much of the Old Testament distilled into one sentence—"Be holy, as I the LORD your God am holy"—that shows up as James's concern that we remain morally pure. But moral purity can't exist alongside injustice, and justice cannot flourish where holiness is compromised by pride, greed, or indifference, and so the other half of truly godly religion is the practical concern of the invisible, providing for them and preventing abuse of them. "When justice is pervasively trampled upon, then the very foundations of liveable society crumble . . . because justice is fundamental to the very nature of the Lord."[33]

Repeatedly throughout the Scripture, when God makes a statement regarding his own work in justice, it is followed by an assertion such as "You shall also," something we saw in the Deuteronomy 10 passage. For instance, while God may protect the widow, orphan, and foreigner, he does not leave this as a simple statement of his character. Instead, the text immediately follows with "You shall also . . ." (v. 19). While in this case it refers to the foreigner in their midst, it provides yet another instance wherein the Israelites are reminded of their own position outside of God's choice of them, living as foreigners and slaves. Such a reminder should leave no place for pride in their interactions with others. God's people were to worship him by how they structured their society. But it is not simply the *imitation* of God that is at work, however, in the commands to "be holy as I am holy." They were—and are—those who act according to his nature because they were created in his *image*.

Humans in the *Imago Dei*

From creation onward, all humans were created by God in the *imago Dei* ("image of God") to rule in his creation as his representatives, which makes the kingship discussion of immediate relevance for all humans.[34] While recognizing the difficulty of translating *rdh* in Genesis 1:26, it is

[33] Wright, *Old Testament Ethics*, 253.

[34] Dexter E. Callender, *Adam in Myth and History: Ancient Israelite Perspectives on the Primal Human* (Winona Lake, IN: Eisenbrauns, 2000), 62, comments, "Just as Yahweh is responsible for the creation and maintenance of such fertility, so is the king. The image of gardening is a royal image."

nevertheless the "destiny of *human beings* to rule over the cosmos; it is not the destiny of the ancient gods. It is, moreover, the destiny of human beings *all together* to rule; it is not just the destiny of the god-king in the city state."[35]

As discussed above, when God created the earth, he created the whole earth to be his temple. So, for instance, Psalm 72:19 exclaims, "Blessed be his glorious name forever; may his glory fill the whole earth. Amen and Amen." Just as God's glory had filled the tabernacle and the temple in Israel's journey and settlement, the goal was that the whole earth would be the temple of God, filled with his glory. Isaiah sees a glimpse of the fulfillment of this prayer in Isaiah 6: "I saw the Lord sitting on a throne, high and lofty; and the *hem of his robe filled the temple.* Seraphs were in attendance above him. . . . And one called to another and said: 'Holy, holy, holy is the Lord of hosts; *the whole earth is full of his glory*'" (vv. 1–3). Much like with Revelation, where what is heard and what is seen are two different realities,[36] here what Isaiah sees is the robe filling the temple, but what he learns is the reality that the whole *earth* is filled with God's glory.[37] What Isaiah hears from the seraphs is not simply a prayer that earth *would* be filled, but that it indeed *is* reality. The earth is God's temple, made for his glory.

In ancient temples, the image of the god resided in the innermost part of the temple. And it was through this statue that the god was heard to speak and communicate with its followers. Through rituals, "a divine image may be completely transformed into its referent" such that "when the image attains life, it becomes the vehicle through which the reference is manifest. More than a representation, then, the similative image becomes its referent."[38] Priests would dress the statue—worship of the god happened via the image. In the image, people drew near and came to know the god.

---

[35] Provan, *Seriously Dangerous*, 84; emphasis original. This is a remarkably egalitarian reality, one affirmed in Psalm 8, wherein "each and every individual human person has been raised to the status of *divinity and royalty* from the status only of a *slave*." Ibid.

[36] Cf. Gordon Fee, *Revelation*, New Covenant Commentary (Eugene, OR: Wipf & Stock, 2010), 79–80, who calls the Lion/Lamb contrast in Rev. 5:5–6 "one of the great moments in Christian theology. . . . The only lion in heaven is in fact the Slain Lamb. It is difficult to emphasize adequately the theological import of this dramatic replacement of images. . . . No lion ever appears in Heaven. But the Lamb is there all the way through, even at the end."

[37] Oswalt, *Isaiah*, 181, comments, "This statement indicates that God's presence (his glory, Ex. 40:34) is not restricted to temple. But it is also a way of saying that the earth's abundance is merely a reflection of this God's being."

[38] Randall W. Garr, *In His Own Image and Likeness: Humanity, Divinity, and Monotheism* (Leiden: Brill, 2003), 144, cited in Catherine Beckerleg, "The 'Image of God' in Eden: the Creation of Mankind in Genesis 2:5–3:24 in Light of the *mīs pî pit pî* and *wpt-r* Rituals of Mesopotamia and Ancient Egypt," PhD thesis submitted to Harvard University (September 2009), 168.

But in Jerusalem's temple, while the presence of God rested there, there was no image placed. Instead, God placed his image in his temple at creation! Catherine Beckerleg suggests that "Adam and Eve resemble God, yet they are not God. No explanation of what constitutes the likeness is given. Rather, it seems that the son resembles his father, and, by analogy, humans correspond to God, simply because he was created by his father. Thus correspondence is intrinsic to being human and is passed on by the parents, who themselves are created in the image and likeness of God, to their children at birth."[39] But the image was marred in the fall.[40] Genesis 9 reveals that while humanity's rule was in some ways lost when man was expelled from the garden, the *imago* remains.[41] And so God calls a people, first Abraham out of Ur, then Israel out of Egypt, and teaches them to know him. By experiencing his compassion and mercy, they learn he is the God who hears the cry of the oppressed and acts on their behalf, who forgives when people repent from their rebellion. By receiving the law, they are trained to act in accordance with his holiness.[42] And the intent of Israel's relationship with God is the purpose covenanted with Abraham, that through this people "all the families of the earth shall be blessed" (Gen. 12:3). Israel's witness is to be one through which all people are drawn to acknowledge Yahweh as Lord and worship him, and thereby they—and we—fulfill our roles as being his image in the world. The world is to learn *who* God is and be drawn to worship him *via his people*, his image bearers (cf. Isa. 55:4–5).

God's people are to engage with him in his work of restoring and redeeming his creation. Beckerleg suggests that the "nature of the divine-human relationship as it is presented in Gen. 1 has three major components which are intimately related to one another: kinship, kingship, and cult."[43] We are children of Yahweh, placed in his creation to rule

---

[39] Beckerleg, "The 'Image of God,'" 171. She quotes Claus Westermann, *Genesis 1–11: A Continental Commentary*, trans. John H. Scullion (Minneapolis: Fortress, 1994), 356: "It [correspondence] is something given to humans by the very fact of existence."

[40] Beckerleg, "The 'Image of God,'" 292, notes, "Mankind was designed to dwell in the divine presence, that is, with God in his most holy place. The fact that Adam and Eve were expelled from the garden, however, highlighted one of the most significant differences between Gen 2:5–3:24 and the comparative texts: the opening of the eyes cost them their status as co-rulers over creation and their filiation with the divine."

[41] Provan, *Seriously Dangerous*, 81, notes regarding Gen. 9:6 that "once again 'man' is *'adam* here. . . . In spite of the havoc wrought by evil throughout Genesis 3–8, in Genesis 9 human beings are still the image bearers of God."

[42] Wright, *Old Testament Ethics*, 40, argues, "The commands of God are not autonomous or arbitrary rules; they are frequently related to the character or values or desires of God. So to obey God's commands is to reflect God in human life. Obedience to the law and the imitation of God are not mutually exclusive categories: the one is an expression of the other."

[43] Beckerleg, "The 'Image of God,'" 186. Meredith Kline, in *Kingdom Prologue: Genesis Foundations for a Covenantal Worldview* (Overland Park, KS: Two Ages, 2000), 45, notes a parallel in the birth of Seth in Gen. 5:1–3: "In this passage a statement of Adam's creation in the likeness of God is directly juxtaposed to a statement that

on his behalf, in his way, to lead the worship of him. God recognizes his people because they are the ones who act like him, and as such there is a certain necessity—but more than necessity, *inevitability*—that the people of God *will* act like God in bringing justice and relief to the oppressed. God's impartial justice, which defends the defenseless from all who would subjugate them, runs contrary to human desires to "lord it over" those we can dominate (e.g., Matt. 20:25). Separate from knowing God's character, however, there can be no such thing as justice. Rather, we will wander into the territory of the judges, where each one does what is right in his own eyes, defining justice according to our own desires.

As his image bearers in his temple, humans inhabit a unique place in creation, and those who have been brought into relationship with him are the "first fruits of his creatures" (James 1:18), born again by God's will and grace. As new creations, filled with the Holy Spirit, believers have a chance to live according to how humans were originally intended to live on earth: as representatives of God in his creation. Richard Hays notes that the "church embodies the power of the resurrection in the midst of a not-yet-redeemed world," a "critical framework that pronounces upon our complacency as well as upon our presumptuous despair."[44] Believers have been gifted with the Holy Spirit to guide and empower (cf. John 14:16, etc.), and so obedience in this area is not simply a matter of "works" to show how "holy" one is but rather becomes a process by which we allow the Spirit to shape us into the image and likeness of God.

It is for this reason, then, that the Psalms indicate that "only those people who mirror the integrity, compassion and purity of God can legitimately come to worship at all (Pss. 15 and 24)."[45] In the same way, when God speaks of the worship he desires, the ritual purity demanded is meant to inculcate a purity among his people that will allow them also to *live* purely in the world, such that they will worship according to his requirements "to do justice, and to love kindness, and to walk humbly with your God" (Mic. 6:8). As God's image placed in his creation/temple and given life and breath by God, we are indeed the ones through whom God touches his creation. This explains, therefore, why he is so concerned that his people *do* reflect his character of justice and mercy for the oppressed, for we are the ones through whom he has chosen to work (cf.

Adam begat a son in his own likeness and image. Clearly we are being advised that there is a similarity between these two processes, both of which result in products like their authors."

[44] Richard B. Hays, *The Moral Vision of the New Testament: A Contemporary Introduction to New Testament Ethics* (San Francisco: HarperCollins, 1996), 198.

[45] Wright, *Old Testament Ethics*, 41.

James 2:1–13). Margaret Miles cautions, "We, in our fascination with intellectual insight, often forget that to be Christian is to affirm an incarnational orientation to life whereby what we do is as important as what we think."[46] Indeed, if we take seriously our life as made in the *imago Dei*, we will seek to think *and act* as God's in-breaking into his creation. We do not do this, however, solely on the basis of God's covenant people and his instructions to them, nor on deductions based on our identity as his image bearers. We learn how to live as image bearers through the imitation of the one who was himself fully God and yet fully human, who by his life and work established God's kingdom (society) on earth.

Jesus as the Ultimate Revelation of the Love of God

Jesus himself provides the ultimate self-revelation of God in his life, ministry, death, and resurrection. This revelation, now God in flesh, ties together the themes of Yahweh's self-revelation and humanity's worship and what it means to be the image of God in creation in the clearest possible demonstration. We, the image bearers, gain a clear model of how God himself would act on earth, a model exemplifying a self-giving love that refuses to make demands of one's own rights (cf. Phil. 2:5–11). In his demonstration of "total obedience to his Father," Jesus "models the free and glad obedience of love," an obedience expressed "nowhere more remarkably than in depicting himself as a slave who serves others."[47] As John teaches us through his Gospel, the glory of God was revealed as Christ was raised on the cross.[48] While we cannot duplicate Christ's redemptive work on the cross, Christians are "consistently called to take up the cross and follow in the way that his death defines," and when "'imitation of Christ' is understood in these terms, the often-proposed distinction between discipleship and imitation disappears. To be Jesus' disciple is to obey his call to bear the cross, thus to be like him."[49] Christ, in his life and even in his self-sacrificial, obedient death, reveals to humanity what it is like when God walks in his creation.

To begin, Jesus makes very clear that he is a unique revelation on earth of who God is, albeit one that does not fit presumed categories. For instance, in Matthew 11:25–27 Jesus begins by celebrating God's

[46] Margaret R. Miles, *Fullness of Life: Historical Foundations for a New Asceticism* (Philadelphia: Westminster, 1981), 162–63.

[47] Bauckham, *God and the Crisis of Freedom*, 20.

[48] Cf. the title and cover image of Richard Bauckham's *Gospel of Glory: Major Themes in Johannine Theology* (Grand Rapids, MI: Baker Academic, 2015), on which the title is paired with an image of Christ being raised upon the cross.

[49] Hays, *Moral Vision*, 197.

will to make himself known not to the elites but to the powerless, the "infants." Whether in the infancy narratives, where it is shepherds and foreigners who come to worship (Luke 2; Matthew 2), or the centurions who exhibit faith (Matt. 8:5–13 par. Luke 7:2–10; Matt. 27:54 par. Mark 15:39), or the lengthy conversations with and startling acknowledgments of women (Matt. 9:2–22 par. Mark 5:24–34; Luke 8:43–48; Matt. 26:6–11 par. Mark 14:3–9; Mark 7:24–30; Luke 7:36–49; John 4:6–29; 8:2–11, etc.), all through the Gospels Jesus interacts with the widow and the unclean woman, the orphan and the children, the foreigner, and the working class with grace and great mercy, revealing something of God's character to those who encounter him. And what is revealed? "No one knows the Son except the Father, and no one knows the Father except the Son and anyone to whom the Son chooses to reveal him" (Matt. 11:27). According to this shocking statement, now the *only* way to know God is through Jesus. In John 10:30 we hear the startling statement, "The Father and I are one." For this statement, the crowd seeks to stone him, and Jesus replies, "I have shown you many good works from the Father. For which of these are you going to stone me?" (v. 32). Jesus startlingly equates *his* works with those of the Father; to see how he acts is to see God act. Later, in conversation with his disciples in 14:6–13, Jesus makes this even clearer:

> Jesus said to him, "I am the way, and the truth, and the life. No one comes to the Father except through me. *If you know me, you will know my Father also. From now on you do know him and have seen him.*" Philip said to him, "Lord, show us the Father, and we will be satisfied." Jesus said to him, "*Have I been with you all this time, Philip, and you still do not know me? Whoever has seen me has seen the Father. How can you say, 'Show us the Father'*? Do you not believe that I am in the Father and the Father is in me? The words that I say to you I do not speak on my own; *but the Father who dwells in me does his works.* Believe me that I am in the Father and the Father is in me; but if you do not, then believe me because of the works themselves. Very truly, I tell you, the one who believes in me will also do the works that I do and, in fact, will do greater works than these, because I am going to the Father. I will do whatever you ask in my name, so that the Father may be glorified in the Son.

Jesus' very works speak to the truth of his revelation of God: he acts as God acts; therefore we know God because we know Jesus. Philip, in failing to understand, thinks of Jesus merely as a mediator who points to God rather than as God's self-revelation come in the flesh.

Jesus understands his work as revealing the Father, and this is made clear right from the missional summary of Luke 4:16–21, where he is handed the Isaiah scroll and reads from it, concluding, "Today this scripture has been fulfilled in your hearing" (v. 21). The summary statement of Isaiah 61:1–2, however, is of a profoundly topsy-turvy world order whereby good news comes to those who least expect it:

> The spirit of the Lord GOD is upon me,
> because the LORD has anointed me;
> he has sent me to bring good news to the oppressed,
> to bind up the brokenhearted,
> to proclaim liberty to the captives,
> and release to the prisoners;
> to proclaim the year of the LORD's favor,
> and the day of vengeance of our God;
> to comfort all who mourn.

What Christ came to do was partly to inaugurate a new age in God's work of loving and protecting the vulnerable.[50] The "good news" is about salvation from sins but is also a much more programmatic, holistic revelation of God's protective love for the defenseless.[51]

This reality of Christ's mission as revelation of God ties to how humanity should worship God. There are two facets to this. First is obedience to living according to what has been revealed by God, to live for justice for the oppressed because of his great love for them. As Jesus says in John 14:21 and 23–24, "They who have my commandments and keep them are those who love me," and, "Those who love me will keep my word, and my Father will love them, and we will come to them and make our home with them. Whoever does not love me does not keep my words; and the word that you hear is not mine, but is from the Father who sent me." As we love Jesus and love God, we will act according to his revealed will and offer him the worship of defending the defenseless and protecting the widow, the orphan, the foreigner. Christopher Wright observes that the "prophets observed people whose lives lacked ethical integrity coming to worship. . . . But for the prophets, there could be no peace-

[50] This hymn is, of course, very like Mary's hymn in Luke 1:46–55. One can see from her Magnificat why she was chosen to raise Jesus and can also hear echoes of her praise in James.

[51] Hays, *Moral Vision*, 116, observes, "By evoking these texts at the beginning of his ministry, Luke's Jesus declares himself as the Messiah who by the power of the Spirit will create a restored Israel in which justice and compassion for the poor will prevail. All of Jesus' miracles and healings throughout Luke's Gospel are therefore to be read as signs of God's coming kingdom, in which the oppressed will be set free."

ful coexistence between sacred rites and social wrongs."[52] Jesus expresses the same disdain in Matthew 23:23: "Woe to you, scribes and Pharisees, hypocrites! For you tithe mint, dill, and cummin, and have neglected the weightier matters of the law: justice and mercy and faith. It is these you ought to have practiced without neglecting the others." Warnings such as this, as well as all the eschatological teaching in chapters 24 and 25, "define significant ethical *norms* having to do primarily with just and merciful treatment of others," reinforcing "Matthew's earlier emphasis on mercy as the hallmark of the kingdom of God."[53] As Jesus reveals the Father, he reaffirms that God's people should be shaped to worship God as God desires worship—with both pure hands *and* a pure heart, not tainted by greed and idolatry. Burridge notes that in the various power struggles with the political and religious leaders, "It was *religious leaders*, the ones with high ethical standards and the guardians of morality, who found him uncomfortable and with whom Jesus finds himself constantly in conflict."[54] Those who look to have Jesus fit into their prescribed place for itinerant teachers find that somehow they are missing the key, but the humble find themselves encountering God.

In this context, then, it is worth quoting 1 John 4:19: "We love because he first loved us." According to the Johannine epistles, love of God is shown in how we love our neighbor, and we love our neighbor *because* we have received God's love and realize that God loves them as well. And, of course, the parable of the good Samaritan (Luke 10:25–37) rules out any definition of *neighbor* that does not include the hurt, the vulnerable, the weak.

There is one other aspect of how the revelation of God in Jesus informs our worship that ties to our identity as image bearers, and that is how John's Gospel presents the glory of God as the cross. Throughout the Gospel, Jesus warns that he must be lifted up. In 3:14 he likens his death to the healing brought by Moses when he "lifted up the serpent in the wilderness." In 8:28 he warns the Pharisees, "When you have lifted up the Son of Man, then you will realize that I am he, and that I do nothing on my own, but I speak these things as the Father instructed me," strengthening his identification with the Father, much to their dismay. And then, finally, the most triumphant statement is in 12:32: "I, when I am lifted up from

[52] Wright, *Old Testament Ethics*, 374.
[53] Hays, *Moral Vision*, 107.
[54] Richard A. Burridge, *Imitating Jesus: An Inclusive Approach to New Testament Ethics* (Grand Rapids, MI: Eerdmans, 2007), 62; emphasis original. Burridge expresses surprise that despite Jesus' teaching a "rigorous ethical teaching," he finds himself in a "struggle against those who cannot live up to his standard."

the earth, will draw all people to myself." This last one ties his death not simply to the work of redemption from sin but to the prophetic promises begun in the covenant with Abraham—that through Israel, "all the families of the earth shall be blessed" through Abraham, the "ancestor of a multitude of nations."[55] How is this promise fulfilled? At the cross—the most devastating moment in human history turns out to be its triumph. And so believers should fall down and worship, as did Moses when he met God's extreme mercy and compassion face-to-face.[56]

This leads to the tie to the third theme, that as we learn how to worship God for who he is revealed to be, we come to learn what it means to be fully human. As John presents the cross as *the* central moment of history, the moment in which God's glory is fully revealed, so does Paul in Philippians 2:6–11. Christ emptied himself all the way, not merely to death but death *on the cross*, the most humiliating moment. But Paul uses this to teach us something of the imitation of Christ: "Let the same mind be in you that was in Christ Jesus" (v. 5). We do not learn simply about how lavish, how abounding, how outrageous is the love of God for his people that he would come and die for his lost humanity, although we do learn that. "What the New Testament means by 'love' is embodied concretely in the *cross*."[57] We learn in Christ's death who *we* are to be as a people as we love God and our neighbor in humility, obedience, and self-sacrifice.[58]

This takes to the next level what was revealed in John's Gospel in the foot-washing moment, where, "having loved his own who were in the world, he loved them to the end" (13:1) and proceeds to wash their feet as a servant to reveal how deep his love is willing to go into their brokenness. He does this and then explicitly states, "You also should do as I have done to you" (v. 15). Burridge notes, "As the supreme demonstration of

[55] N. T. Wright, *Paul and the Faithfulness of God* (Minneapolis: Fortress, 2013), 1006, summarizes his discussion of Romans 4 by saying, "We do not have to regard Abraham as 'our forefather according to the flesh,' Paul is concluding, because he is the father of us *all*, Jew and Gentile alike, in accordance with the promise of Genesis 17:5. . . . This is so important that Paul, unusually, repeats it in the next verse. . . . This is the way the one God always intended to work (and this is what Abraham always believed that he would do) in order to include Gentiles in his 'seed.' What this always meant, and still means for Paul, is something about the character of the one God himself. . . . The character of 'faith' alters depending on what sort of God one believes in."

[56] Charles Wesley captures this in his hymn "And Can It Be That I Should Gain?" He laments: "Died he for me?, who caused his pain! / For me, who him to death pursued? / Amazing love! How can it be / That thou, my God, shouldst die for me?" and in stanza 3: "He left his Father's throne above / So free, so infinite his grace; / Emptied himself of all but love; And bled for Adam's helpless race; / 'Tis mercy all, immense and free, / For, O my God, it found out me!"

[57] Hays, *Moral Vision*, 202.

[58] Ibid., 197: "The image of the cross should not be used by those who hold power in order to ensure the acquiescent suffering of the powerless. . . . The New Testament writers consistently employ the pattern of the cross precisely to call those who possess power and privilege to *surrender* it for the sake of the weak (see, e.g., Mark 10:42–45, Rom. 15:1–3, 1 Cor. 8:1–11:1)."

his love, he then takes the towel and basin and washes his disciples' feet in the manner of a servant" so that we might come to understand "Jesus as the bringer of divine love."[59] He then teaches his followers, "I give you a new commandment, that you love one another. Just as I have loved you, you also should love one another" (v. 34). This command is worked out as we humble ourselves, taking the role of a servant and caring for the weak. As we have been loved, so we should love, and in so doing we image Christ and the Father into our world.[60] Paul himself understood this, such that his admonition to "'work for the good of all' in Gal. 6:10 may be said to derive from the narrative of 'the Son of God, who loved me and gave himself for me' (Gal. 2:20, cf. 1:4)."[61] Christians, of all people, live in the grace of God's love for us, and so we live accordingly out of a humble love for others who cannot save themselves.[62]

Implications for God's People

This *imago* reality is why New Testament authors are concerned that Christians live according to the holiness of God. God's people were—and are—to participate in the process of *shalom* making. Cornelius Plantinga describes *shalom* as "the way things ought to be"—"the webbing together of God, humans, and all creation in justice, fulfillment, and delight is what the Hebrew prophets call *shalom*. . . . In the Bible, shalom means *universal flourishing, wholeness, and delight*."[63] Notice the interplay not just of personal peace and delight but of justice as well, whereby all may flourish. God makes clear in Deuteronomy 30 that to live according to his commands is not impossible but rather a setting of the world to the right order, the way they were *made* to behave:

> Surely, this commandment that I am commanding you today is not too hard for you, nor is it too far away. It is not in heaven, that you should say, "Who will go up to heaven for us, and get it for us so that we may hear it and observe it?" Neither is it beyond the sea, that you should say, "Who will cross to the other side of the sea for us, and get it for us so

---

[59] Burridge, *Imitating Jesus*, 343. He adds, "Jesus is the revealer who not only teaches us the truth of God, but also shows us what the divine love is like, so that we can imitate him and so participate in the divine life" (345).

[60] See also the commands such as Luke 6:36, "Be merciful, just as your Father is merciful."

[61] Longenecker, *Remember the Poor*, 310.

[62] There is no better phrasing of this than Eph. 2:8–10: "By grace you have been saved through faith, and this is not your own doing; it is the gift of God—not the result of works, so that no one may boast. For we are what he has made us, created in Christ Jesus for good works, which God prepared beforehand to be our way of life."

[63] Cornelius Plantinga Jr., *Not the Way It's Supposed to Be: A Breviary of Sin* (Grand Rapids, MI: Eerdmans, 1995), 10; emphasis original.

> that we may hear it and observe it?" No, the word is very near to you; it is in your mouth and in your heart for you to observe. (Deut. 30:11–14)

God seems to teach that this law is something his image bearers can actually keep in relationship with him. He gave his law so that his image bearers might represent him well in his created temple, contrary to Luther's despair about law keeping, which is in truth "metonymy for any and all attempts to secure one's righteousness through a reliance on one's own works, which by definition are done 'from our own natural powers' apart from God's grace and forgiveness."[64] Believers, however, have the Spirit poured upon us, so we are living at least in the inauguration of Jeremiah 31's great promise:[65]

> I will put my law within them, and I will write it on their hearts; and I will be their God, and they shall be my people. No longer shall they teach one another, or say to each other, "Know the LORD," for they shall all know me, from the least of them to the greatest, says the LORD; for I will forgive their iniquity, and remember their sin no more. (Jer. 31:33–34)

The model of Jesus shapes a holy people into his humble likeness, people who *know* God and live according to the Spirit in their midst, and therefore love what and who God loves and passionately hate injustice and oppression. In doing so, we will simply receive the implanted word that has the power to save our souls (James 1:21), allowing it to transform us. This is not hard, per se; we are being shaped to the very likeness of our God!

Christians must stand in the same position as Israel did in the sense that we are to be the walking, talking, embodied image of God, through whom the world does—or does not—see the very character of our God. And if our God is the one who is compassionate and merciful, then what adjectives should be first on people's lips when they speak of Christians? If our Lord is the one who executes justice for the oppressed and provides a refuge for the homeless and foreigners, then that is what the church should be about. What does it mean that God is just? It means he will not allow oppression to have the final word in this story of ours, and we need to acknowledge that it is often through his people that he works. Gary Haugen of International Justice Mission reflects, "Over time I have come

[64] Scott Hafemann, "Yaein: Yes and No to Luther's Reading of Galatians 3:6–14," in *Galatians and Christian Theology: Justification, the Gospel, and Ethics in Paul's Letter*, ed. Mark W. Elliott et al. (Grand Rapids, MI: Baker Academic, 2014), 118.

[65] Wright, *Paul and the Faithfulness of God*, 1507, observes, "The crucified and risen Messiah, and the outpoured Spirit, meant here as elsewhere a transformed and transforming fulfillment of the Isaianic promises."

to see questions about suffering in the world not so much as questions of God's character but as questions about the obedience and faith of God's people. . . . The problem may not be that God is so far off; the problem may be that *God's people* are far off."[66]

To develop any sort of Christian, biblical theology of social justice, this *must* be based in the character of God as revealed in his Word, wherein God's description of *his* ideal society is laid out. The God of the Bible is an uncomfortable one, demanding that his people act like him, even to their own cost, as it was to his cost. All through the text, God distances himself from the prideful and the public-holy,[67] instead associating with the downcast, repentant, helpless, the oppressed.[68] Instance after instance of this truth should lead God's people toward understanding justice as not simply part of the work that God engages in but the outflow of his very character. The God who "opposes the proud, but gives grace to the humble" (James 4:6; quoting Prov. 3:34; cf. 1 Pet. 5:5) hears the cry of the poor and warns the oppressor of imminent judgment (James 5:1–6; cf. Isaiah 58).[69]

First John teaches that the character of God has vital impact on the nature of Christian worship. Robert Yarbrough observes, "No trait is more inherent to God as depicted in 1 John than the active will to love."[70] And so with the iterations in 1 John 4 that "God is love" (and not, by the way, that "Love is god"[71]),

> John is stressing God's nature as the reason Christians must love others if they are to "remain in God." As a communicable attribute of God, God's indwelling love in the life of the believer causes him or her to love others, that is, to live with others by the moral standard of God's light, for the opposite of love is sin. When a person is born again as a child of the Father, the Father's traits become increasingly apparent in that person's life. If God is generous, self-giving, and compassionate, those

[66] Haugen, *Good News about Injustice*, 100.

[67] E.g., Deut. 8:14; 2 Chron. 32:25; Pss. 36:11; 40:4; 94:2; 101:5; Prov. 15:25; 21:4; Eccles. 7:8; Isa. 2:12; 28:1, 3; Ezekiel 28; Obadiah 3; Hab. 2:4; Zech. 10:3; Matt. 3:7; 6:1; 23:2–36; Luke 1:51; 2 Cor. 10:5.

[68] This principle is epitomized in the parable of the Pharisee and the tax collector in Luke 18:9–14, which concludes, "All who exalt themselves will be humbled, but all who humble themselves will be exalted."

[69] Hays, *Moral Vision*, 36–37, comments, "Does grace undo ethics? Paul himself was forced to worry about this problem, because his detractors were already asserting that his gospel did away with Law and order, removing the necessary restraints on human sinfulness. . . . It is a peculiar irony that in the modern—and 'postmodern'—world, Christianity has come to be regarded as narrow and moralistic. Originally, it was quite the reverse: figures such as Jesus and Paul were widely regarded as rebels, antinomians, disturbers of decency."

[70] As quoted in Karen H. Jobes, *1, 2, 3 John*, ZECNT (Grand Rapids, MI: Zondervan, 2014), 198.

[71] Cf. Stanley Hauerwas, *Vision and Virtue: Essays in Christian Ethical Reflection* (Notre Dame, IN: University of Notre Dame Press, 1981), 124: "The ethics of love is often but a cover for what is fundamentally an assertion of ethical relativism."

> who claim to know him as their Father must also be. The children of God must love as God loves.[72]

John, in his Gospel and epistles, teaches the children of God to imitate the character of their father. God will bring about justice, not necessarily on our time but very likely through his people. The image bearers of God are to reveal their creator's character in a world desperately in need of compassion and mercy as well as a model of holiness. Richard Hays observes, concerning the Sermon on the Mount, "The point is that the community of Jesus' disciples is summoned to the task of showing forth the character of God in the world."[73]

We are to be a cross-shaped people who are not focused on our rights, in whom "Jesus Christ becomes the animating force in our lives. However mysterious such claims appear, they show that there is a deep connection in Paul's thought between Christology and ethics: to be in Christ is to have one's life conformed to the self-giving love enacted in the cross."[74] If we do not ground our attempts at justice and mercy in the character of our God, we will lose our focus and become idolaters, worshiping our own imagination's best idea of justice and fairness rather than bearing the image of our God faithfully. But in the end, as Bruggemann celebrates, "It will finally be about God and us, about his faithfulness that vetoes our faithlessness. . . . It is in receiving and not grasping, in inheriting and not possessing, in praising and not seizing. It is in knowing that initiative has passed from our hands and we are safer for it."[75] We do not create justice; we learn what it is in our God. God is the just and the justifier, the Lord compassionate and merciful, and we are his people, commissioned to bear his image and character into the world.

---

[72] Jobes, *1, 2, 3 John*, 198.
[73] Hays, *Moral Vision*, 329.
[74] Ibid., 32.
[75] Brueggemann, *Prophetic Imagination*, 65, 78.

SELECTED BIBLIOGRAPHY

Agan, C. D. "Jimmy," III. *The Imitation of Christ in the Gospel of Luke: Growing in Christlike Love for God and Neighbor*. Phillipsburg, NJ: P&R, 2014.

Anderson, Francis I. "Yahweh, the Kind and Sensitive God." In *God Who Is Rich in Mercy*, 41–88. Edited by D. B. Knox. Grand Rapids, MI: Baker, 1986.

Bray, Gerald. *God Is Love: A Biblical and Systematic Theology*. Wheaton, IL: Crossway, 2012.

Calvin, John. *Suffering: Understanding the Love of God*. Edited by Joseph Hill. Darlington, UK: Evangelical Press, 2005.

Carson, D. A. *The Difficult Doctrine of the Love of God*. Wheaton, IL: Crossway, 2000.

———. *The Gagging of God: Christianity Confronts Pluralism*. Grand Rapids, MI: Zondervan, 1996.

———. *Love in Hard Places*. Wheaton, IL: Crossway, 2002.

Chapell, Bryan. *The Promises of Grace: Living in the Grip of God's Love*. Grand Rapids, MI: Baker, 2001.

Chute, Anthony L., Christopher W. Morgan, and Robert A. Peterson, editors. *Why We Belong: Evangelical Unity and Denominational Diversity*. Wheaton, IL: Crossway, 2013.

Coppedge, Allan. *The God Who Is Triune: Revisioning the Christian Doctrine of God*. Downers Grove, IL: IVP Academic, 2007.

Dodds, Michael J. *The Unchanging Love of God*. Washington, DC: Catholic University of America Press, 2008.

Edwards, Jonathan. *Charity and Its Fruits*. Carlisle, PA: Banner of Truth, 1969.

Fairbairn, Donald. *Life in the Trinity*. Downers Grove, IL: IVP Academic, 2009.

Fernando, Ajith. *Reclaiming Love: Radical Relationships in a Complex World*. Grand Rapids, MI: Zondervan, 2012.

Frame, John M. *The Doctrine of God*. Phillipsburg, NJ: P&R, 2002.

Furnish, Victor P. *The Love Command in the New Testament*. London: SCM, 1973.

George, Timothy. *The Mark of Jesus: Loving in a Way the World Can See*. Chicago: Moody, 2005.

Gilchrist, John. *The Love of God in the Qur'an and the Bible*. Summerfield, FL: Jesus to the Muslims, 1989.

Glueck, Nelson. *HESED in the Bible*. Cincinnati: Hebrew Union College Press, 1967.

Green, Michael. *To Corinth with Love*. Dallas: Word, 1988.

Gruenler, Royce. *The Trinity in the Gospel of John: A Thematic Commentary on the Fourth Gospel*. Grand Rapids, MI: Baker, 1986.

Jeanrond, Werner G. *A Theology of Love*. London: T&T Clark, 2010.

Jones, David Clyde. *Biblical Christian Ethics*. Grand Rapids, MI: Baker, 1994.

Kelly, Anthony J. *God Is Love: The Heart of Christian Faith*. Collegeville, MN: Liturgical Press, 2012.

Köstenberger, Andreas J. *A Theology of John's Gospel and Letters: The Word, the Christ, the Son of God*. Biblical Theology of the New Testament. Grand Rapids, MI: Zondervan, 2009.

Kreeft, Peter. *Knowing the Truth of God's Love: The One Thing We Can't Live Without*. Knowing the Truth. Ann Arbor, MI: Servant, 1988.

Lewis, C. S. *The Four Loves*. New York: Harcourt Brace, 1960.

McIntyre, John. *On The Love of God*. London: Collins, 1962.

Miller, Paul E. *Love Walked among Us: Learning to Love Like Jesus*. Colorado Springs: NavPress, 2001.

Moffatt, James. *Love in the New Testament*. New York: Richard R. Smith, 1930.

Moloney, Francis. *Love in the Gospel of John: An Exegetical, Theological, and Literary Study*. Grand Rapids, MI: Baker Academic, 2013.

Morgan, Christopher W., and Robert A. Peterson, editors. *Hell Under Fire: Modern Scholarship Reinvents Eternal Punishment*. Grand Rapids, MI: Zondervan, 2004.

Moroney, Steven K. *God of Love and God of Judgment*. Eugene, OR: Wipf & Stock, 2009.

Morris, Leon. "Love." In *Dictionary of Jesus and the Gospels*. Edited by Joel B. Green, Scot McKnight, and I. Howard Marshall. Downers Grove, IL: InterVarsity, 1992.

———. *Testaments of Love: A Study of Love in the Bible*. Grand Rapids, MI: Eerdmans, 1981.

Newlands, George M. *Theology of the Love of God*. Atlanta: John Knox Press, 1980.

Nygren, Anders. *Agape and Eros*. Translated by Philip S. Watson. London: SPCK, 1957.

Oord, Thomas Jay. *Defining Love: A Philosophical, Scientific, and Theological Engagement*. Grand Rapids, MI: Brazos, 2010.

Packer, J. I. *Knowing God*. Downers Grove, IL: InterVarsity, 1973.

Piper, John. *Desiring God: Meditations of a Christian Hedonist*. Portland, OR: Multnomah, 1986.

———. *God's Passion for His Glory: Living the Vision of Jonathan Edwards*. Wheaton, IL: Crossway, 1998.

———. *Think: The Life of the Mind and the Love of God*. Wheaton, IL: Crossway, 2011.

Popkes, E. E. "Love, Love Command." In *Dictionary of Jesus and the Gospels*, 535–40. 2nd ed. Edited by Joel B. Green, Jeannine K. Brown, and Nicholas Perrin. Downers Grove, IL: InterVarsity, 2013.

Post, Stephen G. *Christian Love and Self-Denial: An Historical and Normative Study of Jonathan Edwards, Samuel Hopkins, and American Theological Ethics*. Lanham, MD: University Press of America, 1987.

Reeves, Michael. *Delighting in the Trinity*. Downers Grove, IL: IVP, 2012.

Ryken, Philip Graham, and Michael LeFebvre. *Our Triune God: Living in the Love of the Three-in-One*. Wheaton, IL: Crossway, 2011.

Schaeffer, Francis A. *The Mark of a Christian*. 2nd ed. Downers Grove, IL: InterVarsity, 2006.

Segovia, Fernando F. *Love Relationships in the Johannine Tradition: Agapē/Agapan in I John and the Fourth Gospel*. SBLDS 58. Chico, CA: Scholars Press, 1982.

Strange, Daniel. *The Possibility of Salvation among the Unevangelized*. Carlisle, UK: Paternoster, 2000.

Tolsma, Neil. *This Is Love: Tracing the Love of God throughout the Biblical Story*. Phillipsburg, NJ: P&R, 2012.

Vanhoozer, Kevin, editor. *Nothing Greater, Nothing Better: Theological Essays on the Love of God*. Grand Rapids, MI: Eerdmans, 2001.

Volf, Miroslav, et al. *A Common Word: Muslims and Christians on Loving God and Neighbor*. Grand Rapids, MI: Eerdmans, 2010.

Vos, Geerhardus. "The Scriptural Doctrine of the Love of God." In *Redemptive History and Biblical Interpretation*, 425–57. Edited by Richard B. Gaffin. Phillipsburg, NJ: P&R, 1980, 2001.

Wells, David F. *God in the Whirlwind: How the Holy-love of God Reorients Our World*. Wheaton, IL: Crossway, 2014.

Wright, Christopher J. H. *Old Testament Ethics for the People of God*. Downers Grove, IL: IVP Academic, 2004.

NAME INDEX

SUBJECT INDEX

SCRIPTURE INDEX

THEOLOGY IN COMMUNITY

FIRST-RATE EVANGELICAL SCHOLARS
take a multidisciplinary approach
to key Christian doctrines

OTHER BOOKS IN THE SERIES

Suffering and the Goodness of God
The Glory of God
The Deity of Christ
The Kingdom of God
Fallen: A Theology of Sin
Heaven

For more information, visit www.crossway.org.